SELLING THE SIGHTS

SELLING THE SIGHTS

The Invention of the Tourist in American Culture

WILL B. MACKINTOSH

New York University Press

NEW YORK

NEW YORK UNIVERSITY PRESS
New York
www.nyupress.org

References to Internet websites (URLs) were accurate at the time of writing. Neither the author nor New York University Press is responsible for URLs that may have expired or changed since the manuscript was prepared.

Library of Congress Cataloging-in-Publication Data

Names: Mackintosh, Will B., author.
Title: Selling the sights : the invention of the tourist in American culture
 / Will B. Mackintosh.
Description: New York : New York University, [2019] | Includes
 bibliographical references and index.
Identifiers: LCCN 2017054989 | ISBN 9781479889372 (cl : acid-free paper)
Subjects: LCSH: Tourism—Social aspects—United States—History—19th
 century. | Tourists—United States—History—19th century. |
 Travelers—United States—History—19th century. | Popular culture—United
 States—History—19th century.
Classification: LCC G155.U6 M3 2019 | DDC 306.4/8190973—dc23
LC record available at https://lccn.loc.gov/2017054989

New York University Press books are printed on acid-free paper, and their binding materials are chosen for strength and durability. We strive to use environmentally responsible suppliers and materials to the greatest extent possible in publishing our books.

Manufactured in the United States of America

10 9 8 7 6 5 4 3 2 1

Also available as an ebook

Contents

Introduction: A Physiology of Travelers

In the spring of 1847, the well-known British engraver Frances Delamotte decided to publish a popular illustrated volume on the subject of "travelling and travellers." Being more an artist than a writer, Delamotte asked his friend E. L. Blanchard, a famous writer of Drury Lane pantomimes, to supply the text. Blanchard complied, and in an astonishing six weeks he produced a slim, lighthearted work that he dubbed a "physiology . . . of travelling and travellers." In it, he sought to present "an animated picture of that unceasing movement which is constantly impelling mutable humanity forwards and backwards, upwards and downwards, left and right, over the solid, or fluid, or gaseous portions of the world." He gave his book the bombastic but prescient title *Heads and Tales of Travellers & Travelling: A Book for Everybody, Going Anywhere.* The *Sunday Times* called it "exactly one of those books that every one ought to read," and many evidently did, because it remained in print on both sides of the Atlantic for a decade.[1] It was an ephemeral piece of commercial entertainment, but the topic was well chosen and the timing was right, and its authors were amply rewarded.

Delamotte's proposed subject of "travelling and travellers," and the "physiology" template that Blanchard used to structure the book, were not chosen thoughtlessly. By the middle decades of the nineteenth century, the speed, distances, and modes of travel were all exploding, thanks to technological and market innovation and to relative peace in the Atlantic world after Napoleon's fall at Waterloo. Contemporary observers noticed that travel was becoming more central to people's lives, as an economic pursuit, as an educational experience, and increasingly as a form of leisure. In recognition of this growing importance, Blanchard declared, "There is indeed a wide field open" thanks to the "numberless varieties of locomotion . . . which civilization, chance, and conveyance-companies have provided, at different time[s], for the exportation of the biped species."[2] This sense of the vast new possibilities of travel, created by modern business enterprises and used by an increasingly "mutable humanity," demanded a new accounting and a new cataloging to make it comprehensible. A "physiology" did just that; a genre with roots in France in the 1830s, "physiologies" were textbooks that classified human bodies and expressions into readily understandable categories, which promised to help readers understand the interior character of strangers in an increasingly anonymous society. "Physiologies" offered a delineation of cultural types that taken together characterized the growing and restless societies of the nineteenth century. Blanchard's "physiology" was a winkingly comedic take on a serious genre and on a social and cultural phenomenon that was attracting considerable attention from the more buttoned-up social analysts of his day.[3]

As befit a physiology, Blanchard dissected the traveling body politic and analyzed its constituent parts. He examined different modes of travel, categories of destinations, and, most importantly, types of travelers. He drew distinctions between the disciples of "pedestrianism" and the new breed of commercial travelers. From both, he distinguished "tourists" as a kind of traveler "who merely travels for the sake of travelling."[4] It was the tourist who had pride of place as the subject of Blanchard's first chapter, which suggests the outsized significance of this relatively new category of people on the road. But Blanchard's work was a literary pantomime—lighthearted, comical, and topical—rather than a serious work of social analysis. This book takes seriously the project that Blanchard undertook facetiously, by explaining the origins and cultural significance of the distinctions he made among travelers at midcentury, and by explaining the emergence of a new category, the tourist, in nineteenth-century American culture.

At the opening of the nineteenth century, few observers made sharp linguistic or cultural distinctions between the different types of travelers they observed on the roads, rivers, and seas of the early American republic. The word "tour" had been used in English to describe traveling since the mid-seventeenth century, and it spawned the word "tourist" around the turn of the nineteenth century.[5] In 1800, leading British

"It has often been a matter of pleasant entertainment to me to watch the varied features of those who are to be my travelling companions, and endeavour to divine by physiogomy the various motives that have changed their stationary condition."

WASHINGTON IRVING.

FIGURE I.1. Frances Delamotte's visual physiology of traveling types, from the frontispiece of *Heads and Tales of Travellers & Travelling*. Courtesy of the University of Michigan Library.

lexicographer Samuel Pegge wrote, "A Traveller is now-a-days called a Tour-*ist*."[6] For Pegge, the two terms were equivalent, if not synonymous, and in fact they were treated as such in the earliest years of the neologism. The first appearance of the term "tourist" in an American imprint was in a 1798 novel by John Davis, a British literary entrepreneur who came to the United States in the 1790s hoping to make a name for himself on the nascent American literary scene. Davis celebrated the "pedestrian tourist" who dared to walk from New York to Philadelphia, but his compound noun shows he did not distinguish between "tourists" and practitioners of "pedestrianism," as Blanchard would fifty years later. During that intervening half century, "tour" and "tourist" became more clearly distinguished from the general terms "travel" and "traveler," such that Blanchard could treat them as self-evidently different social phenomena.[7]

The meanings of the terms "traveler" and "tourist" began to diverge in the 1820s, as an emerging national market economy began to reshape the availability of geographical knowledge, the material conditions of travel, and the number and variety of destinations that sought to profit from visitors with money to spend. These interrelated developments, all pushed by a generation of ambitious boosters and entrepreneurs, began to transform the critical steps of travel—including choosing a place to go and obtaining the knowledge and the means to get there—into commodities that could be produced in volume and sold into a potentially national marketplace of consumers. The commodification of these components happened gradually and unevenly across the territory of the United States and the decades of the nineteenth century: certain print genres of geographical knowledge were more efficiently produced by industrial publishing firms than others; some routes of travel supported large-scale transportation businesses before others; and accessible destinations with appealing natural features attracted more visitors than did obscure and featureless resorts. The routes and technologies deployed by both the print and transportation industries tended to spread westward and southward from the major northeastern port cities, and thus their commodification took place earlier in the Northeast and the Old Northwest than they did in the Deep South and the Old Southwest. Because the commodification of print and travel was gradual and uneven, so too was the movement toward distinct meanings for "traveler" and "tourist" to which it gave rise. The term "tourist" was used by some authors to disparage British travelers in the early decades of the century; some guidebooks still hailed their audience as "travelers" on the eve of the

Civil War; and some observers continued to treat them as synonyms, especially when writing casually. But by the time Blanchard's literary burlesque hit the shelves of American booksellers in 1847, pleasurable travel experiences were widely available for purchase by elite and middling Americans, and the consumers who bought such experiences were generally termed "tourists" and understood to be a separate and identifiable subset of the traveling public.

The growing nineteenth-century distinction between "travelers" and "tourists," and the association of the latter with the consumption of commodified experiences, created new cultural fault lines that all travelers had to navigate. Some travelers became enthusiastic consumers of commodified experience and increasingly embraced the label of "tourist," celebrating those experiences for the pleasure they provided and for the social and cultural benefits they accrued. Others rejected both the label and the commercialized travel products that defined it, seeking instead to define themselves in opposition to "tourists," as "travelers" whose journeys were more original, useful, and meaningful than the predictable itineraries of tourism. Both groups sought to harness their travel to their ambitions for social and cultural status, but they chose different strategies for doing so. However, these two cultural positions were also mutually constitutive: a tourist was not a traveler, and a traveler was not a tourist. This fundamental opposition and the market relations that underlie it, rooted in the economic and cultural conditions of the early nineteenth century, continue to shape our understanding of the meanings of travel to this day.

Tracing the tourist's emergence as a distinct cultural figure shows how deeply the emerging national market economy impacted the cultural structures of nineteenth-century American life. This analysis is deeply underwritten by the theoretical framework of "commodification," the socioeconomic process that takes place when the value of a good is established by its exchangeability—which is to say its availability for sale in the marketplace—rather than through its utility.[8] Although the concept has deep and important roots in Marxist political theory and anthropological analysis, it has been most concretely defined for historians of the nineteenth-century United States by William Cronon, who characterizes it as the transformation of the idiosyncratic products of nature into standardized, interchangeable commodities that could be exchanged in increasingly distant and anonymous markets.[9] Commodification is a complex process, equal parts material and conceptual, so tracing its effects is a delicate and messy process. It also was not, to use Ann Blair's term, an "actors' category"; the word was not used during the early American republic, and thus analyzing the world of nineteenth-century Americans using commodification as an explanatory framework is to see it in a way that was not theirs.[10] Both the term and the process it describes have taken on a negative connotation in modern usage, both because Marxists have connected them with exploitation and because we associate commodities with inauthenticity. As a result, this book uses "commodification" carefully and advisedly as an analytical term, with attention to the complexity of the process; to the sometimes sharp divide between "actors' categories" and modern scholarly language; and to the need to control for and explain the negative connotations that many modern readers associate with it.

Notwithstanding the delicacy with which the term must be used, it offers powerful insight into the lives of nineteenth-century Americans. Historians have detailed the myriad ways in which market relations restructured labor, families, knowledge, the nation-state, and class relations over the course of the century. As the material stuff of life was slowly commodified, American culture became increasingly dominated by an emerging bourgeois middle class, formed in the counting-houses of the market economy, in the loving homes of nuclear families, and in the pulpits of liberal Protestantism. But historians have not always extended the same perceptive analysis of commodification to the leisure activities of this middle class, at least not in the years before the Civil War. Analyzing the ways in which tourists were increasingly distinguished from travelers shows us that market-oriented Americans consumed *commodified experiences* as well as commodified goods in the early nineteenth century, and that their relationship to these commodified experiences was central to their own understanding of their social position. Tourists consumed nascent commercial cultural products—an experience with a price tag—that ideally embodied the standardization of idiosyncratic individual experiences of travel into predictable and interchangeable experiences of summer leisure. Ambitious Americans bought these experiences—or shunned them—in order to express their cultural values and their social standing. Putting tourists and their detractors at the center of an analysis of nineteenth-century American culture reveals a deep ambivalence at the heart of the economic and cultural processes that commodified experience. Market relations were becoming the most significant force in American culture, but many Americans remained—and remain—skeptical of their social effects.

The emergence of the tourist in nineteenth-century American culture becomes more significant when it is situated within the broader history of leisure travel. Although tourism in its modern commodified form was a product of the nineteenth century, travel for the purposes of pleasure, diversion, and personal gratification has a longer history, particularly on the other side of the Atlantic. As Blanchard's London byline suggests, it is impossible to discuss Americans' ideas about leisure travel without considering those of their British forebears and contemporaries. As with so many other facets of culture in the early national period, American discourse about travel emerged in imitation of and reaction to both a shared seventeenth- and eighteenth-century Anglo-American past and modern nineteenth-century British discourse. As the broad transatlantic circulation of Blanchard's book suggests, British traditions of and ideas about leisure travel were broadly apparent to Americans because the print cultures of the two nations were so intertwined. Even though this book traces the emergence of the tourist in American culture, the story it tells is necessarily transatlantic because Americans were so aware of British precedents and analogues.

At the turn of the nineteenth century, when lexicographers like Samuel Pegge thought the term "tourist" was synonymous with the term "traveler," the term "tour" was generally applied to the British phenomenon of the "Grand Tour."[11] The Grand Tour was an extended trip through continental Europe, made by aristocratic young British men as a part of their preparation for taking leadership roles at home. The practice had its roots in the mid-sixteenth century; the Grand Tour's typical routes and preoccupations began to take form in 1549, when English linguist and historian William Thomas published *The History of Italy* after a four-year tour of the Italian states. Michael Brennan argues that by the beginning of the seventeenth century, "the educational efficacy of continental travel for young Englishmen with high ambitions for public and diplomatic service in later life was firmly established in ways which would remain valid for the next two hundred years."[12] The term "Grand Tour" was first coined in 1670 by Richard Lassels, a Catholic priest and tutor, in his *Voyage of Italy or a Compleat Journey through Italy*, and this codification in language and practice set the stage for what would become the heyday of the Grand Tour in the eighteenth century.[13]

At its peak of popularity, the Grand Tour led across the English Channel, to Paris by way of the Loire Valley, and then on to Italy by way of Geneva. The aristocratic youth who made the tour would then spend time in the cities of Rome, Florence, and Venice, before returning home through Austria, Germany, and Amsterdam. A proper Grand Tour could take as many as five years—usually right after graduation from Oxford or Cambridge—and was accompanied by at least one tutor or chaperone. These tutors were supposed to keep their charges' attentions focused on the explicit goals of the Grand Tour, which included schooling in the languages and manners of refined continental society, enhancing their classical learning through exposure to the sites of antiquity, and cultivating aesthetic taste through the appreciation and acquisition of art. The tutors also enabled, if not encouraged, their charges to pursue temporary relationships with continental women, presumed to be less morally upright than British women of their own class, so that they could return home and enter into a respectable marriage.[14] The term "tour" as a description of a broad, looping journey for pleasure and personal fulfillment thus entered the English language closely associated with this aristocratic rite of passage.

European continental tours that echoed the Grand Tour became more accessible to the rising British bourgeoisie after the Seven Years' War and especially after the end of the Napoleonic Wars in 1815, as the Industrial Revolution built new fortunes in Britain and as peace and prosperity made European travel pleasurable again.[15] But even in its later, more popular incarnation, the Grand Tour was largely a British phenomenon. Relatively few Americans traveled to Europe before 1860, and although the number steadily climbed in every decade save the 1830s, it remained at less than 1 percent of the population. The majority of this small group were not leisure travelers, although as Daniel Kilbride has demonstrated, many business travelers managed to fit in some touring when they went to the trouble of crossing the Atlantic. And trouble it was; transatlantic passage was expensive, unreliable, time-consuming, and potentially dangerous. Indeed, participation in even the increasingly commercialized version of the Grand Tour undertaken by the nineteenth-century British bourgeoisie was prohibitively costly for all but the wealthiest Americans through the Civil War.[16] International travel, and especially international travel for pleasure, was an experience few nineteenth-century Americans could reasonably expect to have in their lifetimes.

Just because few Americans ever took a Grand Tour in the British sense does not mean that they were not well aware of the practice. From the late eighteenth century onward, American readers were avid consumers of travel books. In 1789, the Library Company of Philadelphia advertised more than two hundred volumes under the heading of "Voyages and Travels," out of a collection of "eight thousand, the selection of which, has in general been calculated to promote the more important interests of society." In 1806, over 11 percent of the holdings of the Charleston Library Company in South Carolina were travel accounts.[17] Americans also wrote travel accounts, especially after the American publication of Washington Irving's *The Sketch-Book of Geoffrey Crayon* in 1820, which "helped raise the stature of travel writing in a nation struggling for self-identity and literary respect, and . . . demonstrated the viability of a heretofore unrecognized publishing market."[18] Many authors mined this profitable vein in the antebellum decades, writing and publishing mountains of travel narratives.[19] Books relating to travel were one of the most popular and prolific genres of American print culture during the first half of the nineteenth century, second in quantity only to religious publications.[20]

But Americans of the early republic did not only read and write about travel in distant Europe. A broader and more diverse cross-section of Americans traveled extensively within North America. Alexis de Tocqueville famously painted the Americans as a people on the move, as a nation of "happy men, restless in the midst of abundance."[21] They traveled for business and for migration, and increasingly for pleasure and to experience firsthand the continent they inhabited. The growing amount of travel for leisure was apparent in 1860, when a contributor to the *Yale Literary Magazine* observed, "We are a nation of travelers." Americans of all classes traveled, "for if you can get neither to Niagara, nor Trenton, nor the Springs, giving up broader and more comprehensive views, you pay your last quarter to bask in the sunshine of the Elysian Fields at Hoboken, or borrow a dime to muse over the waters of the Spuyten Duvil Creek [*sic*] at Harlem."[22] Americans of the early republic were enthusiastic travelers as well as readers and writers of travel, and their restless inclinations were ripe for anatomization by observers like Blanchard.

Leisure travelers first became visible on the North American landscape in the decade after the Revolution, although their numbers were small, their destinations were limited, and the crowds were both tiny and elite. Virginia plantation owners, who were always among the most attentive students of elite British social practices, began to gather at mineral and hot springs in the Piedmont and in remote mountain valleys as early as the 1760s. By the 1780s, well-known Virginians like Thomas Jefferson and George Washington were visiting and promoting destinations like Warm Springs and Bath, later Berkeley Springs. New Yorkers were close behind; by the 1790s, pleasure excursions up the scenic and historic Hudson River valley brought travelers to Ballston, a small but growing settlement of lodging houses and hotels clustered in a shady valley around a group of mineral springs.[23] These early destinations could host only a few members of their regional elite and attracted attention mostly from their regional press, but they were nevertheless a visible manifestation of leisure travel on the landscape of the new United States.

The early seeds planted at Berkeley Springs and Ballston Spa began to grow vigorously in the beneficial social and economic climate following the close of the War of 1812. Beginning in the 1820s, a rapidly growing number of Americans undertook travel for pleasure and personal fulfillment within the borders of their own country. Indeed, it is this decade that scholars have generally identified as period of the "birth of American tourism," as the title of one recent study has put it. By the 1820s, springs resorts had proliferated across the landscape of western Virginia and were being knit together by a network of turnpikes and stagecoaches. Ballston was already being supplanted by neighboring Saratoga Springs, a village with more springs, more hotels, and growing crowds. New types of destinations appeared on leisure travelers' itineraries. Americans had long celebrated the natural wonder of Niagara Falls, but the opening of the Erie Canal in 1825 made a summer excursion to them a practical undertaking. Ruined forts and overgrown battlefields from the Revolutionary War dotted upstate New York, and travelers sought them out for their romanticized historical and nationalist associations. A tragic but spectacular landslide that killed an entire family in New Hampshire in 1826 drew attention to the majestic scenery of the White Mountains, which brought a growing stream of visitors by the end of the decade. In the mid-1820s, boosters began to collectively label these northern destinations the "Fashionable Tour" or the "American Grand Tour." This route led north out of New York City and up the Hudson and Mohawk valleys, with stops at Saratoga Springs and Niagara Falls. It then swung north through Montreal and Quebec, and returned to New York by way of the White Mountains and Boston. Like the old British Grand Tour, the American Fashionable Tour was more a set of destinations and social practices than a fixed route, and the term similarly applied to a broad, looping journey undertaken by the social elite for pleasure and personal fulfillment.[24]

The trends of the 1820s intensified in subsequent decades. New destinations proliferated on the roads to the Virginia springs and along the Fashionable Tour. Leisure travelers struck out for new territories, as well; they were exploring the Ohio River valley by the 1830s, and the Great Lakes by the 1840s. Small towns like Bedford, Pennsylvania;

White Sulphur Springs, Ohio; and Avon, New York offered themselves as pleasant stops on a tourist's itinerary. As the United States developed an increasingly integrated national market economy, a growing bourgeois upper middle class commanded the time and financial resources necessary to travel for pleasure. By the 1850s, no one spoke of the "American Grand Tour" in the singular sense of the 1820s, since tours and tourists seemed omnipresent. Thus when Blanchard anatomized the traveling public at midcentury, his American readers would have broadly recognized his dissection of the "tourist" as a distinct species of traveler because they were common figures on their bookshelves and a visible presence on highways and byways across much of the nation.

Historians who have studied American tourism have generally agreed on its broad chronological and geographical contours, but this consensus masks a complex and variegated literature.[25] The existing scholarship on early American tourism is both richly developed and curiously isolated. Since the 1980s, innovative studies have proliferated exploring questions of nation, region, and class through early tourism. Much of the historiography focuses on the relationship between tourism and the creation of national identity in the early United States. Scholars such as John F. Sears, Marguerite Shaffer, Richard Gassan, and Thomas Chambers have discussed the ways in which visits to places of natural and cultural interest worked to produce a distinct national identity for the United States across the nineteenth century. Related work by scholars such as Dona Brown and Charlene Boyer Lewis has explored the ways in which distinctly regional tourism fostered regional identities that were often in tension with the nationalist project.[26] Another important strand in the literature of tourism and identity is related to class, specifically the question of the "emergence of the middle class." Scholars like Chambers, Cindy Aron, Jon Sterngass, and Catherine Cocks have all argued that many different varieties of tourism were important to drawing and policing the boundaries of the "new middle class" and were often in turn shaped by their preoccupations.[27] In each case, historians have interpreted tourism as a site at which nineteenth-century Americans worked out new understandings of the changing world around them.

As many of these scholars have found, studies of the history of tourism quickly stumble over a fundamental problem: who was a tourist, and who was not? They deal with this problem in a variety of ways: by restricting the scope of their studies so that the definition becomes clear in a very specific time or place; by formulating provisional definitions that allow their work to move forward; or by simply treating the category of the tourist as self-evident according to some modern understanding of the word. This problem of defining tourism is exacerbated by historians' tendency to see tourism as exceptional, as a time apart from ordinary life, and therefore as a sort of climate-controlled historical laboratory for the exploration of broader themes. Sterngass, for example, reads resort life using the Turnerian concept of "ritual liminality" and argues that resorts served as "laboratories in which visitors could experiment with new or different ideas about the value of the work ethic, the significance of luxury in a democratic republic, the proper roles of men and women, and the relationship between community and privacy."[28] This analytical impulse, common in studies of early American tourism, stresses tourism's separateness, which has severed it from the broader context of American mobility captured by observers like Tocqueville.

Selling the Sights solves this problem by analyzing the history of tourism broadly and in relationship to the diverse landscape of travel that characterized the early American republic. Rather than deploying a provisional definition of tourism so it can be used as a tool for answering other cultural questions about the nineteenth-century United States, this book takes the very definition of tourism itself as one of its central questions. As earlier historians have found, no fixed definition of tourism emerged either in the nineteenth century or afterward. Rather, contemporaries identified tourists in more tangential ways. They tended to define them by their relationship to the market; tourists were travelers whose experiences were fundamentally mediated by the marketplace. And they increasingly defined them by who they were not; tourists were not "true travelers," who avoided generic commercial experiences and instead sought experiences that they could frame as original, meaningful, and useful.[29] Importantly, neither of these means of identifying tourists was stable. The boundaries of the marketplace, as well as the line between "travelers" and "tourists," were both fuzzy, and they were drawn strategically according to the social and cultural agenda of each observer. Understanding this history turns the ambiguity of tourism from an analytical problem into a historical explanation: identifying "tourists" was a means by which nineteenth-century Americans came to grips with the market and sought to delineate what it was and what it was not. At the same time, distinguishing "tourists" as figures on the roads of the early republic was a means by which nineteenth-century Americans expressed how they valued or did not value the cultural products of the market. Finally, tracing the emerging definition of tourism helps us to explain the opprobrium that has adhered to the term, because it allows us to witness how a broader cultural discomfort with the processes of commodification became adhered to the figure of the tourist over the course of the nineteenth century.

This analysis offers definitional clarity to historians working on the history of tourism in the United States, but it also offers historical specificity to the sociologists and other theoreticians of tourism who have worked to describe the relationship between tourism and capitalism. Much of the contemporary field of tourism studies is built on the work of Dean MacCannell, for whom "tourist attractions are an unplanned typology of structure that provides direct access to the modern consciousness or 'world view.'" Tourists are therefore the ideal ethnographers of modernity, whose consumption of the spectacles of work and leisure allow them to contemplate its "unifying consciousness." MacCannell's "modernity" is specifically postindustrial capitalism, which is why an act of leisure is the most important act of understanding.[30] Similarly, John Urry uses the concept of the "tourist gaze" to mark and distinguish acts of tourism, which are characterized by a particular way of seeing that overlays commercially produced images and myths onto travel destinations.[31] Thus, while the most influential theorists in the field have identified the necessary relationship between tourism and capitalism, *Selling the Sights* shows how that relationship was born, in tourism's moment of origin, out of the historically specific social, cultural, and economic conditions of the first half of the nineteenth century.

If this book brings the insights of the scholarship on nineteenth-century capitalism to bear on the analysis of tourism, then it also brings new insights from the study of tourism to the lively current literature on the cultural history of capitalism. Twenty-five years ago, Charles Sellers's magisterial "market revolution" paradigm described a wholesale transformation of the American economy, and of American attitudes toward the economy, in the years after 1815. His analysis of the development of national markets in Jacksonian America showed how the production and distribution of a wide range of agricultural and handicraft products was increasingly controlled by a capitalist business elite rather than by individual producers. For Sellers and other historians of the market revolution, this spreading divide between production and consumption had important social, political, religious, and cultural effects in the antebellum period.[32]

Building on Sellers's insight, a new historiography of capitalism has emerged, which privileges analysis of the ways in which "capitalism helped to transform personhood in the nineteenth century," as Joanna Cohen has recently put it.[33] This vibrant literature pays special attention to the ways in which the economic practices of capitalism spilled into everyday life, by creating and foreclosing possibilities and by supplying overwhelmingly powerful economic metaphors for facets of life not previously considered economic. It is from this scholarship on the lived experience of capitalist transformation that this book draws its theoretical framework of commodification. Attention to commodification has directed historians' attention to absorption of ever-larger realms of human existence into "the market" and has produced some of the most original and illuminating recent histories of the nineteenth-century United States, from Cronon's famous analysis of the commodification of nature and the creation of Chicago, to Walter Johnson's analysis of the commodification of human beings and the creation of slave markets, to Jonathan Levy's analysis of the commodification of contingency and the creation of a modern corporate capitalist order.[34] In this tradition, *Selling the Sights* is an analysis of the commodification of experience and the creation of modern industries of leisure.

As productive as this line of analysis has been, historians are only beginning to understand how early national markets began to commodify less tangible but still saleable goods, like a pleasant evening at the theater or indeed an enjoyable summer's day at the springs. Historians of urban popular amusements have begun to redeem the term "culture industry" to describe "the specific effects of corporate capitalism on specific cultural industries at specific moments in time," and they have traced the emergence of such culture industries as early as the 1830s in the showrooms of P. T. Barnum and on the minstrel stages of T. D. Rice.[35] The economic complex of innkeepers, steamboat lines, guidebook publishers, railroad corporations, and local boosters that created the tourist was just such a culture industry, and by interpreting the early American tourist industry through the lens of commodification, *Selling the Sights* shows that the commodification of experience was both broader and more tightly integrated into middle-class Americans' lives than just in the showrooms of Barnum or on the stages of the touring circuit. A wider range of entrepreneurs than historians have previously understood, operating in both urban and rural environments, sought to transform unique experiences of leisure travel into predictable, interchangeable, marketable commodities which they could sell into a national market of potential tourists and from which they could thus derive profit. Experimentation with the alchemy of the commodification of experience took place in remote mountain valleys in Virginia, not just in the pleasure palaces of Broadway and the Bowery. As a result, the identities of Americans prosperous enough to afford such commodities were fundamentally reshaped, as they were forced negotiate new meanings associated with their consumption.[36]

This new history of tourism also forces us to reconsider the chronology of American capitalism. Historians tend to associate the commodification of experience with the turn of the twentieth century, albeit with important precursors in the nineteenth century. The attention that cultural historians have paid to circuses, dime novels, vaudeville, professional sports, department stores, dance halls, Coney Island, and moving pictures all point to a general historical consensus that Americans increasingly came to define themselves through the consumption of experience in the closing decades of the nineteenth century.[37] But paying attention to tourists in the opening decades of that century, particularly in the context of the larger world of travel and mobility, shows that this process was much older and much more centrally woven into the emergence of bourgeois identities than we have previously understood. As much as tourists were the products of national and regional culture, or of the processes of middle-class formation, they were also products of the emerging market economy and the commodified experiences it produced. If, as Dean MacCannell would have it, tourists are definitionally modern and tourism is the fundamental social practice of modernity, then understanding tourists as some of the earliest consumers of commodified experience helps us to understand the history of modernity, or at least the originating connection between capitalism, commodification, and lived experience in the production of modernity.[38]

As with any historical change in the deep structure of culture, the commodification of travel experiences and the creation of the tourist was a slow, gradual, and uneven process over time and across space. Thus, as with any cultural history, the change over time traced by *Selling the Sights* is gradual, nonlinear, and always contested, but nonetheless real and meaningful. Such change is best analyzed thematically rather than strictly chronologically. Roughly grouped into a discussion of causes and a discussion of effects, the five chapters of this book consider different aspects of the commodification of travel and creation of the tourist. They do so by drawing from sources in which travelers and tourists wrote about themselves, including letters, diaries, and published travel accounts, and from sources in which observers wrote about the world of travel around them, including guidebooks and prescriptive literature, social commentary, periodical literature, fiction, and advertisements. As befits a cultural history, *Selling the Sights* focuses more on the meanings nineteenth-century Americans made about travel than on the material experience of travel itself. The universe of possible meanings available to them was shaped by a larger discourse about the meanings of travel and the meanings of different kinds of travelers. This discourse can be found in the print sources that circulated widely and the set cultural parameters within which individual tourists could situate themselves. As a result, the chapters that follow largely though not exclusively build their arguments from the rich archive of print objects that were increasingly omnipresent in the world of nineteenth-century tourists.

The first three chapters trace the cultural and economic processes that drove the commodification of three critical components of tourism: the universe of print materials that taught tourists where to go; the various transportation technologies that got them there; and the entertainments that occupied them at their destinations. Chapter 1, "Describing the Terraqueous Globe: Tourists and the Culture of Geographical Knowledge," traces how the commercialization of the print industry changed the print culture of geographical knowledge between the 1790s and the 1860s. In the earliest years of the American republic, when a group of authors, editors, and educators began to craft the first specifically American geographical texts, they did so as part of a late-Enlightenment intellectual culture that sought to catalogue comprehensive, universal knowledge and to publish it in encyclopedic form for the parlors, libraries, and schoolrooms of the new nation. Beginning in the 1810s and 1820s, a generation of local boosters began to use a still decentralized print infrastructure to craft new geographical texts, including gazetteers and guidebooks, designed to drive migration to, investment in, and for some, visitors to their hometowns. The volumes that they published were narrower and more specific than their Enlightenment predecessors, and they were ultimately intended as promotional tools. At the same time, a subset of printers in Philadelphia and New York began to specialize in publishing geographical texts, which were both tailored to particular audiences and generalized for sale in an increasingly national marketplace for books. These two trends came together in the 1850s as industrial-scale generalist publishing firms, mostly in New York, entered and quickly dominated the market for geographical texts. Their business incentive was to repackage existing geographical knowledge for as many audiences and for as large a market as possible. By midcentury, the changing conditions of the marketplace for print had transformed the American culture of geographical knowledge from one of authorial craftsmanship and universalist ambitions to one of mass production and market specialization. This history drove the creation and evolution of guidebooks for tourists, of geographical knowledge packaged for specific experiences, aimed at the largest possible market of interchangeable leisure travelers.

During the same years, a parallel process of commodification was reshaping the industries that provided transportation to American travelers, and was also more significantly reshaping the experience of being transported. Chapter 2, "Yesterday the Springs, To-day the Falls: Tourism and the Commodification of Travel," applies this analysis to the historical development that historians have usually known as "the transportation revolution."[39] At the beginning of the nineteenth century, transportation on the American continent was largely a self-produced affair. Travelers generally had to identify their route, assess its conditions, and figure out how to acquire the necessary carriage, food, and shelter along the way. But after 1815, a series of technological and business developments enabled transportation entrepreneurs to begin to provide all those necessary components of travel as a complete package, allowing individual travelers to become consumers of premade travel rather than producers of their own travel. Stagecoaches, turnpikes, and steamboats in the 1810s and 1820s, canals in the 1820s and 1830s, and finally railroads in the 1830s and 1840s provided the underlying technology that allowed easy and reliable transportation to be supplied on a mass scale. Entrepreneurs sold this transportation using new market mechanisms like the ticket, a paper representation of future transportation that could be bought and sold on the open market. This basic shift, from improvisational producers of unique journeys to comfortable consumers of ticketed transport, fundamentally reshaped travelers' experiences of and expectations for travel. They expected commodified travel to be fast, comfortable, and affordable, and to increasingly be a source of leisure and even pleasure, rather than just utility. This market habit of mind with which travelers approached the problem of transportation mostly produced celebrations of the conveniences of commodified travel, although a minority bemoaned the inevitable creeping sameness of its itineraries. Either way, the commodification of travel created the market for mobility in which tourists could shop.

Chapter 3, "I Find Myself a Pilgrim: Commodified Experience and the Invention of the Tourist," turns its attention to the destinations that these leisure travelers sought out through their guidebook reading and ticket purchasing. Beginning in the 1820s with the same cohort of local boosters who were reshaping the print culture of geographical knowledge, a largely rural group of entrepreneurs began to offer different kinds of pleasurable experiences for sale to potential leisure travelers. The specific experiences they offered varied depending on what they perceived to be their unique local strengths, and as a result they varied from lively social experiences of belonging to a regional or national elite, to intense aesthetic experiences of spectacular landscapes, to bucolic summer experiences of idealized rural life. Both the kinds of experiences available for purchase and the number and variety of localities that sought to market such experiences proliferated over the subsequent decades, creating a lively national market for leisure travel by the middle of the century. These innovations represented the very earliest attempts at the creation of the domestic tourist industry, which in the nineteenth century consisted of an often-disconnected group of cultural entrepreneurs who increasingly sought to profit from the idea that experiences could be bought and sold in the marketplace. That this industry began to form at all shows that such commodified experiences had a lot of satisfied consumers, and significant traces of this satisfaction remain in both published and unpublished accounts of the pleasure tourists took from their destinations. They enjoyed them, generally, in precisely the ways that their proprietors intended for them to be enjoyed. However, like with commodified travel, commodified leisure experiences also had their detractors. A small but growing number of travelers began to doubt the value of commodified experience, which was by its very nature controlled, standardized, and predictable. The emerging marketplace for commodified leisure was the economic and cultural context in which the distinct modern meanings of the terms "tourist" and "tourism" were forged, complete with their modern ambivalence about the value of touristic experiences.

The final two chapters consider the cultural effects that this dichotomy produced as it hardened, especially in the decades before the Civil War. Together, they begin to articulate the opprobrium American observers displayed when they discussed tourists and tourist practices. *Selling the Sights* does not assume that the term "commodification" has a negative connotation, nor does it seek to tell the story of commodification as one of declension. Instead, these chapters propose to explain how one particular kind of commodified good—tourist experiences—came to get its negative connotation. These chapters incorporate more print sources that were British in origin, like Blanchard's 1847 physiology. The material processes that commodified tourist experiences were largely and necessarily American in their scope, scale, and origins. Reactions to the emergence of tourism, however, were broadly transatlantic, because parallel material processes were having similar effects in Britain at around the same time, and the strong transatlantic links in Anglo-American literary and intellectual culture meant that American reactions were shaped by and in response to British discourses.

Chapter 4 takes up this ambivalence and tracks its emergence through the transatlantic proliferation of literary satires aimed at tourists. Entitled "I'll Picturesque It Everywhere: The Archetype of the Tourist in Satire," this chapter identifies a diverse group of literary authors who used caricatures of tourists in their work. Spread across the first half of the nineteenth century and writing in English on both sides of the Atlantic, these satirists aimed their wits at social groups as diverse as the ambitious English bourgeoisie, condescending European travelers in America, and country hayseeds on their first trip to the city. Although their diversity prevents them from being labeled as a coherent genre, nevertheless these satirists of tourism identified overwhelmingly similar negative characteristics of tourists to heighten and exaggerate for comic effect. Tourists were ambitious, banal, formulaic, and ignorant. Their unoriginality, superficiality, and fondness for cliché made their claims to social and cultural importance ridiculous. Even though these authors wrote in different times and places, for different audiences, and with different satirical targets in mind, their comic renderings of tourists were sufficiently similar that a distinctly negative tourist archetype had formed by midcentury. Critically, those midcentury satirists increasingly associated tourists' negative characteristics with the consumption of commodified experience. It was this broadly understood caricature of the tourist-consumer that Blanchard tapped into when he wrote that the great majority of tourists traveled not "in the true spirit of locomotion" but instead "because others have gone out of town before them, and they like not lingering behind." For Blanchard, tourists who were driven by such banal social mimicry had no real engagement with their own journeys. He wryly noted that "the meditative fly that coolly perambulates the map of Europe suspended in your study, and stalks from the North Pole to the Mediterranean, before you have time to whisk him off with your handkerchief, scarcely scampers over the whole continent with more speed."[40] In the hands of masterful midcentury satirists like Blanchard and especially Mark Twain, the term "tourist" came to have a negative connotation that that was deeply rooted in tourists' status as consumers of experience.

Chapter 5, "Traveling to Good Purpose: The Invention of the True Traveler," considers those travelers who wished to avoid the opprobrium of the tourist's increasingly negative connotation. Much as the term "tourist" came to have a meaning distinct from its onetime synonym, so too was the term "traveler" used in an increasingly specific and oppositional sense. As tourists became increasingly identifiable on American byways, a new subgenre of travel writers emerged who promised to teach travelers how to, in the words of Theodore Dwight, "travel to good purpose," in order to avoid the taint of being superficial tourists. Beginning in the 1830s, Americans could read advice on traveling to good purpose from a variety of British and American essayists and educators. These writers agreed that travelers to good purpose could transcend the tourist label by shunning commodified experiences, by preparing themselves morally and intellectually for their journey, by cultivating consistent and exhaustive habits of observation and record keeping on the road, and by sharing the original knowledge that their travel produced through correspondence or scientific publication. Parents or guardians who took their children with them for the purpose of educating them could also claim that they were traveling to good purpose. These "travellers to good purpose" pushed back strongly against the association of tourism with decadent consumption; instead, they sought to position themselves as useful producers, a form of social and cultural worth that was uniquely powerful in the nineteenth century. But this task was a profoundly gendered one. Much writing on the subject suggested that in order to qualify as purposeful, travel had to have explicitly scientific means and ends, supported by the institutional structure of a publication, college, or learned society. By the 1830s and 1840s, such institutionally supported science was increasingly a masculine preserve, and as a result productive travel seemed closed to women travelers. Some women travelers vigorously opposed this discursive exclusion and sought to carve out a feminine-gendered space for purposeful travel that centered on observation of and education in morals and manners. Eager to distance themselves from the archetype of the tourist, such travelers to good purpose articulated their own social and cultural worth by positioning themselves as producers. Thus, by the eve of the Civil War, tourists and travelers were distinct figures in American culture, defined oppositionally and valued hierarchically, and forged in the heat of the emerging national market.

As a Saratoga society correspondent might have put it in the 1850s, it has been de rigueur for late twentieth- and early twenty-first-century scholars of tourism to quote Daniel Boorstin, whose 1961 essay "From Traveler to Tourist: The Lost Art of Travel" was a biting high-culture critique of tourists in the twentieth century. "The traveler was active; he went strenuously in search of people, of adventure, of experience," Boorstin explained. "The tourist is passive; he expects interesting things to happen to him. He goes 'sight-seeing.'"[41] Boorstin articulated with great clarity, if also with enormous condescension, the basic organizing dichotomy that undergirds all modern discussions of travel and assessments of the value of travel in American society, from the most rarefied sociological theory to the most disposable visitor's pamphlet. At its most fundamental level, this book seeks the origin of this organizing dichotomy in the years between the end of the Revolution and the beginning of the Civil War. It lies in the emergence of a national market economy in the early nineteenth century; in the dynamics of commodification that allowed inventive entrepreneurs to sell standardized leisure experiences to a potentially continental market of middle-class strangers; and in the social and cultural value systems that led some Americans to embrace commodification's promise and others to reject its limitations. The dichotomy that Boorstin treated as fundamental in the twentieth century was in fact created by the fault lines of emergent modern market capitalism in the nineteenth century. Though we might not realize it, our impulse to anatomize "mutable humanity" into tourists and travelers has long been a part of living within and through that modern market capitalist world.

1 / Describing the Terraqueous Globe: Tourists and the Culture of Geographical Knowledge

In 1793, a Massachusetts minister named Jedidiah Morse published a "system of Geography" to which he gave the somewhat paradoxical title *The American Universal Geography*. Although the juxtaposition of words in his title seems jarring, it precisely captured Morse's intellectual project and that of other geographers writing at the birth of the new nation. His book promised geographical information that was tailored to the needs of an independent United States, but more importantly, it sought to encompass the whole world between its covers. Writing in a moment that was shaped by the political and intellectual frameworks of the late Enlightenment, Morse presented himself as reluctant philosopher who sought to share his encyclopedic knowledge with a domestic audience. His geography took seriously the goal of being both American and universal at the same time.

Almost sixty years later, the largest American publishing firm, Harper and Brothers, issued a slim volume with the considerably more prosaic title *Harper's New York and Erie Rail-road Guide-book*. Although it was Harper's first foray into the burgeoning genre of guidebooks, it too was entirely typical of its moment. As its title suggested, it offered limited and focused geographical information designed for maximum utility for travelers along one particular rail line. It was produced on mechanized printing equipment by a large firm that made its publishing decisions according to its calculation of supply and demand in the market. It was written and illustrated to fill this demand by content producers who were already members of Harper and Brothers' stable of authors and illustrators. In short, it was a standard product of the booming midcentury culture industry.

The wide gulf between Morse's geography and Harper and Brothers' guidebook was representative of the fundamental structural and intellectual changes that reshaped the distribution of geographical information over the first half of the nineteenth century. Early national Americans lived in what Matthew Edney has called "later Enlightenment elite cartographic culture." In this culture, "production of *knowledge* depended not only on the measured survey and observation of the landscape but also on the reconstitution and interpretation of the resultant data to create a single corpus of geographic knowledge." This data could be rationalized through the use of "reason," which would "reconcile conflicting observations of points or view so that all phenomena could be systematically described within a single 'archive.'"[1] But by midcentury, the intellectual project of universal geography had retreated to the cheap textbooks and rote memorization exercises of common school classrooms, and to the professionalizing discipline of academic geography. Most geographical information available on booksellers' shelves came instead from large commercial concerns that sought to publish only what their customers would buy, no more and no less. The new business techniques and national market orientation of these publishers drove significant innovation in the formats and genres through which this information was delivered, leading to a world of geographical publishing that was both more varied and more specialized than the heavy tomes of Jedidiah Morse.

The emerging dominance of culture industry practices led to an explosion in geographical publishing in the 1840s. Ever-larger quantities of geographical information were produced and distributed to an American audience with a seemingly limitless reading appetite, in both new and established genres. But this explosion in information availability was not evenly distributed across space. Some regions, routes, and resources were covered extensively by commercially produced texts, while other fell into or remained in obscurity. This unevenness was a direct result of the increasing market sophistication of the big New York and Philadelphia publishing houses; they sought to print only what they could produce cheaply and what would reliably sell to the largest possible audience. Although big midcentury commercial publishers like Harper and Brothers lacked modern market research techniques, they nevertheless understood their product well enough to focus on heavily traveled areas, like those along the route of the New York and Erie Railroad. The sheer quantity of geographical information available in the American market-place of print grew enormously, but its scope also narrowed, especially compared to the goal of universality espoused by Morse's generation.

In many ways, this deep structural change in the mechanisms of geographical knowledge production and distribution was not unique. The emergence of large, integrated commercial publishers that sought to dominate national book sales reshaped countless cultural and intellectual endeavors across the nineteenth century.[2] Although it was reflective of broader trends, the commodification of geographical information has its own specific history that was shaped by the processes of gathering, producing, and sharing knowledge about space. The first authors and printers who moved away from Enlightenment universality were a generation of local businessmen and boosters who sought to deploy geographical information strategically in order to drive growth in their hometowns and home states beginning in the 1810s. Around the same time, a distinct group of entrepreneurs, printers, and engravers began to specialize in publishing geographical texts, first in Philadelphia and then in New York. This specialization allowed them to produce these expensive print objects more efficiently and distribute them more widely. However, that very innovation made the new genres pioneered by the local boosters and geographical specialists appealing to the large generalist industrial publishers that emerged in the 1840s and 1850s. By the eve of the Civil War, all of these groups produced geographical knowledge for sale to American readers who benefited from its unprecedented scale and variety of forms.

As with other culture industries, the tumbling rush of affordable entertainment existed alongside an imperative for standardization. But since much of this new geographical print was produced for use by travelers on the roads, rivers, and rails of the United States, this standardization shaped the real possibilities for travel on the ground. A variety of profit motives drove the creation of specialized guidebooks and gazetteers that enticed travelers onto the road with simple instructions and enticing descriptions of picturesque scenery and lively destinations. But these commercially produced texts enabled travel over a relatively limited set of routes, to a relatively limited set of destinations—both of which were selected by the logic of the market—which served to foreclose possibilities at the same time that new ones were produced. This new kind of travel, both enabled and limited by the commodification of geographical information, was undertaken by what contemporaries increasingly called "tourists." The promoters, geographers, printers, and publishers who propelled this process of commodification did not invent tourism, but they did create the conceptual paradigms and material conditions of knowledge production that made it possible. The emergence of tourism and the growth of the print industries were inextricably linked in that tourists' experiences were profoundly mediated by the changing conditions of print.

If the mid-nineteenth-century American geographical publishing industry was shaped by the innovative and disruptive forces of the culture industry, then its forebears at the turn of the nineteenth century were still deeply rooted in an earlier Enlightenment culture of geographical knowledge. The content of these early national geographies was shaped by the politics of the postrevolutionary moment, but the framework of the genre was still derived from imported prerevolutionary texts. The authors and printers who produced this boom shared with their Enlightenment forebears a number of fundamental assumptions about the purposes and processes of geographical knowledge production. They understood their work to be the product of individual publicly minded thinkers, who worked cooperatively but who nevertheless had distinct and identifiable intellectual voices. Their tone was collaborative because they understood themselves to be engaged in a collective project of knowledge production with universality as its goal, by which they meant both the acquisition of universal knowledge as well as its wide distribution toward the ends of universal geographical literacy. They imagined that this universal absorption of universal knowledge would happen in a sedentary context, in homes and classrooms, and that its production would also be largely, albeit not exclusively, a sedentary intellectual project. And even though their geographical ambitions were limitless, the means by which they produced their volumes were profoundly local, since early national printers mostly produced and distributed their wares on a limited scale. The content of these early geographies may have been "Americanized," but the larger culture of geographical knowledge in which they wrote was deeply rooted in the vernacular transatlantic Enlightenment.[3] Above all, they sought to build a nation of enlightened citizens, not mobile travelers.

Jedidiah Morse was the first and most prominent geographical author in the early republic, but he was far from the only one. Beginning in the late 1780s, American authors penned large numbers of new maps, schoolbooks, works of geography, and even geographically inspired novels designed to feed a voracious public appetite for geographical texts with an American accent.[4] They created "Americanized" versions of old British geographies and generated new texts that were patterned on British examples.[5] While teaching at a school for young women in New Haven in the 1780s, Morse felt the need for a concise, accurate, and affordable text "to facilitate the acquisition of geographical knowledge" of the new nation. He began to collect relevant information for a fresh American geography, from "a great variety of authors, miscellaneous papers, and verbal information," intending at first to circulate it in manuscript form. However, upon "the advice of several worthy gentlemen," Morse decided to publish his work in order to "exhibit it to public view." In doing so, Morse hoped not only to supply the school market with "a concise, accurate and comprehensive description of the terraqueous globe" but also to supply individuals with a cheap volume for home use.[6] The result of his labor was *Geography Made Easy*, a textbook printed in 1784, which launched his career publishing geographies in a variety of formats for both juvenile and adult audiences, and which inaugurated a lively trade in published geographical knowledge in the early republic. Early national Americans bought up geographical monographs, geographical grammars, gazetteers, and atlases in a range of formats, from slim primary textbooks to weighty library volumes.

This endeavor of producing universal geographical literacy attracted a diverse cohort of contributors. Morse's geographical publications turned into a veritable franchise that outlived the man himself, who died in 1826. *Geography Made Easy* survived in print in various forms until the 1820s, with multiple editions issued almost annually along the east coast. *The American Universal Geography*, a more comprehensive two-volume text intended for the home audience, was first published in 1793 and remained in print until 1819, in both full-length and abridged editions. *The American Gazetteer*, a reference text Morse created by restructuring the content of his *American Universal Geography* into alphabetical order in 1797, was similarly widely distributed along the coast and in the interior, and remained in print until 1810. Morse also developed *Geography Made Easy* into a series of other volumes for classroom use, including *Elements of Geography* in the 1790s, and *A New System of Geography*, a schoolbook that combined a geographical grammar and an atlas, that he produced with his son in the 1820s.[7]

Morse's prodigious output competed with texts from a wide range of other geographers. A Philadelphia author, engraver, and publisher named Joseph Scott loomed similarly large in the 1790s and 1800s, with a series of variously titled gazetteers, an atlas, and a textbook for classroom use.

Like Morse, Scott embraced the rhetoric of universality, with titles like *The New and Universal Gazetteer; Or, Modern Geographical Diction-ary*, published in 1799. Other writers participated in more limited ways. Benjamin Workman, a prodigious almanac author, published a text-book entitled *Elements of Geography* from the early 1790s to the 1810s. Caleb Bingham, a publisher and bookseller in Boston, offered *A Short but Comprehensive System of the Geography of the World* during the first decade of the nineteenth century. Nathaniel Dwight, a Connecticut doc-tor, minister, and textbook pioneer, contributed to Bingham's text and published other school texts of his own. Even Susanna Rowson, better remembered as the author of early national bestseller *Charlotte Temple*, published "universal" geographies in 1804 and 1818. This list is hardly comprehensive, but it suggests how vibrant the print culture of universal geographical knowledge was in the first decades of the new nation.[8]

Despite their variety, these early producers and distributors of geo-graphical knowledge all positioned themselves prominently in their own texts. Geographies from this period generally included extensive introductory material in which the author addressed the reader directly, explaining the scope of the work, its intended purpose, and the methods used to compile the information contained therein. As a result, these works had a personal air to them; they were products of individual, iden-tifiable seekers of knowledge. As such, these texts looked backward to an eighteenth-century intellectual culture in which individual philosophers dedicated themselves to collecting, arranging, and distributing knowl-edge in order to contribute to the common good.

Early national geographical authors positioned their texts as pre-cisely such contributions to the common good by characterizing their own decision to publish as reluctant. As we have seen, Morse claimed to have inaugurated the genre in 1784 only because "several worthy gentlemen" encouraged him to do so. Rowson struck a similar note in 1806. She had been encouraged to submit her manuscript entitled *An Abridgement of Universal Geography* to the press, but she "feared the implication of arrogance and presumption." But like Morse, she allowed herself to be persuaded by "the flattering persuasions of several friends."[9] Morse even offered to give up his first gazetteer project in 1797. In his introduction to *The American Gazetteer*, he described a moment when he learned that "Capt. Thomas Hutchins, then Geographer General of the United States, contemplated a Work of the same kind." Morse was concerned about competing with Hutchins, who, "being from the nature of his office, [was] far more competent to the task," and so he "resigned

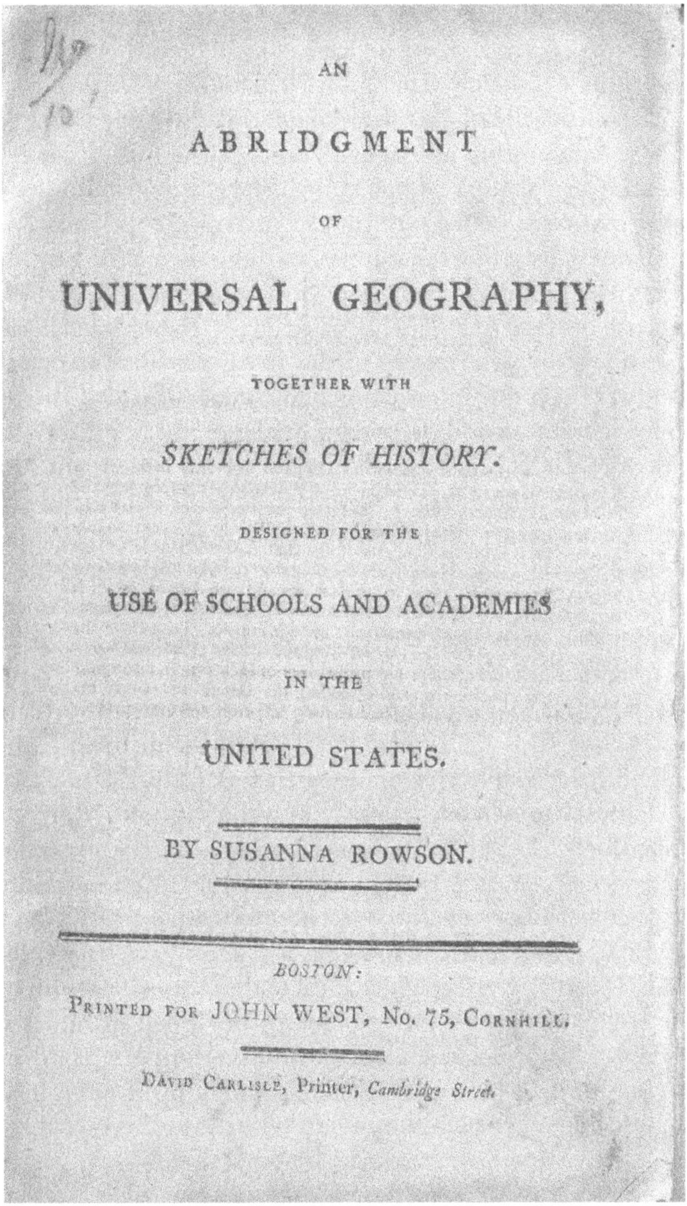

AN

ABRIDGMENT

OF

UNIVERSAL GEOGRAPHY,

TOGETHER WITH

SKETCHES OF HISTORY.

DESIGNED FOR THE

USE OF SCHOOLS AND ACADEMIES

IN THE

UNITED STATES.

BY SUSANNA ROWSON.

BOSTON:

PRINTED FOR JOHN WEST, No. 75, CORNHILL.

DAVID CARLISLE, Printer, Cambridge Street.

FIGURE 1.1. The title page of Susanna Rowson's *An Abridgment of Universal Geography* (1806). Note the prominence of her name below the title. Courtesy of the William L. Clements Library, University of Michigan.

his pretensions, and made him a tender of all the materials he had collected." Hutchins, though, would have none of it, and "with a kindness
and generosity which flowed naturally from his amiable and noble mind,
Capt. Hutchins declined the offer, relinquished his design, and put into
the hands of the Author all the collections he had made, together with
his maps and explanatory pamphlets, which have contributed not a little
to enrich this Work."[10] This performative disavowal of personal ambition
was meant to suggest that these authors wrote only for the public benefit.

Nevertheless, authors like Morse and Rowson were careful to maintain a sense of their individuality as scholars. They personalized their
work with lengthy descriptions of the efforts they had undertaken to
collect timely, accurate information about national space. These efforts
were often literally embodied, in that the author's personal travel under-
wrote their research. "To those who are but partially acquainted with the
geography of the United States," Joseph Scott wrote in his 1795 gazetteer,
"I think it is necessary to observe, that I have travelled through many
of the states myself, and have been in several of the towns throughout
the Union."[11] Similarly, Morse emphasized his travel experience when
establishing his authority. His gazetteer was published after Scott's,
which allowed Scott to claim the distinction of issuing the first American gazetteer, but Morse noted that he had contemplated such a project
before Scott did. This contemplation took place on the road. "The design
of compiling and publishing an American Gazetteer, was conceived,"
Morse claimed, "as early as the year 1786, while [I] was travelling through
the United States, for the purpose of collecting materials for [my] *American Geography.*"[12] With this simple introduction, Morse reminded his
readers that he had personally collected information around the United
States; that his geographical knowledge was already proven in print; and
that even if Scott's gazetteer had made it to the presses before his own, he
was the originator of the idea. And indeed, Morse had already reminded
his readers of his own acquaintance with American geography in 1789.
"Four years have been employed in" compiling his *American Geography*, a period during which Morse had "visited the several states in the
Union."[13] Morse and Scott may have claimed that they were interested
only in contributing to the common stock of knowledge, but they were
still individual, embodied geographers with a keen sense of professional
rivalry.

Although disputes about precedence like that between Morse and
Scott in the 1790s did occur, most authors nevertheless conceived of
the early national print culture of geographical knowledge as a project

of collective knowledge formation.[14] Ultimately, relatively few authors cited their time on the road like Morse and Scott; more commonly, they named each other, and their predecessors, as their most important sources of information. In *American Geography*, Morse claimed to have "maintained an extensive correspondence with men of Science; and in every instance . . . endeavoured to derive his information from the most authentic sources." Morse "also submitted his manuscripts to the inspection of Gentlemen in the states which they particularly described, for their correction."[15] In the eighteenth century, the categories of "Gentlemen" and "men of Science" were not distinct from each other; for authors immersed in Enlightenment intellectual culture, "men of Science" were invariably "Gentlemen," and together they represented a national intellectual community collectively dedicated to perfecting geographical knowledge. Joseph Scott took advantage of his residence in the national capital, Philadelphia, to gather information for his 1795 gazetteer. He "received [his] information from several of the members of Congress," an easily accessible network of "enlightened gentlemen" with widely distributed local knowledge. He stressed that these "gentlemen" showed a "politeness" in assisting him that was "unaccompanied with that fastidious pride, and sullen haughtiness, which too often characterize the European legislators." Scott also consulted with officials of the executive branch. He gathered military information from the secretary of war, trade information from the commissioner of the revenue, and "necessary and useful information" from "Mr. Patton, of the Post-Office."[16] Lucky to be in Philadelphia, Scott was surrounded by "gentlemen" ready for intellectual collaboration.

A national community of learned citizens was not only a resource for authors like Morse and Scott; it also described their intended audience. Although Morse situated himself in a community of "gentlemen," he imagined his audience to include refined young people of both sexes. In his first edition of *Geography Made Easy*, he included an elaborate dedication addressed "To the Young Gentlemen and Ladies, Throughout the United States." He extended his "ardent Wishes for their Improvement" in "a Science, no longer esteemed as a polite and agreeable Accomplishment only, but as a very necessary and important Part of Education."[17] Morse aspired to grow this national community of learned citizens by spreading universal geographical knowledge. Universality was variously defined; sometimes it meant knowledge of the entire world, and sometimes it meant, as the title of an 1833 textbook would have it, *Rudiments of National Knowledge*.[18] In either case, the goal was to offer generalized, comprehensive geographical literacy rather than specialist knowledge. Broad geographical literacy was an old Enlightenment goal; as Thomas Salmon put it in his 1754 *New Geographical and Historical Grammar*, the purpose of geographical publishing was to acquaint every "rational creature" with "the State of the World about him, and the Manners, Customs, and History, of the several Nations his Cotemporaries [*sic*]."[19] Training for geographical literacy began in childhood; Morse's *Elements of Geography* recommended a "'Geographical Catechism,' for the use of children under 8 years of age."[20] Mature readers faced an equal imperative to understand the world around them, through comprehensive geographies like Morse's and reference texts like gazetteers that kept such information directly at hand. *The American Geography* of 1789 was intended "to accommodate Schools and private Families," because "every citizen ought to be thoroughly acquainted with the geography of his own country, and to have some idea, at least, of the other parts of the world."[21] These early texts sought to teach general geography to an expanding community of learned citizens, in a socially and politically useful manner.

Gazetteers were the most common geographical reference texts in period, and they were similarly "universal" in their coverage. Gazetteers had their origins in early eighteenth-century geographical indexes designed to accompany newspaper reading.[22] Joseph Scott championed the genre's potential for universality, comparing it to a "great . . . landscape, when the shades are judiciously disposed, and fully drawn." His 1795 *United States Gazetteer* was written to increase Americans' geographical literacy beyond "their personal knowledge of Geography [which is] confined to a few places." This universal knowledge would help citizens fulfill "the indispensible [*sic*] duty which every man owes to himself, to become acquainted with the geography of the country wherein he resides."[23] This common emphasis on broad acquaintance was characteristic of a print culture of geographical knowledge populated by "encyclopedists" who valued comprehensive breadth of knowledge over depth of specialization.[24] Claims of universality were not always about the scope and content of the work—after all, many geographies claimed to be "universal"—but rather about the Enlightenment intellectual tradition in which they situated themselves.

Morse and Scott's peregrinations notwithstanding, the early national geographical encyclopedist, whether author or reader, was ultimately a sedentary figure. Authors were more likely to have sat in their studies consulting earlier geographical works than they were to have "sedulously explored" the United States, as Morse put it in 1790.[25] "In leading my young travellers round the globe," Rowson wrote, "I collected from the authors with whom I was most acquainted, particularly Guthrie, Walker, and Morse, every thing which I thought could engage attention or awaken curiosity."[26] Rowson's entire engagement with "universal" geography was through the written word. And in describing her students as "young travellers," Rowson spoke metaphorically. Her slim volume, like most of its competitors, was designed for home or schoolhouse use. It was organized into sections, ordered from most general to most specific, and included a series of geographical and historical exercises to help students retain what they read. Her contemporaries similarly pitched their texts to armchair travelers. Morse's *Geography Made Easy* sought to "bring this valuable branch of knowledge home to common schools, and to the cottage fire-side."[27] At the turn of the century, universal geographical knowledge was a domestic pursuit, suitable for the schoolroom, the library, and the "fire-side," not for the muddy thoroughfares of the new nation. Of course some early national Americans traveled, but they did so without the practical or conceptual support of the print culture of their era, which looked backward to the eighteenth century as much as it did forward to the nineteenth.

The American print culture of geographical knowledge began to move decisively away from the paradigm of universality in the 1810s. The demographic and economic growth that the United States experienced after 1815 brought a new generation of geographical authors and publishers to the marketplace, many of whom were motivated more by economic boosterism than by the production of universal knowledge. The broader landscape of American publishing entered a period of rapid innovation and consolidation as Philadelphia and New York entrepreneurs deployed capital and technology on an unprecedented scale to build a national market for industrially produced books. The introduction of these new market pressures into the print culture of geographical knowledge changed the kinds of books that were produced. Authors and publishers increasingly packaged and repackaged geographical knowledge that could be efficiently produced and distributed on a national scale; in other words, they published what was easy to gather and would be widely popular. This new economic and cultural configuration transformed the print culture of geographical knowledge from one inflected by Enlightenment preoccupations to one that was dominated by textual commodities produced by and for an increasingly national market of readers.

In the 1810s and 1820s, the turn away from universal geographical knowledge was driven by a generation of regional boosters who saw publishing geographies as a way to drive local economic development.[28] In some cases, these boosters were the same authors and printers who had sold universal geographical literacy to turn-of-the-century readers, but increasingly they were joined by a cohort of more locally rooted authors who used local print jobbers and smaller regional publishers to offer gazetteers and guidebooks to their own backyards. These generally slim, ephemeral volumes were produced to inform a wider regional and national audience about the economic strengths and aesthetic charms of their regions, in order to attract investment and visitors. The regions most commonly covered by these texts unsurprisingly mirrored the geography of print infrastructure in the early republic, with New York, Pennsylvania, and New England receiving the most treatment in early years, and with coverage spreading into the Old Northwest in the 1820s and 1830s. The South and Southwest produced very few booster geographies through the Civil War, a reflection of print infrastructure's relatively slow spread in the slave states.[29] These boosters were the first to pursue an openly nonuniversal geography, and in doing so they created new genres that recruited leisure travelers for the first time.

These authors and printers first turned to publishing slimmer, more focused gazetteers in order to promote knowledge of and development in their own regions. "Universal" gazetteers like Morse's and Scott's continued to be widely available in updated editions, but in the 1810s and 1820s they were joined by a raft of state-level gazetteers that expressed more utilitarian goals. For example, in 1819, John C. Pease and John M. Niles, brothers-in-law and publishers of the *Hartford Times*, undertook *A Gazetteer of the States of Connecticut and Rhode-Island* because of the "general utility" of such a volume. In it, they proposed to introduce "the people of the several States" to "their local resources and advantages; the most important interests, whether of agriculture, manufactures or commerce; the most conspicuous departments of industry, and the prevailing local characteristics."[30] They sought a "general diffusion of information" that would not only serve national unification but that would also "contribute to the general improvement."

The promotional thrust of this generation of gazetteers was generally framed by this kind of noble intention, but their content trumpeted the region's geographical blessings, inhabitants, and economy. Horatio Gates Spafford's 1813 *A Gazetteer of the State of New-York*, a pioneering state-level work, included voluminous descriptions of the state that painted it in the most flattering economic light. About New York's rivers and canals, Spafford claimed that "no portion of the United States enjoys such facilities for inland navigation, as the State of New-York; combining, in all consideration, the objects and the means of intercourse." Its roads were "certainly very good, and conveniently disposed," which supported the "improved state of our manufactures, and their rapid increase in extent and variety within a few years." His description of the state's agricultural potential was long and loving, a potential quickly being exploited by the combination of a diverse population of "ancient inhabitants" and "the New-England people, [with whom] have come their improved agriculture, their enterprize, their ingenuity in the arts, and their social habits." Striking what would become an increasingly common note for New York boosters, Spafford claimed that the "Mineral Waters of this state . . . are universally acknowledged to excel in richness and variety."[31] Whatever their claims to interest in the "general improvement," authors like Spafford were clearly more invested in the improvement of their home states.

Spafford, Pease, and Niles were pioneers in what would become a flood of state-level gazetteers in the 1820s and 1830s. These texts were mostly authored by residents of the states they covered, who were generally businessmen who had a direct interest in attracting attention, visitors, immigrants, and investment to their states. For example, John Kilbourn opened a bookstore in Columbus, Ohio, around 1812, just after the town had been established to serve as the capital of the new state. In 1816, he published *The Ohio Gazetteer: Or, Topographical Dictionary, Containing a Description of the Several Counties, Towns, Villages and Settlements in the State of Ohio*, the first book published in the new settlement and one that remained in print under various titles for more than twenty years. Later editions made its boosterish intent even more clear; in 1826, it became *The Ohio Manual* and in 1837 *The Ohio Gazetteer and Travellers Guide*.[32] As a businessman established in the state capital, Kilbourn was deeply interested in Ohio's future, and he shaped his geographical work to further that interest. Similarly, Alphonso Wetmore, an early resident of Missouri and U.S. Army paymaster, worked as a trader along the Santa Fe Trail in the late 1820s. In 1837, he wrote a *Gazetteer of the State of Missouri* that was published in St. Louis and that sought to incentivize similar investment in the state.[33] A glance at *Trübner's Bibliographical Guide to American Literature* from 1859 shows that Kilbourn and Wetmore were not unique cases; the catalogue listed more than a dozen state-level gazetteers published between the 1810s and the 1850s.[34] Their authors included printers, ministers, and teachers—professions that had participated in the print culture of geographical knowledge from the earliest days of the United States—but also included merchants, lawyers, and land agents, who were all newcomers to the print culture of geographical knowledge.[35] These new authors wrote to encourage development in the territories and states where their livelihoods lay. They were less interested in universal knowledge than in furthering specific economic interests.

With their strict alphabetical organization, gazetteers were blunt instruments with which to drive migrants, investment, and visitors to a region. By their very nature, reference works resisted promotional arguments, a shortcoming that was tacitly acknowledged by their authors' tendency to integrate them into larger "emigrants' guides" in the 1840s and 1850s. For example, John Newhall's *A Glimpse of Iowa in 1846* was penned by a sometime merchant and full-time promoter of settlement in the new territory and locally printed in Burlington, along the Mississippi River. It organized its information under the usual gazetteer headings derived from natural and political divisions, but it also included chapters with titles like "What productions are most profitable to cultivate," "Prospects for mechanics and laborers," and "Persons best qualified to emigrate."[36] If eighteenth-century gazetteers had been intended as universal geographical references for curious readers, then by the middle of the nineteenth century many of their successors had abandoned that purpose in favor of providing selected geographical morsels as promotional advertising.

In the more thickly settled eastern regions, local boosters had to rethink their geographical publishing strategy more thoroughly. Rather than seeking emigrants, local boosters in upstate New York, western Virginia, and the White Mountains of New Hampshire sought to attract leisure travelers who would patronize a growing network of inns, hotels, and attractions by publishing cheap, disposable, and up-to-date guides to their regions' infrastructure and destinations. As a strategy of local economic development, attracting temporary visitors had different ends and deployed different means in print. These eastern boosters sought to bring cash-bearing customers to local businesses that supplied services, rather than producers and laborers for farms and industry. Even though their texts similarly described the natural and man-made features of their area, including landscape and infrastructure, they tended to emphasize beauty, convenience, and refinement rather than productive capacity and ease of investment. The resulting slim volumes represented the emergence of a new genre in the print culture of geographical knowledge: the guidebook.[37]

This innovation first appeared in the Erie Canal district of upstate New York in the 1820s, where the conditions were ripe for local boosters to turn to promoting recreational travel. The region was filling up from the rush of settlement that followed the Iroquois cessions of the 1790s, bringing with it a cohort of ambitious newcomers who sought novel ways to profit from the landscape. It was the epicenter of intensive infrastructure development, with the establishment of steam navigation on the Hudson in the 1810s and the commencement of construction on the Erie Canal in 1817.[38] The growing towns served by these transportation facilities also quickly developed the network of printers, publishers, and booksellers necessary to support a local print culture of geographical knowledge.[39] Finally, some of these towns were located near significant natural features that could be advertised, particularly the scenery of the Hudson valley, the mineral springs of Saratoga County, and the cataract at Niagara Falls. This combination of natural and cultural features and intensive capital investment created an environment that fostered booster creativity.

The first such booster to experiment with this new formula for promotion was Gideon Davison, a printer and newspaperman who arrived in the still raw settlement of Saratoga Springs in 1819. He had trained as a printer in his native Vermont and in New York City, and he came to the burgeoning springs town to make his fortune. He set up a print shop, began issuing the *Saratoga Sentinel*, created a reading room and a lending library in the Pavilion Hotel, and eventually became a wealthy man through local real estate investments. Saratoga had neither fertile farmland nor convenient water access, the most important prerequisites for commercial success in the 1820s, but it did have good mineral springs in an era in which Americans with access to wealth and leisure time were increasingly interested in the health-giving properties of such water and in the social possibilities of spa towns.[40] Thus, rather than publishing a promotional gazetteer like his contemporary Horatio Gates Spafford, Davison issued *The Fashionable Tour; Or, A Trip to the Springs, Niagara, Quebeck, and Boston, in the Summer of 1821*. Historians of tourism agree that *The Fashionable Tour* was the first clearly identifiable American guidebook, offering advice about routes and destinations that was explicitly aimed at leisure travelers, and regularly reissued with updated information.[41] Davison's guidebook remained in print through the mid-1840s, a period of rapid growth in Saratoga and of its emerging dominance as a leisure destination.[42] The growing number of visitors drew a significant permanent population, to the benefit of early investors like Davison.[43]

Guidebooks like Davison's differed from gazetteers like Spafford's in critical details of content and organization. Rather than describing the natural and social features that made New York an appealing place to settle or invest, guidebooks described, in Davison's phrase, "sources of interest and delight to the stranger."[44] On this earliest version of the Fashionable Tour, these "sources of interest" included the scenery of the Hudson, Mohawk, St. Lawrence, and Champlain valleys, and of the Catskills and the Berkshires; the springs towns of Saratoga County; Niagara Falls; and battlefields from the French and Indian War, the Revolutionary War, and the War of 1812. The individual entries were dominated by qualitative description rather than the quantitative tallying of gazetteer entries. The destinations were arranged geographically rather than alphabetically or thematically, along the route of travel that Davison's readers would take, and were interwoven with practical transportation information like tables of distances and steamboat schedules. The earliest guidebooks were slim, disposable volumes, with spare descriptions and only the most general information about the practicalities of travel, but they eased the progress of early leisure travelers along the still underdeveloped routes of upstate New York by offering a coherent outline of a Fashionable Tour and at least a rough guide to the practicalities of such a tour. It met an emergent demand for leisure travel with a polished product that sought to increase that demand and direct it toward upstate New York.

Davison was the first booster to issue a guidebook in order to entice travelers to his town, but his idea was quickly adopted by other regional businessmen looking to build on Saratoga's success. In 1830, the young New York firm of J. & J. Harper printed Robert Vandewater's *The Tourist, Or Pocket Manual for Travellers*, another cheap, slim, disposable volume that covered much of the same territory as Davison's, offering practical route information and "scenes and objects worthy of notice, and calculated to excite curiosity." Vandewater's interest in this geographical material was revealed by his preface, in which he bragged that "the Compiler having long been connected with one of the North River steamboats, has had the best opportunities of obtaining correct information."[45] Vandewater served throughout the 1830s and 1840s as the New York City agent for a line of canal packet boats running between Manhattan, Utica, and Oswego, and unsurprisingly, his guide favored destinations along that line of travel.[46] Like Davison's, Vandewater's "pocket manual" first guided its readers up the Hudson valley, although it offered considerably more detail about boats and schedules and relatively less

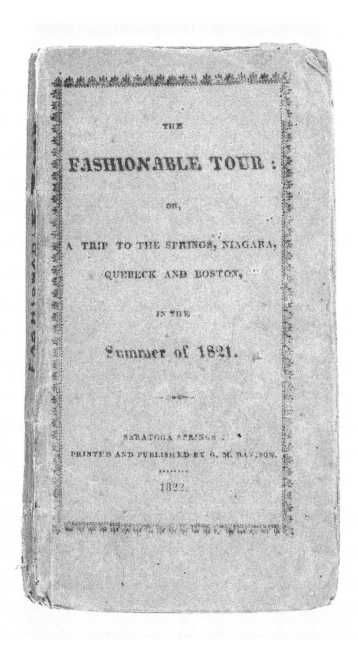

THE

FASHIONABLE TOUR :

OR,

A TRIP TO THE SPRINGS, NIAGARA,

QUEBECK AND BOSTON,

IN THE

Summer of 1821.

SARATOGA SPRINGS :
PRINTED AND PUBLISHED BY G. M. DAVISON.

1822.

FIGURE 1.2. Gideon Davison's first guidebook. Courtesy of the American Antiquarian Society.

description of riverside scenery. But at Albany, it turned its readers westward along the Erie Canal, depicting canalside attractions in more detail en route to Niagara. Vandewater did include a brief chapter on the route to and attractions of Saratoga, an acknowledgment of the springs' growing appeal, but it was tacked on the end as a postscript. The main point of the guidebook was to entice leisure travelers to follow the route served by Vandewater's packet boats, an evidently successful strategy, since the guidebook was regularly reissued for a decade after its original publication.

A similar strategy was deployed by Samuel De Veaux, an early and prominent business and political leader in the village of Niagara Falls. After moving to western New York in 1803 at the tender age of fourteen to work for the prominent land speculators Oliver Phelps and Nathaniel Gorham, De Veaux pursued mercantile opportunities around the region before settling at Niagara in 1817. By the mid-1830s, his interests in trade and real estate had made him the richest person in the area, which he parlayed into positions of political and ecclesiastical leadership.[47] In 1839, he wrote *The Falls of Niagara, Or Tourist's Guide to This Wonder of Nature*, which was published locally in Buffalo. De Veaux's guide was less technical than Vandewater's, intended instead to answer "every inquiry . . . that is usually made by strangers." De Veaux also thought that "his small publication [would] form an agreeable present from those who visit the Falls, to their friends and children at home, when they return refreshed from their pleasant and amusing tour."[48] The resulting volume combined local history anecdotes and chatty advice about seeing the Falls and touring the vicinity, and drew attention to the richness of the natural and historical destinations in the area. In 1841, De Veaux reissued his work with another Buffalo firm under the title *The Traveller's Own Book, to Saratoga Springs, Niagara Falls and Canada*, with added material on the Fashionable Tour route and Saratoga, but like both Davison and Vandewater, he ensured that his readers' paths led through the village where his business interests lay.[49]

The boosters of upstate New York were earliest and most aggressive in their use of guidebooks to attract paying visitors, but promoters in other regions began to make similar efforts in the 1840s. National interest in the scenery of the White Mountains of New Hampshire began to grow after a spectacular landslide killed a family high in Crawford Notch in 1826; the national press coverage and fictionalized retellings that followed the disaster at the Willey House created an opportunity that local entrepreneurs seized in subsequent decades.[50] Printers in the mountains, in Concord, the state capital, and in Boston began to issue guidebooks to the region in the mid-1840s to bring travelers' business to their doorsteps.[51] For example, John Spaulding, a partner in the new Tip-Top Summit House on Mount Washington, published *Historical Relics of the White Mountains: Also, a Concise White Mountain Guide*, in 1855. This guidebook, like De Veaux's, combined colorful local tales, natural history, and practical guidebook information to attract visitors to the area and ultimately to Spaulding's establishment on the mountaintop. The book was printed locally by John R. Hitchcock, who would take over management of the Mount Washington summit houses from Spaulding in 1861, which suggests that it was a thoroughly homegrown attempt to build a local economy around leisure travelers.[52]

In western Virginia, local boosters initially had to look farther afield to have their guidebooks printed and distributed. The region's main appeal for leisure travelers were the wide variety of health-giving mineral springs scattered across its mountain valleys, so its most prominent boosters were hotel owners and doctors, who were sometimes the same person.[53] In 1839, Thomas Goode, a doctor and proprietor of the Virginia Hot Springs, had a collection of case studies and testimonials attesting to the efficacy of his water entitled *The Invalid's Guide to the Virginia Hot Springs* printed in Richmond.[54] Goode's slim volume was not a guidebook because it assumed that his readership would know where the Hot Springs were located and how to get there, but it foreshadowed later, more comprehensive guides like William Burke's 1842 *The Mineral Springs of Western Virginia: With Remarks on Their Use, and the Diseases to Which They Are Applicable*. Like Goode, Burke was a doctor and the proprietor of Red Sulphur Springs, and he pitched his book toward health-seekers and those who "want that calm repose, that freedom from restraint, that omission of conventional uses, which render the society of our Virginia Springs so delightful."[55] Burke's book guided his readers to more than just his own establishment, although he could not resist denigrating the competing White Sulphur water. He also provided more information about getting to Red Sulphur than to any of the other hotels, a choice that was perhaps influenced by his personal stake in the Salt Sulphur and Red Sulphur Springs Turnpike Company.[56] Finally, John J. Moorman, the resident physician of the much larger establishment at White Sulphur Springs, compiled a similar work in 1847, which combined extensive analyses of the waters with abbreviated route information for tours that all terminated at his place of employment.[57] Both Burke and Moorman wrote several fresh editions of their guidebooks in the 1850s as the

Virginia springs entered a new period of popularity, and each new version contained relatively more geographical information and relatively less analysis of the waters, making them increasingly resemble northern boosters' guidebooks.[58]

Unlike upstate New York and New Hampshire, western Virginia had extremely limited print infrastructure in the 1830s and 1840s; indeed, as late as 1856, contemporary estimates showed that the value of all the books printed in upstate New York was roughly equivalent to the value of all the books printed in the entire South, and the same was true for rural New England outside of Boston.[59] As a result, early Virginia promotional guidebooks were less likely to be wholly locally produced affairs. Burke's 1842 guidebook was published by the emerging national firm Wiley & Putnam in New York, and Moorman's 1847 guidebook was printed in Philadelphia. By the 1850s, the print infrastructure of Richmond had grown sufficiently that western Virginia boosters could produce and distribute their guidebooks relatively locally, and indeed most guides that focused on the Virginia springs were produced in that city until the outbreak of the Civil War temporarily impeded leisure travel in the Old Dominion in 1860. Thus the business strategy pioneered by Davison in Saratoga in the 1820s, which sought to drive local economic development by attracting leisure travelers with time and money to spend, was replicated in subsequent decades by entrepreneurs across the eastern landscape who had local scenery and history that could be sold. The result was the rise and dominance of a new genre of printed geographical knowledge, one that encouraged active travel in search of leisure rather than the contemplative study of geography.

The era of booster dominance of gazetteer and guidebook publication ultimately did not last long. By the 1840s, the commercialization and industrialization of book production that was remaking the broader landscape of American print culture was having an effect on the production of geographical knowledge. Large firms in the major publishing centers of Philadelphia and New York increasingly took over the publication of geographical knowledge. As with the boosters' texts, the scope and content of their publications were not dictated by the old Enlightenment goals of universality, but they were also not driven by the promotional particularities of local economies. Instead, their catalogues were shaped by the logic of the emerging national market for mass-produced books; they published what they could produce at the lowest cost and sell in the largest quantities. Within the print culture of geographical knowledge, the greatest efficiencies could be found publishing guidebooks for routes and destinations that were already established and made popular by the booster texts, which meant that, by the 1850s, guidebooks were more widely available than ever but also more similar to each other than ever.

The centralization and ultimate mass production of the print culture of geographical knowledge happened slowly and unevenly. It was initiated by smaller firms located in major publishing centers that sought to carve out a space for themselves in the increasingly national marketplace for print by specializing in map printing. The first of these specialist firms was founded by John Melish, a Scottish immigrant who settled in Philadelphia in 1812. Before choosing Philadelphia, Melish had made two tours of the United States, which he wrote up and published once he settled down. This experience introduced him to Philadelphia's vibrant community of skilled engravers, two of whom produced maps for his travel narrative. Within a couple of years, Melish had become a prolific publisher of maps and atlases in his own right. He was a publisher in a more modern sense than most of his contemporaries, because while he planned, financed, and distributed his wares, he neither engraved them nor printed them himself, relying instead on the deep well of skilled labor available in Philadelphia.[60] Melish died in 1822, before guidebooks had emerged as an identifiable genre, but nevertheless beginning in 1814 he experimented with a road book entitled *The Traveller's Directory through the United States*. This handbook "was compiled by the author principally with the view of guiding strangers and travellers in their progress through the country." Melish saw such a guide as a conscious extension of his emerging specialization in geographical publishing because, "having systematically engaged in the promulgation of geographical knowledge by the publication of maps, [he] has also been induced to bend his attention to the necessary *descriptions*."[61] Although Melish's directory was not the kind of experiential guide for leisure travelers that Davison would publish almost a decade later, it revealed the emerging business logic of cartographical publishers who wanted to extend their existing specialization into potentially lucrative new markets. Melish had already collected all the relevant geographical data, so publishing a road book represented an opportunity to repackage that data for a new audience, and perhaps drive sales of his existing maps as well.

Although Melish's publishing career was brief, the engravers and printers with whom he worked in Philadelphia built on his model in the 1820s and 1830s. Henry Schenck Tanner, an engraver who worked on Melish's maps and atlases in the late 1810s and 1820s, formed a partnership that undertook map and atlas publishing on its own account in 1819. In 1834, he began publishing *The American Traveller*, a "small volume" that contained a "very concise statement of such facts in relation to the several states, their population, number of counties, area, forms of government, cities, towns, roads, canals, distances, &c. as would be most likely to prove useful to, or the deserve the notice of the traveller." This guidebook ran to ten editions, the last of which was published in New York after Tanner moved his firm there in 1843.[62] Similarly, Samuel Augustus Mitchell came to Philadelphia from Connecticut around 1830 in order to turn his teaching career into one publishing geographical texts. Although he was neither a cartographer nor an engraver, Mitchell's skill as a manager and an editor allowed him take over Tanner's establishment and build it into a business that at its peak employed hundreds of workers and sold tens of thousands of geographical texts annually. He embraced cutting-edge technologies like steel engraving and lithography, and used the large print runs that they enabled to expand his market and drive prices down. Like his contemporaries, he experimented with new publications as a way to build on his emerging dominance in the market for printed maps. His *Mitchell's Traveller's Guide through the United States* contained mostly route tables, destinations, and distances, but it worked well as an adjunct to Mitchell's maps, which was doubtless the point. It was an effective enough extension of Mitchell's geographical expertise that it remained in print as *Mitchell's New Traveller's Guide through the United States and the Canadas* through the Civil War.[63]

Entrepreneurs like Melish, Tanner, and Mitchell made Philadelphia the center of large-scale geographical publishing in the early republic, but as Tanner's late-career migration showed, the center of the national publishing industry was rapidly shifting to New York in the 1830s and 1840s. The seeds of a geographical publishing community existed in New York in the 1820s in the person of bookseller and publisher A. T. Goodrich, an "active though minor figure in New York literary circles" best known as James Fenimore Cooper's first publisher and epistolary confidant.[64] But literature was a sideline for Goodrich; rather, he identified his shop at 124 Broadway as a "geographical establishment."[65] Upon Melish's death in 1822, Goodrich purchased his engraving plates, copyrights, and existing stock, and at the same time he became the first retailer in New York to carry Gideon Davison's pioneering *The Fashionable Tour*.[66] In 1826, Goodrich published the second edition of Theodore Dwight's *The Northern Traveller*, an early competitor to Davison's guidebook, and by the 1830s he had built up an extensive catalogue of maps, gazetteers, and guidebooks. In 1839, Goodrich published his own guidebook, *The North American Tourist*, which tutored its readers on "the regular routine in going east or west." These "routines," Goodrich was careful to note, began "from the vicinity of the fashionable hotels" and passed through locations of "fashionable resort in summer."[67] Like his Philadelphia contemporaries, Goodrich published guidebooks as a natural extension of his geographical specialization.

Goodrich's successors in New York geographical publishing in the 1840s and 1850s operated on a scale beyond what any of the earlier generation of Philadelphia-based publishers, with the exception of Mitchell, could have imagined. A native of New England, John Colton came to the city around 1830 and slowly began to build a business as a map publisher by purchasing existing copyrights and reissuing older maps. Over the next decades, Colton grew his business by moving aggressively into emerging market segments, like railroad maps in the 1850s and Civil War maps in the 1860s. This business savvy allowed the Colton firm to stay in business, under the direction of his sons, into the 1890s.[68] Like Mitchell's firm, Colton's focused on maps and atlases, but it also published various guides, gazetteers, and "views" as supplements for users of those maps. Also like Mitchell's guidebooks, Colton's were assembled from the firm's existing geographical material.[69] At the same moment that Colton was establishing his map business, a young printer from Troy named John Disturnell moved to New York to open a bookstore and publishing firm focused on maps, handbooks, and guidebooks. Like Goodrich before him, Disturnell saw an opportunity to open a "Geographical and Statistical Library" on Broadway, and also like Goodrich, he took advantage of existing geographical publishing talent by partnering with Henry Tanner's son. Although not a cartographer or engraver himself, Disturnell was "a good salesman, industrious and aggressive," who quickly built up a significant catalogue of maps, handbooks, route guides, and guidebooks.[70]

Disturnell made a more consistent effort than did the other geographical specialists to target his guidebooks specifically at the leisure travelers cultivated by the booster authors. Right at the beginning of his career as a New York geographical publisher, in 1835, Disturnell published both *The Picturesque Beauties of the Hudson River and Its Vicinity* and *The Hudson River Guide* (often bound together with *New-York As It Is, in 1835*). The former contained engravings and picturesque descriptions of Hudson valley scenery, and the latter provided practical advice so tourists could see these sights for themselves.[71] In 1836, Disturnell combined these functions into *The Traveller's Guide through the State of New York, Canada, &c: Embracing a General Description of the City of New-York; the Hudson River Guide, and the Fashionable Tour to the Springs and Niagara Falls.* This book repackaged Disturnell's existing material for travelers on the Fashionable Tour, a group of potential consumers already identified and labeled by Gideon Davison more than a decade earlier.[72] Disturnell diversified his engagement with the tourist guidebook market in the 1840s and 1850s. He continued to publish guides to the New York Fashionable Tour under the generic title *The Picturesque Tourist*, but he added regional subguides for the northern states, for the New England or eastern states, for the Great Lakes or western states, and for Canada.[73] He also published guides to specific categories of tourist destinations, like his 1855 *Springs, Water-Falls, Sea-Bathing Resorts and Mountain Scenery of the United States and Canada.*[74] In the 1850s, he supplemented these thicker tourist guides with a series of slimmer "Railroad and Steamboat Guides" that provided updated route, fare, and timetable information for all the latest transportation improvements.[75] Of all the Philadelphia and New York firms that specialized in geographical publishing during the first half of the nineteenth century, Disturnell's most aggressively sought to repackage its geographical information for leisure travelers.

As the tangled history sketched above shows, the world of specialized geographical publishing was overlapping and fundamentally interconnected. A community of publishers in Philadelphia and New York shared business partners, engraving talent, printing plates, and publication credits. The New Yorkers' shops clustered almost within sight of each other along Broadway in the blocks above Trinity Church.[76] The clubby nature of the geographical publishing industry was embodied in the 1851 establishment of the American Geographical and Statistical Society (AGSL). The organizing meeting was held at Disturnell's so-called "Geographical and Statistical Library," which may have given the organization its name. This investment in the institutional organization of the geographical community paid off handsomely for publishers like Disturnell, because the AGSL gave them ready access to jobbing geographical authors who could supply content for their proliferating catalogues. For example, John Calvin Smith, a map engraver and a member of the early governing board of the AGSL, wrote gazetteers and guidebooks for the Tanner firm, for Disturnell, and especially for John Colton from the late 1830s to the late 1850s. Richard Swainson Fisher, a doctor who served as the secretary and librarian of the AGSL in the late 1850s, penned countless descriptive geographies, school textbooks, and guidebooks for J. H.

Colton from 1849 into the 1860s.[77] Thus, by the 1850s, the national print culture of geographical knowledge was embodied by a tightly knit group of specialist publishers, engravers, and jobbing authors in New York who used their knowledge of American geography to dominate an increasingly national market for geographical print and who had learned to repackage that knowledge into a wide variety of genres and formats to meet the diverse needs of different consumers.

But even in the decade of their triumph, the specialist publishers began to face the threat of even larger, better-capitalized firms with unparalleled national market reach. The centralization of talent and resources that the specialists built on lower Broadway and in the American Geographical and Statistical Society created a resource that nonspecialist publishers could use to break into the guidebook market. For example, George Putnam, who established the large industrial publishing firm that became G. P. Putnam's Sons, served on the first governing board of the AGSL in the early 1850s.[78] Putnam had dabbled with guidebooks as part of his earlier partnership with John Wiley, including William Burke's aforementioned guide to the Virginia springs in the 1840s, as well as the first American guidebook to Europe in 1838.[79] After 1850, Putnam's independent and rapidly growing firm focused on guides for American tourists in Europe, publishing titles like Roswell Park's *A Hand-Book for American Travellers in Europe* in the 1850s and the *Galignani's New Paris Guide* series in the 1870s.[80] Similarly, John Calvin Smith, who was a prolific author of guidebooks and gazetteers for John Disturnell, compiled a gazetteer for the dominant industrial publisher of the day, Harper and Brothers, in 1855. The advantages in scope and scale that the geographical specialist publishers had built for themselves—advantages that allowed them to repackage the same geographical knowledge into multiple formats and sell it to an increasingly national audience—were ready to be exploited by even bigger and better-capitalized generalist firms by the 1850s.

Although G. P. Putnam's Sons and Harper and Brothers both dabbled in guidebook production, it was the firm begun by Daniel Appleton that entered the market most aggressively. Beginning in the mid-1840s, the Appleton concern published a series of guidebooks that quickly mushroomed into a range of comprehensive regional guides issued on an annual or nearly annual basis. The Appletons' investment in the guidebook market was initiated by George S. Appleton, one of Daniel's sons who ran an affiliated publishing and bookselling establishment in Philadelphia in the 1840s and 1850s.[81] In 1846, he issued *The American Guide Book, Being a Hand-Book for Tourists and Travellers through Every Part of the United States*, which promised to fill the "obvious want of a good Guide Book that travellers might have in hand as a companion for their tour." Like many of his specialist contemporaries, Appleton's guidebook was intended to be "complete in itself," so as to "preclude the necessity of resorting to any other Guide Book . . . [and] to preclude the necessity of using local guides."[82] As his title and preface implied, Appleton sought the widest possible market for his work rather than the promotion of a specific region. Authorship was attributed to Willis Pope Hazard, who was George Appleton's "chief assistant and salesman" in Philadelphia.[83] Hazard was a professional book dealer, not a geographer, who compiled works as necessary to support Appleton's publishing ventures as well as, by 1849, his own "Hazard's Cheap Book Store" in Philadelphia.[84] His catalogue of authored works reflected the broad sweep of his business interests and included books on beauty regimens and agricultural improvement and children's literature, as well as guidebooks. The Appletons' foray into guidebook publishing was driven by a business analysis that identified a gap in the national marketplace for books, and they sought to fill that hole using their available authorial resources as efficiently as possible. The production of *The American Guide Book* involved neither geographical specialists nor local boosters; it was entirely the production of an ambitious publishing firm hoping to exploit a fertile field for growth.

This strategy was amazingly successful, especially once the main Appleton firm in New York got involved in the late 1840s. By the 1850s, D. Appleton & Company, already well on its way to becoming one of the largest industrial publishing firms in the United States, was issuing multiple tourist guidebooks in yearly editions. At the beginning of the decade, the flagship *Appletons' New and Complete United States Guide Book for Travellers*, which covered all of English-speaking North America, was joined by *Appleton's Northern and Eastern Traveller's Guide* and *Appleton's Southern and Western Travellers' Guide*. The former guided tourists through the destinations of the old American Grand Tour, as well as around New England, the middle states, and Canada, and the latter covered the Virginia springs and emerging destinations around the Great Lakes and in the Mississippi valley. By the end of the decade, the firm had stopped offering separate regional guides but had supplemented their national *Appleton's Illustrated Hand-Book of American Travel* with a guidebook more focused on the practicalities of transportation, entitled *Appletons' Illustrated Railway and Steam Navigation Guide*. The company produced these guidebooks in enormous quantities and issued new additions almost annually.

FIGURE 1.3. View of West Point from *Appleton's Northern and Eastern Traveller's Guide* (1851). Note the visual similarities between this engraving and the image of West Point from the *Hudson River Portfolio* in chapter 3. Courtesy of the University of Michigan Library (Special Collections).

Willis Hazard had moved on to his own business ventures by the 1850s, so the Appletons had to look beyond their own firm for writers to research and compile their multiplying guidebook titles. Like other publishers looking to compete in this market as efficiently as possible, they tapped the existing pool of geographical specialists in their urban publishing centers. Most of their output in the early 1850s was attributed to Wellington Williams, a Philadelphia engraver who published a few maps under his own name but who appears to have made his living largely by compiling geographical material for large publishing firms in his home city and in New York. Later in the decade, the Appletons turned to Thomas Addison Richards, a New York–based landscape painter and travel writer, to establish their long-running *Appleton's Illustrated Hand-Book of American Travel*.[85] Employing Richards represented a different strategy than employing Hazard or Williams; rather than using obscure authors to churn out guidebooks quickly and cheaply, the firm used a compiler whose name was already popularly associated leisure travel and the consumption of scenery. It was a savvy strategy; Richards's guide remained in print in new editions well after the Civil War and spawned a host of postwar spinoff Appleton guides to cities and regions, as well as summer and winter resorts. The firm continued to dominate the domestic guidebook market from the 1850s until the end of the century.

The Appleton firm was emblematic of guidebook publishing in the 1850s not only because of its remarkable scale and success with the genre but also because of how it arrived at its dominance. Of all the founders of major industrial publishing companies at midcentury, the Appletons were the only family who did not get their start as printers or booksellers. Daniel Appleton, the founder of the firm, was a dry goods merchant in Massachusetts who moved to New York City in 1825 to participate in the booming wholesale and retail market in dry goods that resulted from the opening of the Erie Canal. He only moved into publishing in the 1830s, when his mercantile experience demonstrated the potential profitability of selling books across his adopted city's rapidly expanding economic hinterland.[86] He approached publishing like he approached the dry goods market more generally: he identified specific market opportunities and pursued them with an eye to economy of scale. Appleton established himself as a publisher in the 1830s by issuing books of religious inspiration, a strategy that stemmed not only from his religious faith but also from his analysis of the book market. Similarly, in the 1840s, the Appleton firm identified a growing market for Spanish-language school books in the independent nations of Latin America. They arranged for the translation of their English-language readers and launched a market strategy that allowed them to dominate the Spanish-language export business for a century.[87] The Appletons' analysis of the potential demand for domestic guidebooks in the early 1850s, and their aggressive moves to dominate that market, were entirely in keeping with their understanding of the publishing business as a series of national and international markets that could be captured by smart strategy and the judicious application of capital.

The steam presses of Appleton & Company crystallized a process that had been under way since the 1830s: they made guidebooks, and the information they contained, into commodities. From their roots in the efforts of local boosters beginning in the 1820s, guidebooks were increasingly produced by national-scale publishers who identified and sought to fill a demand among travelers for conveniently formatted information that would help guide their travel. As a result, the content of tourist guidebooks changed dramatically. They became larger and more generic in order to fulfill the needs of a larger audience over a longer span of time. Gideon Davison's *The Fashionable Tour* laid out a single route through New York, Canada, and New England in the 1820s. It did so in considerable detail, and appropriately so, considering the primitive transportation facilities and neophyte tourists of the era. By contrast, Richards's *Appleton's Illustrated Hand-Book of American Travel* offered a selection of routes all over the country and offered general advice about which routes to choose based on the time of year and length of time available. Rather than promoting a particular tour, Richards offered a menu of possible excursions and exhorted his readers to "*Go somewhere, if you can*, all of you."[88] His "Skeleton Tours" offered less guidance than Davison's *Fashionable Tour*, but since there were more of them, more widely distributed, they could appeal to a wider national audience. The selection of tours that guides like Richards's contained were in a very real sense a product of market analysis, produced and distributed according to a commercial logic that sought to sell the same handful of texts to the largest numbers possible.

As the Appletons' guides show, the world of American geographical publishing was very different in the 1850s than it had been in the 1790s. The visions of universal geographical enlightenment that had inspired the geographical authors of Jedidiah Morse's generation held no appeal for the big industrial publishing firms that were the most vital and aggressive force in the midcentury national book market. This is not to say that the value of sedentary geographical knowledge for its own sake was completely abandoned; it lived on, in somewhat sclerotic form, in the burgeoning demand for geographical textbooks, which was largely filled by Mitchell in Philadelphia by the 1840s. His *System of Modern Geography* dominated the national market for primary school geography texts until well after the Civil War with few changes. Universal geographical knowledge also appeared in more modern guise in the emergence of geography as a professional scholarly discipline. By the end of the nineteenth century, the AGSL had evolved into the American Geographical Society, a professional scholarly organization, and universities had begun to establish formal geography departments. According to Susan Schulten, the 1880s and 1890s saw "a reconceptualization of geography as a more analytic, scientific body of knowledge" defined in opposition to "a loose and idiosyncratic body of gazetteer knowledge."[89] The dream of creating a comprehensive corpus of geographical knowledge did not disappear, but it retreated from the commercial marketplace to a more

stable perch in the ivory tower. Similarly, although the rise of local boosters had contributed to the erosion of the Enlightenment culture of geographical knowledge in the 1810s, the large national firms of the 1850s
showed little interest in such locally specific texts with such parochial
agendas and such limited potential markets. Again, geographical publishing as a strategy of local development did not disappear completely;
local gazetteers, for example, continued to be produced on a small scale
in local printing centers, especially in the West, well into the 1850s, and
these texts coexisted peacefully with the products of national publishing
firms on booksellers' lists.

Of all the genres of printed geographical knowledge, guidebooks
most clearly embodied the process of culture industry commercialization. From their origins as an innovative form of local promotion in
the 1820s to the dominance of the systematized production regimes of
the Appleton firm in the 1850s, guidebooks most clearly reflected the
consolidation of the industry and the power of the national publishing
market to shape the content of geographical knowledge. In the hands
of these successful culture industry entrepreneurs, geographical knowledge was thoroughly commodified for an audience of prospective travelers. This specific investment in the mass production of geographical
print had real effects on the world outside of books: the traveling public
targeted by publishers like Appleton could easily purchase conveniently
packaged information about the spaces and places they sought to travel
to and through. Of all the audiences for geographical knowledge in the
early republic, including scholars, students, and parlor reference readers,
it was travelers whose print culture was most thoroughly transformed
between the 1790s and the 1850s. At the turn of the nineteenth century, American authors and printers offered only a small handful texts
intended for a mobile readership. By the middle of the century, they
offered a wide selection of guides, covering different parts of the United
States in a variety of formats, and increasingly targeted at leisure travelers. Publishers reacted most strongly and creatively to the emergent
demand for geographical information from such travelers, and those
who would be such travelers.

Indeed, that demand was growing because interest in leisure travel
was growing in the first half of the nineteenth century. As the following
chapters will show, a combination of parallel changes in the production
of transportation; the rise of a largely rural group of entrepreneurs who
sought to sell leisure experiences to summer travelers; and a growing
interest in the social and aesthetic possibilities of resort life created a

ready market for all kinds of guidebooks. A growing group of authors and publishers sought to meet this demand, and also to encourage it by producing geographical knowledge that was tailored to leisure travelers. Their evolving intellectual commitments, social and economic investments, and business models shaped the specific nature of the products they supplied to meet that demand, in ways that were culturally and economically profitable to their producers. As a result, the experiences of leisure travelers were fundamentally shaped by the dynamics of commodification within the print culture of geographical knowledge, producing what would be increasingly considered tourist experiences. They covered a limited number of fixed routes, highlighted a handful of desirable destinations, and articulated an increasingly stable set of cultural meanings for those routes and destinations. The commodification of geographical knowledge undertaken by print entrepreneurs between the 1820s and the 1850s changed leisure travelers' real experience of space on the ground.

2 / Yesterday the Springs, To-day the Falls: Tourism and the Commodification of Travel

In February 1815, a young man named William Richardson embarked on an arduous two-month overland journey from Boston to New Orleans. Like many other ambitious sons of New England farm families in the early nineteenth century, he left home to find his fortune elsewhere. He made his way on a haphazard series of narrowly caught stagecoaches, horses borrowed and bought, ferryboats, and his own two feet. Long-distance travel, especially in the backcountry, was an improvisational affair, which put Richardson "in perpetual anxiety for [his] future welfare and success, which precluded every thought of past difficulties." He worried constantly about finding food, lodging, and a passable route, and about losing his horse, his way, and his sanity. "To sum up the whole," Richardson wrote from the banks of Lake Pontchartrain, "my journey has been tedious beyond description." Thirty years later, now "one of the leading bankers and most influential citizens of Louisville," Richardson left home for New York to embark on a long-desired visit to Europe. He and his wife were whisked up the Ohio, across the mountains, and down through Baltimore and Philadelphia to New York by a series of comfortable and fast steamboats, stagecoaches, and railroad cars. Gone were the anxieties and tedium of thirty years earlier, at least for this prosperous traveler.[1]

The difference in means and intent between Richardson's two recorded journeys in 1815 and 1844 was vast. During these decades, in rapidly developing corridors like the Ohio River valley, a host of technological changes reconfigured the relationship between geographical knowledge, physical movement, and the lived experiences of travel. Travelers at the beginning of the nineteenth century necessarily treated travel as something that they produced themselves, out of the raw materials of geographical knowledge, means of transportation, and provisions for the road. In order to execute his 1815 itinerary, Richardson had to know where to go, how best to get there, and the current conditions along his route. He also had to choose and acquire the means of getting to his destination, including transportation, lodging, and supplies. He acquired these raw materials for travel haphazardly and improvisationally as he went and used them to construct a journey for himself that was as idiosyncratic as it was exhausting.

By the middle of the century, however, an increasing number of travelers treated travel as a service to be purchased. As the century progressed, the materials, labor, knowledge, and relationships necessary to move travelers from place to place were increasingly obscured behind tickets and other market abstractions that represented travel itself as a finished product, a discrete purchasable commodity. As a result, in 1844 Richardson no longer had to engage in a tedious scramble for route information, local geographical knowledge, and fresh supplies to support his journey. Instead, in a booming marketplace for travel between the Ohio valley and the East Coast, he bought tickets from stagecoach, steamboat, and railroad companies that supplied transportation from place to place as a single commodity. Richardson knew little and cared less about the labor, capital, and knowledge that went into providing that travel, because those problems were solved by the businesses that sold him his tickets. Like many of his contemporaries, he was transformed from being a traveler who produced his own means of travel to being a passenger who consumed those means produced by someone else. With so many of the burdens of travel lifted off his shoulders, he was free to enjoy the journey in a way he had not been able to previously. No longer so much work, traveling as a passenger could be a form of leisure.

Historians have described the difference between Richardson's two experiences as a transportation revolution. The term was coined in 1951 by George Rogers Taylor, who used it to describe the effect that technological and financial improvements had on the commercial and industrial development of the United States between 1815 and 1860. The "core of [this] revolutionary change," according to Taylor, was "the cheapening and facilitating of the movement of goods and persons."[2] Technological innovation on the ground began in earnest after the close of the War of 1812, largely financed and constructed by states and by private corporations in the face of institutional weakness and political impasse in the federal government. The first manifestation of the transportation revolution was the turnpike boom, which began in the Northeast in the early years of the nineteenth century and which spread across the South and especially the Old Northwest in the 1810s and 1820s. Privately financed turnpikes turned out to be mostly poor investments, so by the 1830s the boom was over, and many existing turnpikes were abandoned. In their wake, however, they left a road network that was much improved over the colonial era.

The next phase of the transportation revolution came from advances in navigation on inland waterways. Natural waterways were opened to fast and efficient circulation, both upstream and downstream, after Robert Fulton's demonstration of the feasibility of steamboats on the Hudson River in 1807. The natural waterways where the steamboat saw its most intensive development included the Hudson and the other navigable waterways of the eastern seaboard and most notably the extensive navigable branches of the Mississippi and Ohio Rivers and the Great Lakes. Steamboats spread rapidly, especially after New York State revoked Fulton's monopoly of steam navigation on its waters in 1819, until "by 1830 it dominated American river transportation and for two decades thereafter was the most important agency of internal transportation in the country." The natural waterways of the interior were soon supplemented by artificial waterways, which promised inexpensive operation, albeit with a high construction cost. The first and most successful of these projects was the Erie Canal in New York, begun in 1817 and completed in 1825, which linked the Hudson at Albany with Lake Erie at Buffalo. The Erie Canal was an instant success for New York because it provided an efficient means of moving goods and people between the extensive Great Lakes basin and the Atlantic seaboard. States such as Pennsylvania, Virginia, Ohio, and Indiana, jealous of New York's success, soon began their own canal projects, creating a boom in the late 1820s and 1830s. These newer canals were largely unable to replicate the Erie's success, leading to a steep decline in canal building by the 1840s.

These later canals failed at least partly because they had to compete with a newer technology, the railroad. Railroad companies started incorporating in the late 1820s, and the first serviceable passenger railroads opened for short distances in the early 1830s. The Baltimore & Ohio, designed to give Baltimore access to the Trans-Appalachian West and thus compete with the Erie Canal, was the first to open for passenger service in 1830, but its early lead in long-distance passenger service was soon surpassed by the growing railroad networks of Pennsylvania and New York. Although railroad construction proceeded quickly in the early years, the relatively short distances of each individual line and their lack of integration kept them from being truly useful long-distance transportation options for passengers. However, in the late 1840s and 1850s, large corporations like the New York Central and the Pennsylvania Railroad wielded impressive amounts of capital to consolidate, connect, and expand existing lines into extensive long-distance transportation networks. As with the turnpike construction boom two decades earlier, railroad networks generally spread southward and westward from coastal cities, creating a network that by 1860 covered much of the settled United States, albeit with a much heavier concentration of rail connections in the Northeast and Old Northwest. These successive waves of technological and financial innovation made transportation faster, more reliable, and more economical in 1844 than it had been in 1815.[3]

The transportation revolution paradigm, with its focus on technology and infrastructure development, does an admirable job of explaining the very different material conditions of travel that Richardson encountered in 1815 and in 1844. But it does not capture the equally different lived experiences of travel that Richardson recorded at the beginning and in the middle of the century.[4] Those experiences were reshaped by precisely the same processes of commodification that were remaking the print culture of geographical knowledge. Travel was increasingly provided by a capital-intensive service industry that produced a commodity for sale into an expanding market that served a nation that was growing both geographically and demographically. The transportation revolution may have been the iron horse that the market rode in on, but the experience of riding the transportation revolution was shaped by the same separation of production and consumption that characterized other emerging markets for commodities.

In concrete terms, the process of commodification that reshaped the experience of travel between Richardson's two journeys was driven by several distinct but interrelated changes in the production and sale of transportation. At a fundamental level, the technologies and business structures of the transportation revolution alienated the producers of travels from the consumers of travel. The workers who advised travelers; plotted routes; set schedules; anticipated the weather; bought, fed, and drove horses; shoveled coal into boilers; and cooked the dishes that were served in dining cabins became insulated from and mysterious to travelers themselves. Moving people and goods comfortably through space required many different kinds of raw material and many different kinds of labor, which were increasingly acquired and supplied by teams of workers whose efforts were coordinated by the managers of stagecoach and steamboat lines and turnpike and railroad companies. As those workers became more anonymous, their labors became more opaque to those who benefited from them. Instead, travelers interacted with middlemen like tavern keepers who kept stagecoach manifests; with steamboat captains whose tasks included interacting with passengers as much as steering their ship; and with railroad station agents who sold tickets for trains and provided receipts for baggage. From such middlemen they bought paper abstractions that represented a promise of future travel rather than the material stuff of travel itself. The travel represented by such abstractions carried heightened expectations of reliability and uniformity; travelers expected one ticketed trip to be as much like another as reasonably possible, and to be timely, comfortable, and free of annoyance. Each of these processes was distinct and proceeded according to its own economic and cultural logic, but collectively they transformed travel into a commodity.

Like the expansion of the market economy itself, the commodification of travel happened gradually, partially, and unevenly throughout the nineteenth century and across the geographical space of the expanding nation, and individuals' access to commodified travel varied significantly. Transportation developed more quickly in the North and the Old Northwest than it did in the South and the Old Southwest. Investment was most intensive along a handful of popular routes, like the Erie Canal corridor and the Pennsylvania Main Line between Philadelphia and Pittsburgh, which meant that the pleasures of being a passenger were more widely available in the denser and more economically developed sections of the nation. Traveling on the latest conveniences was not usually the cheapest way to go, meaning that the emerging middle class could more readily become passengers than could poor and working people. Recent scholarship has shown that access to new transportation technologies was also profoundly limited by travelers' race and gender.[5] Nevertheless, a growing number of travelers chose to become passengers—consumers of travel rather than producers of travel—and as they began to think about travel as a commodity, they invested their experiences with new expectations of affordability, reliability, and convenience.

With each ticket purchased from an agent, nineteenth-century passengers anticipated that commodified travel would meet a rising bar for speed, ease, comfort, reliability, and affordability. These interlocking expectations worked together to open a new set of possible meanings for travel: that it could routinely serve as a source of pleasure, recreation, and even liberation for a broad swath of the traveling public. Historians of tourism have long pointed out that the transportation revolution provided the necessary infrastructure for the development of tourism, but commodified travel contributed more than just roads and railways. It enabled a consumeristic attitude toward the act of travel that suggested the possibility of the consumption of leisure experiences on the road, which laid the cultural foundation for the birth and growth of the domestic tourist industry. People traveled for a wide variety of personal and economic purposes in the early republic, but the commodification of travel made recreational travel a conceptual possibility for the emerging middle class. Indeed, it was precisely these middling sorts who were best positioned to take advantage of the transportation revolution because the rich could travel anyway and the poor could not afford the tickets. At the same time, this rising American bourgeoisie was the class most shaped by emerging market habits of mind. As a result, most middle-class travelers and observers of travel saw the commodification of travel as a positive development because it offered mobility to an expanding circle of consumers and built new expectations about the liberating possibilities of travel. But at the same time, the evident passivity of being a consumer of travel opened a new avenue of criticism of ticket buyers, which would grow into a stronger critique of tourism as more and more routes could be easily navigated by passengers holding small slips of paper.

In order to show the changing texture of the lived experiences of travelers in the early republic, this chapter considers three examples. The first is William Richardson and his two journeys. The stark contrast between his journeys, separated by thirty years, shows how profound the transition from being a producer of travel to being a consumer of travel really was. The difference between making his own way and purchasing tickets from a series of middlemen fundamentally changed his experience of travel and particularly its possibilities for pleasure. The second and third examples fill in the dichotomous picture drawn by Richardson's journeys. The second example follows Thomas McKenney on a single journey over a long distance in order to illustrate how individual itineraries often crossed market boundaries between different transportation regimes, and how travelers adjusted their expectations about uniformity, reliability, and comfort as a result. Travelers like McKenney regarded tickets as markers of commercial obligation; when they put someone else in charge of their travel, they complained vociferously when their standards were not met. The third example recounts the history of a specific place, Trenton Falls, in upstate New York, to show how entrepreneurs responded to these new expectations in a halting fashion as they sought to attract leisure travelers. The availability of tickets to a particular destination—or the lack thereof—shaped how travelers thought of them and the possibilities they attached to a visit. Taken together, these three examples show how travel became a commodity in the first half of the nineteenth century, and how these processes of commodification invested travel with new expectations and new meanings.

In each case, I will read the relevant travel accounts with a special attention to the language that travelers used to describe their journeys, in order to show how the meanings they assigned to their travel evolved alongside their changing experiences of transportation technology. To be sure, no nineteenth-century traveler described the changes that they saw taking place around them as "commodification," nor did they describe the experiences of ticketed travel as "commodified." These terms embody an analysis that was beyond the perception of contemporary actors, who mostly noticed that traveling became more reliable to plan; more convenient to arrange; more comfortable to ride; and more pleasurable to undertake, even while the entire experience was increasingly alienated from cartographers' presses; ferrymen's bells; horses' sweat; and indeed from the highways and landscapes of the American continent. The sum total of these observations, charted over the space and time of the early American republic, described the changing experience of travel under the structural conditions of commodification.

When departing on his trip from Boston to New Orleans in the late winter of 1815, Richardson faced an immediate problem: choosing the best route. As a child in Massachusetts in the 1790s, Richardson likely would have encountered the geographical grammars of Jedidiah Morse and his contemporaries, and been exposed to their project of universal geographical knowledge. He certainly relied on his broad acquaintance with American geography as he was making his plans. He originally thought a sea route would be most expedient, and that his best opportunity for finding a ship bound for New Orleans lay in New York. However, after taking a stagecoach to New York, he "went to see Mr. Goodhues to ascertain if any vessel would depart soon for N. Orleans and receiving

FIGURE 2.1. Map of William Richardson's 1815 journey. Courtesy of the New-York Historical Society.

a negative answer took a seat in the Pilot stage for Philadelphia and crossed over the river to Pawlus Hook in a small boat." He tried again in Baltimore but found that "the ships are all blocked up with the ice," so he "took a seat in the morning stage for Washington." With his initial route plans in shambles, he sought guidance from his connections in Washington. "Call'd on Mr. Gove from whom I obtained information respecting route to N. Orleans," Richardson recorded. Mr. Gove recommended an overland route through the Cumberland Gap and down the Natchez Trace to New Orleans, a route that was long and hard but evidently preferable to waiting for a ship, probably because of the winter weather and the unsettled condition of maritime traffic in the immediate aftermath of the War of 1812. Richardson settled on this route, though not without later regrets. In Abingdon, Virginia, right before his first encounter with what he called "wilderness," he "saw several gentlemen who had travelled the route I am going, and all gave those most dismal and discouraging description. I now regretted that I had not stopped in N. York and taken water, but here I am and must go on."[6]

Although Morse's grammars might have helped Richardson frame the big choice between traveling by land and traveling by sea, they offered little guidance about which would best fit Richardson's particular needs in 1815. Instead, he made specific route decisions while he was already on the road, through consultation with people he met along his way. He had to make social connections that would supply him with the knowledge necessary to choose a route, even along the relatively populous eastern seaboard. Once he turned west into the interior, he became even more reliant on information obtained from new acquaintances made on the road. Heading west out of Virginia, Richardson traveled with a Mr. Harris and a Mr. Paige, both of whom were traveling to or from homes in Tennessee and were thus able to guide Richardson for a portion of his journey. Once in Nashville, he "rose early and went to the Boat Landing to find a Keel Boat going down to N.O. but was disappointed." This route, which would have entailed floating down the Cumberland, Ohio, and Mississippi Rivers to his destinations, would have been slower but almost certainly easier and safer than taking the Natchez Trace overland. His strategy for navigating the difficult and potentially confusing trails of the Trans-Appalachian interior was to find travel companions with local knowledge. After his disappointment on the Nashville wharves, he "went to all the Public Houses to find company going my way; in this I was again disappointed. I now made preparations to set off alone and at 11, having got my necessary stores, started off, tho against the advice of all who conversed on the subject."[7] Luckily, after only two days' ride, he found another travel companion, a "Mr. Brooks of Tennessee," to help him navigate the difficult "wilderness" between Nashville and New Orleans.

Cultivating local knowledge also helped Richardson with smaller decisions along the road, as he regularly relied on local reports to determine his daily course. On March 25, he "started early as we were told the Buzzard Roost Creek had fallen and could be forded." Two days later, he recorded that "the waters were now so high the mail carriers said it was useless to start, so we concluded to stop till morning."[8] In the early nineteenth century, a journey was often just such a series of improvisations, as decisions were made on the road according to the geographical information that the traveler could obtain along the way, in response to unforeseen circumstances and changing conditions. Richardson improvised on a daily basis, whether making large decisions about route and means of transport, or small decisions about whether or not to attempt to cross a swollen creek. He did not, and could not, purchase this information in the marketplace, for the simple reason that no marketplace yet existed for this kind of geographical knowledge.

Richardson also negotiated his means of transportation on the ground and in the moment. Having abandoned his original plan of traveling by ship, he sought to travel by stagecoach instead. Although initially intending to travel directly from Washington to Staunton, Virginia, he found that the stage had stopped running at Fredericksburg. He ended up in Richmond instead, where he "made enquiries respecting my route to Nashville; found the stage did not start until Thursday and that the distance before me is much greater that I expected." He made use of his time in Richmond by dining with a Mr. Williams, from whom he "procured letters to gentlemen at Abingdon, where I expect to leave the stage, and would want assistance in purchasing a horse." Richardson's expectation of taking the stage to Abingdon—still in the state of Virginia—was once again optimistic; bad roads ended the line in Lexington, and from Lexington to Abingdon he proceeded through a combination of borrowed horses, bribed mail riders, and hired guides. At Abingdon, his letters introduced him to a Mr. Morris, "who assisted me in looking up a horse that would answer my purpose." The horse he purchased in Abingdon would carry him all the way to the shores of Lake Pontchartrain. Not only was Richardson in constant negotiation to obtain his means of transportation along the road; he also had to supply his own provisions. At Nashville he "got [his] necessary stores," which after a day on the road he deemed insufficient. At Dobbins he "laid in some Biscuit and Pork, in addition to what I got at Nashville, as I heard none to be had for 60 miles."[9] Richardson had to acquire both the geographical knowledge necessary for travel and also the most basic supplies to support life on the road. In both cases, the uncertainty that he encountered along the way forced him to improvise.

When circumstances dictated, Richardson was willing to pay individuals who could supply him with both the knowledge and the means to get from one place to another, although he obscured the financial nature of these transactions in his diary. Notably, he hired African American men, both freedmen and those whose legal status he did not record, to serve as guides and porters while traveling in Kentucky, a practice that was not uncommon in such border regions at the beginning of the nineteenth century. In November 1815, on his second trip to New Orleans, he crossed the Ohio River into Kentucky where, having given up his horse, he "had to seek some mode of conveyance to Lexington." At a public house, he "found a black fellow who was going on to Louisville & had a spare horse which I concluded to ride & pay his expenses." Richardson "mounted [the] large elegant white Horse & rode 8 miles—in true

Kentucky stile, with my black boy Gabriel following me." Despite the fact that he was riding Gabriel's horse, he recorded that in Paris he "discharged Gabriel & hired a horse to ride to Lexington." He remained in Lexington until the new year, and on March 1 he "sent for Peter (a free negro whom I have employed to take me to Louisville) and ordered him to bring his horses to Mr. Higgins." This second stage of his journey was also conducted in what Richardson thought to be "true Kentucky stile"; Richardson referred to his hired man as "my man Peter" and praised his "majestic appearance [and] good humor."[10] He employed both of these men because they could supply him with the horses and geographical knowledge necessary to proceed to his next destination. But he also sought to elide the economic nature of these transactions, downplaying his reliance on his guides by highlighting their racial subjugation in the "true Kentucky stile." He recorded his payments to them, but he also emphasized that they rode behind him and served his needs, even when he was relying on them on unfamiliar terrain. Richardson sought to retain his agency as a traveler by dismissing crucial support he received from free blacks.

Although Richardson paid for the materials, supplies, and knowledge necessary for travel, his itinerary was not a commodity because he negotiated the acquisition of individual supplies and discrete pieces of information with individuals along his route rather than buying means and knowledge together in unified transactions. He bought the raw materials for travel rather than travel itself. He was therefore, in a very real sense, the producer of his own travel. His travel diary was filled with assertive, active-voice sentences that captured his pride in his achievement. By 1844, however, when Richardson traveled from Louisville to New York with his wife, the situation had changed dramatically. Largely absent were the individual negotiations made along the route for directions, lodging, and transportation. Instead, Richardson recorded his trip as a series of transactions in which he bought *travel itself,* represented as an abstraction by slips of paper purchased from sales agents. In each of these transactions, the transportation company, whether in the form of a steamboat packet service, a stagecoach line, or a railroad, supplied both the necessary geographical knowledge and mode of transport in return for a fixed fee. Indeed, these transactions with middlemen were the only ones that Richardson recorded, in marked contrast to the constant negotiation in which he engaged in 1815. His 1844 diary reflected his new status as a consumer rather than a producer; gone was the tone of assertive activity, replaced with a breezy and relaxed passive voice.

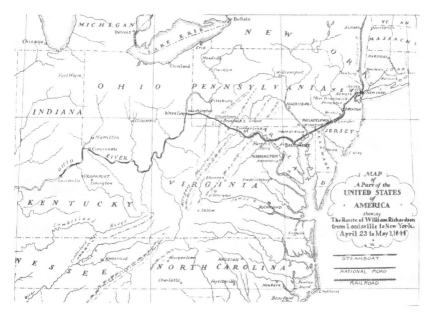

FIGURE 2.2. Map of William Richardson's 1844 journey. Courtesy of the New-York Historical Society.

Richardson and his wife departed Louisville in April 1844 on the mail boat *Pike* on the Ohio River. Their berths on this boat were not a happy accident like that which had eluded Richardson in New York, Baltimore, and Nashville almost thirty years earlier; the *Pike* was a packet boat on a line that ran according to a fixed schedule. The Richardsons purchased tickets in advance expecting to be transported at a fixed time to a fixed destination. They had a small adventure in Cincinnati, where mechanical trouble with the *Pike* required them to find another boat to Wheeling. The excitement of this adventure, however, largely lay in getting up early in order to secure a berth. "Very early," Richardson recorded, "I went on board the 'CUTTER', roused up the Captain who very sluggishly 'turned out' and registered our names for Wheeling. It was lucky for us, I was thus early in securing our berths for very soon an immense crowd were pressing around the Clerk for the same object."[11] Richardson did not need to rely on local contacts or on his own improvisational abilities; all he had to do was get up early and buy his ticket from the agent before his fellow travelers.

After disembarking from their Ohio River steamboat at Wheeling, the Richardsons changed modes of travel several times. They first boarded a stagecoach to Cumberland and then rode a series of railroads, linked by ferries, through Baltimore and Philadelphia to New York, with each transition designed by the transportation companies specifically to eliminate any need for improvisation. At Wheeling, "at half past five o'clock, having taken breakfast, we seated ourselves in the stage" for Cumberland, which was the western terminus of the Baltimore & Ohio Railroad in 1844. Richardson was unquiet; not only was he worried about the "hard ride . . . before us," but he and his wife were also worried that "having so heavy a load, we might fail to reach the Depot at Cumberland in time for the eight o'clock cars." However, the Baltimore & Ohio imposed tight coordination on connecting stagecoach lines, and "true to their promise, the drivers pressed on and set us down in Cumberland just before the cars 'whistle,' roused the multitude to run to their seats in the car." He need not have worried, because this clockwork coordination between forms of transit was included in their fare.[12] Similar coordination was masked by further easy transitions from mode to mode. For example, ferryboats carried train cars across the Susquehanna River in Maryland and also carried passengers to and from trains in New Jersey from both Philadelphia and New York. Richardson did not even mention the first boat ride; on his last morning in Baltimore, "nothing remained for us to do, after breakfast, but to repair to the cars for Philad. At 9 we started. Arrived at Phila. at half past four."[13] That Richardson barely mentioned the other changes from train to boat and back again was a testament to the seamlessness of the transition; in his earlier travels, as we have seen, river crossings were major undertakings that required extensive local negotiation. But now that he was able to purchase a simple comprehensive ticket, those problems of navigation were assumed and solved by the railroad companies that sold him his tickets.

Perhaps the best evidence of Richardson's changed experience of travel lay in the way he concluded his two travel diaries. "Landed at Madam Clarkes in N.O. at 5 o'clock," he recorded in 1815, "Thus my tedious journey is ended."[14] In 1844, however, he ended with a jaunty tally of the cost of the tickets for each phase of his journey. "Expenses of our journey: from Louisville to Cin. One person $3. From Cincinnati to Wheeling—$5. Stage from Wheeling to Philad.—$13. From Phila. to N. York—$4."[15] This accounting divided his trip into geographically counterintuitive pieces. He recorded Philadelphia as a stop but not Cumberland or Baltimore, despite the fact that he changed modes in the former place and spent the night in the latter, while he traveled through Philadelphia without stopping. The geography of his trip did not dictate how he remembered it; instead, he recalled it by how he had purchased his tickets. A long-distance trip was no longer a series of trails to navigate, stagecoach drivers to bribe, rivers to cross, supplies to secure, and shelter to be found. Instead, it was a series of market transactions in which Richardson purchased those services as part of a complete package that moved him from one place to the next. As a result, he recorded his later journey as a pleasurable experience that he bought and paid for rather than as an experience "tedious beyond description."

This precise question of who Richardson paid, and for what, lay at the heart of the process of commodification that made his two trips so different. On both of his journeys, Richardson paid to travel from one place to another, but both the practical and the conceptual contexts of those payments differed sharply between his two journeys. Early in the century, Richardson recorded the paying of "fares," a term that he used to describe the price charged him by innkeepers, stagecoach drivers, or ferrymen for food, lodging, and transportation. These fares were generally negotiated on the spot and paid directly to the provider of the service, a circumstance that sometimes left Richardson feeling taken advantage of as a traveler and a stranger.[16] In each case, the fare represented a specific payment for a specific service rendered by a specific provider, a unique transaction that carried with it all the uncertainty of face-to-face bargaining between strangers. But soon after Richardson made his way to New Orleans in 1815, transportation providers started to develop a more systematic way of doing business. They began to enlist agents to sell spaces on their coaches and boats, which made their services more accessible and predictable. These early middlemen, who were often tavern keepers, sold seats on future runs and kept a list of passengers in a log book, usually called a manifest, for the driver. Occasionally they issued a "ticket," originally a generic term for a small slip of paper, to the passenger as a receipt to prove their place on the manifest. To take an early example, the Stevens family of Hoboken, New Jersey, began to sell passage from New York to Philadelphia in 1823, a journey that required two steamboats, a stagecoach, and multiple transfers. This single transaction included the necessary fares and the transfer of baggage, giving passengers a seamless experience in return for their money.[17]

The practice of giving "tickets" became more common by the 1840s as transportation companies grew larger and more bureaucratic, and by the 1850s interline tickets had begun to smooth the process of transferring between different railroads and steamboat lines.[18] Independent middlemen like the Stevenses were increasingly replaced by ticket agents directly employed by transportation companies. As a result, the term "ticket" increasingly came to indicate a paper representation of future travel. This meaning reflected a wider vernacular shift in the word's usage, which increasingly denoted an exchangeable marker of a standardized item of value that was held elsewhere. For example, the grain elevators operators of 1850s Chicago transformed unique products of nature into interchangeable commodities in their graded silos, which were represented by tickets that could be bought and sold as well as redeemed for grain. Similarly, the circus promotors who pioneered the traveling big top in the 1830s drummed up sales by offering paper admission tickets in advance of their shows.[19] Like Chicago's elevator tickets or a circus admission ticket, the emerging system of stagecoach manifests and railroad tickets meant that travel was abstractly represented by entries in ledgers and slips of paper passed from hand to hand. It could be bought and sold by a network of agents and consumers in a theoretically limitless marketplace, both in the moment and for the future, and ultimately redeemed for a standardized product: a journey from one point to another. The gradual process of transportation market innovation that led to the invention of the ticket by the 1840s marked travel's emergence as a true commodity. As Richardson's two accounts show, that commodity could be consumed as leisure, and even with pleasure, in a way that seemed unimaginable on those gray, rainy days on the Natchez Trace in 1815.

Richardson's experiences of travel were so divergent because his trips were made at very different historical moments, but individual itineraries also crossed the spatial boundaries of the patchwork marketplace for travel in a single historical moment. In 1826, Superintendent of Indian Affairs Thomas McKenney traveled from Washington, DC, to meet with the Chippewa Indians at Fond du Lac in what is now Wisconsin. The trip there and back took almost five months, and the distance to his destination meant that McKenney traveled under a variety of market conditions. The first leg of his journey, from Washington to Detroit via New York City, the Hudson River, the Erie Canal, and Lake Erie, followed some of the most intensively developed transportation corridors of the mid-1820s. However, while the path from Detroit to Fond du Lac via the upper Great Lakes had been beaten for centuries, it was still largely traversed by Native Americans, traders, missionaries, government agents, and self-styled explorers. Neither the volume nor the nature of the traffic on the upper lakes had yet attracted the degree of investment necessary for significant development. Comparing the two halves of McKenney's trip, with Detroit as the dividing line between them, shows how his expectations and experiences were shaped by his status as traveler or passenger, or as producer or consumer of travel, and how they could vary even within a single itinerary.

Upon his departure, McKenney wrote to a correspondent that "in going over some of the grounds, I shall have to tread, of necessity, in paths which have been often trodden before," which would make his account uninteresting. "Indeed," he lamented, "it would be hardly possible to travel through a country, and especially over a public highway, which has been so often and so minutely described, as has so much of the way as lies before me, and between Washington and Buffaloe, by the way of the North river, &c. without recurring to places that every body knows by heart, and even in the order in which they have hitherto been written about." When traveling over this well-beaten ground, McKenney entrusted himself to a series of stagecoaches, steamboats, and canal boats that he expected his readers would know "by heart." He did no inquiring or negotiating; instead, he moved smoothly from one conveyance to the next and from one "recurring place" to the next.[20]

This portion of McKenney's travel narrative, published in 1827 as *Sketches of a Tour to the Lakes,* flowed along in an easy passive voice, as if he had little to do with the execution of his own plans. He described his trip from Baltimore to Philadelphia, made on a combination of steamboats and stagecoaches, as a well-oiled machine on which he was only a passenger. He sailed across the Chesapeake Bay to Frenchtown, "without any variation of the usual appearance of things upon this route . . . and as usual, at the very uncomfortable hour of midnight, where the baggage you know is shifted, with its owners, into stages for Newcastle, distant about fifteen miles, and where, at the hardly less uncomfortable hour of daybreak, we are again shifted from the stages into the steamboat on the Delaware." In this telling, passengers were mere appendages to their baggage, conveyed along the main line of travel up the East Coast. He needed neither route knowledge of his own nor any equipment or supplies to conduct his journey. Instead, he purchased his trip in the jostling marketplace on the Baltimore wharves. Lest his audience mistake his tone of complaint for doubts about the benefits of such commodified travel, he closed his description of this leg of his journey by concluding, "still this accommodation to the public is great."[21]

Where such travel was available for sale, McKenney expected it to work according to fair market rules. On his return trip, he purchased a stagecoach ride from Niagara to Lockport, on the Erie Canal, where he would transfer to a canal packet. Along the way, the driver of his coach became entangled in a dispute with the stagecoach operator, and he retaliated by abruptly quitting his post, abandoning McKenney at an inn ten miles short of his destination. McKenney "suggested to him the propriety of saving his employers from the consequences which must result from such a procedure, and not allow them to be injured in the public confidence by the obstinacy of one of the drivers," but to no avail, and McKenney was forced to cobble together alternate arrangements. He was deeply offended by this breach of contract because he was forced to improvise and produce his own means of travel, when he should have been a simple consumer of the stagecoach company's product. He paid grudgingly for the private wagon "after having paid my fare, of course, at Niagara, to the owners of the stages *for the entire route*." Like many of his contemporaries who were struggling to negotiate a new world of abstract commodities, McKenney sought redress outside of the modern market economy. Rather than using the legal system to force compliance from the stagecoach owners, he deployed an older understanding of the market as a network of personal relationships and reputations in order to shame them into better behavior. He published the stagecoach owners' names in his account, writing that he was "thus particular, that who-ever may see this journal may avoid a line in which there is no security against being left by the way; and no redress against such a grievance, except by resort to the law, which, for my part, I wish to have as little to do with as possible." He expected that buying an abstract representation of travel, like a ticket or a space on a manifest, would be unproblemati-cally redeemed for actual travel by the stagecoach company. As a con-sumer, he expected that he would receive all the value he had paid for, even in western New York in 1826. And when his transaction failed, he chose to address that failure by questioning the entire market structure that undergirded it.[22]

McKenney's heightened expectations of the ease, uniformity, and reli-ability of ticketed travel, and the offense he took at its failure, are thrown into greater relief when compared to his experiences beyond Detroit. There, he relied on Michigan territorial governor Lewis Cass, an expe-rienced traveler in the upper Great Lakes and a fellow member of the expedition, to help him acquire the knowledge, equipment, and person-nel necessary to travel to Fond du Lac. They arranged for canoes and barges, paddled by voyageurs and soldiers, to transport themselves, their party, and their baggage. The party had to rely on its own geographical knowledge, mainly supplied by Cass's extensive experience, to choose its routes and negotiate for supplies. With neither stagecoach nor steamboat tickets available to the upper lakes, McKenney became a more active and improvisational traveler beyond Detroit. The wry, passive tone of his earlier account was replaced by an authoritative yet flexible attitude as Cass and McKenney directed the members of the expedition to best meet the unpredictable challenges of traveling the upper lakes. As they left Detroit, they planned to send their baggage and their party ahead by schooner and to travel by canoe to meet them at Mackinac. On June 17, McKenney was prepared for departure, and he enthusiastically recorded that "we shall proceed as soon as our supplies are off; unless we are detained by the non-arrival of our canoe, which, however, we expect hourly." By June 22, "our canoe not having arrived, we have chartered the schooner Ghent. The want of wind, or the having too much of it, from a wrong quarter, can alone delay us." McKenney and his traveling companions made such decisions on the fly throughout their trip, using their knowledge of local conditions to make new plans when old arrangements failed.[23]

This improvisation often took a democratic form, such as when choosing a camping spot in the face of an unexpected storm on an inlet of Lake Superior. "A council has been held," McKenney recorded, "and it is determined by the majority to be safest to cross over the river for the night." In cases such as these, the party did not purchase the knowledge necessary to execute their journey because a market for such information did not exist. Instead they pooled their common wisdom and experience and made a decision in light of the conditions and equipment available to them while on the road. Such moments introduced significant uncertainty into their journey, but unlike during the incident at Lockport, McKenney made no complaint about changed plans or misplaced baggage because he had different expectations about the nature of travel outside the boundaries of the market for tickets. Whereas he was unable to countenance breach of contract and the resulting improvisation along the developing corridor of the Erie Canal, he accepted such uncertainty and addressed it creatively in the territory beyond Detroit.[24]

Nevertheless, McKenney looked forward to the passing of this uncertain world. "Mackinac is really worth seeing," he enthused to his correspondent at home in Washington. "I think it by no means improbable, especially should steamboats extend their route to it, that it will become a place of fashionable resort for the summer. There is no finer summer climate in the world."[25] McKenney was indeed prescient. Mackinac's charms made it one of the most important destinations for pleasure travel in the upper Midwest, but only after the Civil War, once regular, reliable steamboat service to the island had become firmly established. The operators of such passenger steamboats sold tickets and kept manifests, which made travel around the upper lakes relatively simple, reliable, and predictable for their passengers. Once travel to Mackinac met those expectations, it became a famous stop for leisure travelers from around the Great Lakes.[26]

Mackinac's transformation into a "place of fashionable resort," once passenger tickets became available after the Civil War, was not an unusual historical trajectory. The process of commodification made selling travel for pleasure a viable business venture. Tourist destinations and "places of fashionable resort" were nurtured both directly and indirectly by the marketplace for travel, because the entire experience of visiting them became an act of consumption. This process of economic and cultural development was illustrated in microcosm by the history of Trenton Falls in upstate New York, where it took place on a small scale and over a short period of time. A series of dramatic cataracts located in a deep gorge in central New York State, Trenton Falls was triply favored to become a destination for recreational travelers. It was blessed with "a scenery altogether unique in its character, as combining at once the beautiful, the romantic, the magnificent and enchanting; all the variety of rocky chasms, cataracts, cascades, rapids &c. elsewhere separately exhibited in different regions." It lay only fourteen miles from "the flourishing village of Utica, the great thoroughfare of this region, an internal emporium of business, with a population of cultivated minds and courteous manners," which became an important port on the Erie Canal upon its opening in 1825.[27] Finally, Trenton Falls had savvy investors and skilled promoters in the family of John Sherman.

Trained as a minister at Yale, Sherman left his conservative Connecticut congregation when his theological liberalism led him to accept an invitation to minister to the Unitarian congregation in Oldenbarneveld, New York, in 1806. He became interested in the nearby gorge and falls, and upon his retirement from the ministry in 1823, he bought land near the rim and opened a small hostelry that he called the "Rural Resort." In 1825, using financing supplied by famous New York merchant and diarist Philip Hone, an early guest, Sherman expanded his accommodations into a hotel.[28] The popularity of Sherman's Rural Resort as a destination for pleasure travelers was enhanced by socially prominent and well-connected supporters like Hone and Supreme Court justice Joseph Story, who called Trenton the "falls . . . of great celebrity, and almost universally visited by travellers."[29] But Sherman did not rely only on social connections to bring customers to his hotel. In 1827, he wrote a slim pamphlet entitled *A Description of Trenton Falls* wherein he sang the praises of the scenic gorge and surrounding countryside, which he had printed in Utica. Sherman's ability to spread Trenton Falls' fame, as well as his reputation "as the agreeable and intelligent host, the scholar and friendly gentleman," made the Rural Resort a small but successful destination for pleasure travelers by the mid-1820s.[30]

After Sherman's death in 1828, his son-in-law Michael Moore took over the establishment and continued to expand on both Sherman's facilities and his business practices. He added to the hotel, cultivated his reputation as a host, and collaborated with popular middlebrow author Nathaniel Parker Willis to expand and rewrite Sherman's pamphlet for a wider audience. The new *Trenton Falls, Picturesque and Descriptive* appeared in 1851, at the peak of Willis's celebrity as the embodiment of sentimental bourgeois respectability, and Willis used that fame to boost its scenery and to invite readers to join him as one of the "intelligent traveller[s] and worshipper[s] of the sublimest works of the Creator" who gathered at the Rural Resort.[31] Sherman and Moore carved a destination for pleasure travelers out of their woods and valleys through judicious investment and a smart strategy of cultural positioning and social networking.

It developed slowly, however, because Trenton Falls was still remote and difficult to reach in the early years of its development. A visit to the just-opened Rural Resort required self-reliant travelers who were willing to improvise on the road. In June 1825, a group of six women who comprised the "Bigelow party" were traveling from Boston to Niagara in their own coach. They turned aside from their planned route to visit Trenton, on "the advice of Mr Smith," the landlord of the inn where they had stayed at Little Falls. The party had been charmed by the Smiths' "pleasant neat house embowered in roses" and by "little *William Smith* the landlords only son," and thus allowed themselves to be persuaded by this stranger that they had met along the road. This "deviation" left the party unsettled, because they were "entering a part of the country with which Oliver [the coachman] was unacquainted." One of the diarists recording the trip confided that "this threw a new feeling of responsibility over us." As they proceeded, "the country seemed to be growing more wild + solitary," and they feared that they could not "reach the falls of

Trenton before night." Conditions steadily worsened, and "an universal clamour arose from ladies + coachman against poor Smith." As another of the party recalled, "we had not proceeded far when disappointment and vexation at his misrepresentation almost tempted us to retrace our steps—yet a vague hope of something better carried us on till we were too much advanced to have gained anything by returning . . . the remoteness also of the different settlement, and the ignorance of our driver in regard to the road, caused an anxiety that we could not overcome." Luckily, however, the road flattened out, and "just as the last ray of day-light quitted us, we turned into a wild obscure looking road, cut through woods and fields of black stumps—it seemed to have no end—a glimmering light sometimes cheated us with the hope that we had reached Shermans. At length when we had begun to feel very dismal, a gate was opened for us, and we drove up to a large unfinished house, at the door of which stood Mr Sherman."[32]

The Bigelow party's happily ended misadventure in the wilderness reveals the lack of concrete geographical information about Trenton Falls available in the print marketplace in 1825. Like Richardson in Tennessee or McKenney at Mackinac, they were forced to solicit relevant knowledge on the ground and make snap judgments about its reliability. Not only did they need Mr. Smith's directions, but they also had to decide whether or not he was a trustworthy source. Although they initially found him to be reliable, they soon doubted their judgment and felt "disappointment and vexation at his misrepresentation." But they had no choice but to rely on local informants like Mr. Smith, because information about getting to Trenton was otherwise unavailable. The only guidebook that mentioned Trenton Falls in 1825, Theodore Dwight's *The Northern Traveller,* openly avoided giving specific instructions about how to reach them. "Particular directions should also be obtained before setting out," Dwight wrote, "as the nearest road is very devious, and the country is but thinly populated." Even with proper guidance, the Bigelow party could only reach Trenton Falls by providing their own transportation. Dwight advised that "it will be necessary to get a horse or carriage at Utica, as no stage coach runs that way; and to set off in the morning, as the whole day is not too long for the excursion."[33] Once they arrived, the accommodations at the falls were "unfinished," but for these intrepid travelers at least, these difficulties were compensated for by Mr. Sherman's "air of a Gentleman of the old school."[34] Only those willing to produce their own travel could reach the Rural Resort and experience the charms of its setting and of its host.

Guidance about, transportation to, and accommodations at Trenton Falls all became easier to purchase soon after 1825. From the brief and impractical mention in Dwight's 1825 guidebook, advice on getting to Trenton Falls blossomed in later publications. The third edition of Gideon Davison's pioneering *The Fashionable Tour* added a heading for the falls in 1828, with the advice that "during the warm season, stages also leave [Utica] several times a day (fare $1 going and returning) for" Trenton Falls.[35] Unlike Dwight's refusal to provide directions, Davison's extensive reproduction of stagecoach and canal packet schedules for service to Utica, along with his reference to the Trenton Falls stage, made it possible for prospective passengers to reach Sherman's door without need for local improvisation. John Disturnell's widely available 1836 *Travellers' Guide through the State of New-York* added schedule information for a second stagecoach line that ran to Trenton Falls from Little Falls, following the route that had provoked so much anxiety among the members of the Bigelow party ten years earlier.[36] Within a few years of that harrowing day, the knowledge necessary for a visit to Trenton Falls was available for purchase in the print marketplace, meaning that travelers no longer needed to rely solely on local informants like Mr. Smith.

Along with the increasing availability of published information for travelers, significant investments were made in the infrastructure necessary to transport passengers to the falls. Regular stagecoach service from Erie Canal port towns was itself an enormous advance over the hardscrabble improvisation performed by the Bigelow party, although visitors in the 1830s and 1840s thought the road itself left something to be desired. One traveler in the early 1830s bluntly claimed that "the road leading thither, although short, is one of the worst in America." He sympathized with his fellow visitors, whose "broken vehicles and begrimed faces fully confirmed the general opinion entertained of the danger and unpleasantness of proceeding by this route."[37] Ten years later, another traveler agreed that the falls "are distant from Utica only fourteen miles, in a northerly direction; but the roads are so much worse than the stage-roads in general, that it takes three hours, with the best horses, to accomplish the journey," although, he conceded, "the drive is beautiful, from the extensive and delightful views with which it abounds."[38] The ride to Trenton Falls was not enjoyable, even if leisure was the ultimate goal of such a journey.

The next round of investment came in 1851, when a plank road was opened from Utica to Trenton Falls. Plank roads, built using two stringers laid directly on the ground and decked with heavy planks, were introduced into the United States in 1844 and remained a popular technology for short but heavily traveled routes through the late 1850s.[39] Nathaniel Parker Willis's promotional account bragged that the new road made Trenton Falls only two smooth and comfortable hours from Utica, which boasted regular railroad service by 1851.[40] However, the plank road to Trenton Falls was subject to the same rapid disintegration that limited the utility and longevity of other plank roads. One visitor in 1867 captured the unpredictability of traveling on plank roads: "Sometimes we rolled along with delicious smoothness. Sometimes, where the planks had become uneven, we enjoyed some delightful tossings and bumpings."[41] But when it was in good repair, the plank road made travel to the falls faster, more reliable, and more comfortable, which encouraged Michael Moore to build "very large additions to the building," making it a structure of impressive dimensions with "all the luxuries of a first-class hotel."[42]

The construction of the Black River and Utica Railroad in the 1850s was the last major antebellum transportation investment in this region. This line was completed north through the village of Trenton in 1855, and a spur was built to Trenton Falls in 1856. Like many railroads built in the middle of the nineteenth century, the Black River and Utica was on shaky financial footing, but it made the trip to the falls smoother, quicker, and easier than it had ever been.[43] By the time Willis published the second edition of *Trenton Falls, Picturesque and Descriptive* in 1865, travel time from Utica to the falls had been reduced to an hour.[44] An 1869 guidebook stated that a traveler leaving Albany at seven o'clock in the morning could be at "the Trenton Falls Station, a little after noon," with two simple transfers at Utica and Trenton. This guidebook urged visitors not to miss "one of the most picturesque and lovely spots on the continent," precisely because it was so easy to access. "As these Falls lie only about seventeen miles off the line of railway," the guidebook opined, "with a branch railroad right up to them, they ought not to be passed without a visit."[45] The railroad made access to Trenton Falls faster, cheaper, more comfortable, more predictable, and simpler to visit, which cemented its position as a popular destination for pleasure travelers.

According to Willis's exuberant prose, gone were the days when "the naturalist, the artist, or those who sought salubrious air with domestic comfort and quiet, turned aside at Utica from the confused throng and din of the great thoroughfare; and taking a private conveyance, or the public stage-coach, neither of which were free from annoyances, found themselves, after two or three hours' ride, at Trenton Falls." Now,

HOTEL, 1851.

FIGURE 2.3. Moore's Hotel, in 1851. From Nathaniel Parker Willis's *Trenton Falls, Picturesque and Descriptive* (1865).

"instead of the old mode, the visitor to Trenton Falls takes . . . the cars on the Utica and Black River Railroad, and in forty minutes is within a mile of the hotel, to which comfortable coaches are ready to carry him." Not only was the railroad quick and comfortable, compared to the old mode, it also required less active involvement from its travelers. Willis especially touted the "system of checking baggage" in which the traveler, "on arriving at the hotel, gives the check to the porter, with the number of his room, and he has no further trouble. On leaving the hotel the baggage is checked, the check given to its owner, who retains it till it is rechecked at Utica for other destination[s]."[46] After four decades of investment and development, a visit to Trenton Falls no longer required laborious negotiation and nerve-wracking races against the twilight, looking for the glimmer of Mr. Sherman's door. Instead, it came in the form of paper abstractions like a baggage check, obtained from a managerial middleman, and representing the knowledge, technology, and labor required to deliver passengers and their bags to the hotel's door. With the arrival of the railroad, the expanded hotel, and the "system of checking baggage," a visit to Trenton Falls was a commodity easily purchased at the ticket window of the depot at Utica.

Just as the network of roads and rails that delivered visitors to Trenton Falls grew slowly over decades, so too did travelers' experiences of getting to Trenton Falls change gradually over time. In 1830, a young Bostonian named Henrietta Goddard recorded her trip from Boston to Niagara Falls "with Mother sister + 2 brothers a journey by Stage Coach + Canal Boat." Unlike the Bigelow party, they traveled in public conveyances, even though the network was still relatively skeletal, at least compared to what would come later. On July 24, their canal packet docked at Utica, "& with the same contention as usual between drivers we landed + stopped at Hatch's, dined on gingerbread + beer, took a carriage + went to Trenton, the ride excessively warm, dusty, + disagreeable, found about 5, a very good house, washed, dressed + walked down to see the falls before dark."[47] They did not have to wander the dark woods like the Bigelow party, but the marketplace for travel in central New York was still chaotic and required considerable local negotiation. Indeed, Goddard reported similar scenes of "contention" among packet boat captains and stagecoach drivers at all their stops along the Erie Canal, suggesting that while travel along the Erie Canal corridor was increasingly available as a commodity, it was not yet without improvisation.[48]

During the second half of the 1830s, Utica was linked into a network of east-west railroad lines along the most developed transportation corridor in the state. By the 1850s, these lines were integrated into the New York Central system, which allowed for one-ticket travel across the state.[49] The tighter integration of the Erie Canal route had the paradoxical effect of making Trenton Falls seem further outside the marketplace of travel than it had in the early 1830s because getting there meant venturing out of the network of canals and railroads that smoothed the flow of people and goods from Albany to Buffalo. One of Willis's correspondents recalled the visitors to Trenton Falls in the 1840s as a "somewhat select" group, due to "the expense and difficulty of access." He found this exclusivity appealing, because it attracted "cultivated and charming people" who could appreciate the subtle pleasures of a quiet country vacation in an aesthetically pleasing place. Trenton Falls was exclusive because "in the long corridor of travel between New York and Niagara," it was "a sort of alcove aside—a side-scene out of earshot of the crowd—a recess in a window whither you draw a friend by the button for the sake of chit-chat at ease." The fact that it was "fifteen miles off at right angles from the general procession, and must be done in vehicle for the purpose" made it a relatively expensive side trip for those traveling west along the easy and efficient routes provided by the canal and railroads. As a result, it was "voted a 'don't-pay' by promiscuous travellers, and its frequentation sifted [accordingly."[50] Although the exclusive crowd of the 1840s was delivered to the hotel by stagecoach service, the ease of ticketed travel along the Mohawk valley had the effect of making Trenton Falls seem once again outside the marketplace of travel.

With the arrival of the railroad at the doorstep of Moore's Hotel in the 1850s, Trenton Falls was reintegrated into the state's advanced transportation network, and Moore's Hotel came into its own as a popular destination for pleasure travelers. In November 1856, the *Ladies' Repository* published "A Letter from the Falls" from "our schoolmaster," who had taken advantage of the summer school holidays to whirl "off for the first time in his busy life to see the glorious sights and sounds which his geography has forever so temptingly been dinning in his ears." He had "a rapid transition" from Saratoga Springs to Trenton Falls—"yesterday the springs, to-day the falls"—on the railroad. "After a pleasant ride" along the Mohawk River, he wrote, "we arrived at the point from which Trenton Falls are reached and another rail road ride of sixteen miles, and a stagecoach jolting of one, brought us to the public house, situated amid the lovely scenery about the Falls."[51] Thanks to the convenience and reliability of the railroad, Trenton Falls was not "a sort of alcove aside" for the schoolmaster; rather, it was a stop on the main route between Saratoga Springs and Niagara Falls. He was a passenger who had purchased a ticket, which made it a simple transfer rather than a detour "fifteen miles off at right angles from the general procession." Similarly, Bayard Taylor, a well-known travel writer who visited the falls in 1860, boarded "the Black River train" at Utica, and "in an hour I was put down at the station, where omnibuses were in waiting to carry us to Moore's Hotel, a mile distant." Like the schoolmaster, Taylor's travel to Trenton Falls was a seamless experience, made so by his collection of guidebooks and well-orchestrated railroad service. For him, the fifteen-mile detour to the falls was characterized only by superior scenery rather than by a struggle to move himself through space. Indeed, with omnibuses ready and waiting to meet the train, he was carried to the hotel's very doorstep without considering the details of navigation, transportation, or supplies. Although it may have made for a worse adventure story, Taylor's arrival at the hotel was considerably more leisurely and pleasurable than the Bigelows' search for "a glimmering light" on "a wild obscure looking road."

The pursuit of pleasure made possible by commodified travel to places like Trenton Falls increasingly figured in popular middlebrow fiction as well. N. T. Munroe's short story "Days of Exodus," which appeared in the *Ladies' Repository* just after the Civil War, followed its narrator on a hot July tour of the Catskills, the Hudson valley, and Trenton Falls. Waiting to depart on the train from Albany, the narrator remarked: "How many were travelling! in and out, a perpetual stream of humanity. Some armed cap-a-pie for travelling, with 'ticketed through' on their dress and their faces, others looking unconcerned, and unburdened by shawls or carpet bags. Happy beings! but then they could not be going to Trenton Falls."[52] The pursuit of summer pleasure began with a purchase of a ticket. These leisure travelers—these tourists—were readily identified by "shawls" and "carpet bags," and by a certain appearance of being "ticketed through." In other words, tourists could be identified by markers indicating that they were about to enter into the machinery of travel infrastructure that would lead at the end of the day to being set down at Trenton Falls.

During the transfer between trains at Utica, the narrator consulted her guidebook in order to situate herself: "Utica, so the guide book tells me, is a flourishing city and the great thoroughfare of this region." While observing its hustle and bustle, she was startled by a local man who volunteered interesting information about a nearby bridge. She described this informant as "an animated guide book," who, "not only giving information, but also desirous of gaining it, inquired" whether she was going to Trenton and if she was meeting friends, and provided advice about hotel accommodations at the falls. After leaving Utica, the narrator thought of more questions about traveling to and staying at the falls, but "our guide book had left us."[53] Being part of the "ticketed through" crowd meant that the narrator expected to learn about her surroundings from an anonymous informant on the pages of a guidebook, not from flesh-and-blood people she met on the road. Rather than understanding the guidebook as a commercial version of asking directions along the road, she understood her local informant as anthropomorphic print. By midcentury, this author's expectation that guidance would be purchased in print in the marketplace was so strong that she interpreted people as books come to life.

Although the "animated guide book" had abandoned them, the narrator's party did not lose their way, because their tickets ensured that omnibuses awaited their arrival at the train station. In the midst of this seamless transition from one mode of transportation to the next, the narrator paused to reflect on her fellow-passengers' reaction to being carried along by this well-oiled transportation machine. "I have always noticed [a] peculiarity while travelling," she mused. "People seem to trust themselves to railroads and steamboats with perfect recklessness, but no sooner are they obliged to enter a somewhat rickety stage coach or omnibus, than they instantly begin to think of peril to life and limb. But yet what is a break down in a stage coach to a collision on a railroad or an explosion on board a steamboat!"[54] She might have found it peculiar that travelers made irrational decisions about which modes of transportation to "trust themselves" to, but she did not find it remarkable that, either way, traveling required giving up control to the larger technological and corporate structure of commodified travel. By the postwar era, at least for travel to popular leisure destinations like Trenton Falls, and at least for the relatively well-off writers and readers of the *Ladies' Repository*, transportation was a convenient if passive affair, consumed by passengers rather than produced by travelers. The commodification of travel enabled ever-greater mobility with ever-greater ease and pleasure, but taking advantage of it required giving up any illusion of control.

Munroe's short story could be playfully titled "Days of Exodus" because by 1867 the readers of the *Ladies' Repository* could be expected to understand that the kind of travel she described had leisure as its aim and intention. Its lighthearted tone reflected the growing cultural consensus that the consumption of travel could be an act of pleasure. Those who produced their own travel, like Richardson in 1815, or McKenney on the upper lakes, or the Bigelow party on their detour to Trenton Falls, rarely described their trips as relaxing and amusing experiences. But the passengers who bought commodified travel often did, and they expressed disappointment when the travel they had paid for was not efficient, reliable, and enjoyable. They approached their journeys as consumers in a marketplace, who attached an array of expectations about ease, reliability, pleasure, recreation, and fulfillment to the commodity they purchased. It was this array of consumeristic expectations, increasingly held by the passengers of stagecoaches, steamboats, and railroads, which created both the material and cultural preconditions of the emergence of tourism.

Indeed, midcentury commentators sometimes used the terms "passenger" and "tourist" interchangeably, as did a contributor to the *Southern Literary Messenger* in 1850. This contributor sought to describe one of the "very many scenes of wild and picturesque beauty [that] are often found in Virginia, which no tourist has yet thought it worth while to describe." Specifically, the author sought a raging triple waterfall in the Blue Ridge Mountains, along a side road just off a turnpike. On the hunt, "the passenger is surprised to find a level plain on the summit of a lofty mountain . . . cloven by some terrible convulsion into two parts, which are held together by a tremendous mass of solid granite. Over this rock, the stream, broken into three parts, is precipitated into the abyss below."[55] The author was both being carried along as a passenger in a carriage and being shown one of Virginia's wild wonders. On this tour, these two acts of consumption were fundamentally synonymous. By the 1850s, being a passenger in pursuit of pleasure often meant being a tourist, and vice versa.

The big commercial guidebook publishers that flourished in that decade understood this overlap between the consumers of commodified travel and the consumers of their mass-produced guidebooks. The writers and editors who compiled comprehensive guidebooks for national firms like D. Appleton & Company were relentless cheerleaders of the transportation development, praising it as sound business and a patriotic endeavor of public service. They also realized that the crowds of passengers clutching newly purchased tickets represented a vast national market for their guidebooks, and they subtly reshaped their texts to be more useable in an age of ticketed travel. For example, the editor of *Appleton's Northern and Eastern Traveller's Guide* in the 1850s removed the lengthy tables of routes that had been a standard feature of early guidebooks but that were bulky and of little use to passengers being transported by mechanical means. He also eliminated the standard large foldout map pasted into the flyleaf, which "from the smallness of the scale on which it is graduated, is of very little practical use in a railroad car—and which, from its size, and the necessity of its being opened and re-opened, folded and refolded, is extremely inconvenient in a crowded conveyance, as well as an annoyance to its possessor and his fellow-passengers." Instead, the editor divided his guidebook into a series of routes, following individual lines of railroad and steamboat travel, each with its own small map and list of distances as traveled by modern conveyance. As a result, "with this book in his hand, the Traveller, as he proceeds on his journey in the railroad car, or glides along in the swift and graceful steamboat, can open to the route he is going, and follow it through without trouble or inconvenience." Each route's combination of maps, description, and "all the requisite information respecting hotels, &c., and the charges for boarding—places of amusement—interesting localities in the vicinity, &c., &c." was explicitly organized according to the needs to passengers.

As such texts became more tightly linked to the routes of canals, steamboats, and railroads, they removed ever more of the burden of marshaling specific geographical knowledge from individual travelers, decreased the need for improvisation on the road, and encouraged passengers to think of travel as leisure. Indeed, the conveniently packaged geographical knowledge that guidebooks like Williams's offered for sale in the marketplace came from the same sources as those which spurred the development of travel technology. He gathered much of his information from "a correspondence with individuals connected with the routes," and he solicited "Railroad and Steamboat Companies . . . to forward us the latest information relative to their respective lines, which shall be attended to in our corrected editions."[56] Appleton's celebrated the commercial and national potential of the commodification of travel, and they wrote their guidebook to capture as much of its market as possible. The consumers who bought both railroad tickets and Appleton's guides increasingly became known as tourists.

3 /   I Find Myself a Pilgrim: Commodified
Experience and the Invention of the Tourist

In the late 1850s, the Edinburgh publishing firm Thomas Nelson and Sons was working to build a successful catalogue for its newly established American branch, opened in New York in 1854.[1] Like the other big New York generalist publishing houses whose ranks they hoped to join, T. Nelson and Sons invested in tourist guidebooks for the burgeoning national market. They broke no new ground in terms of format or coverage, a wise strategy for a firm finding its footing in an unfamiliar market. Their titles repackaged existing geographical knowledge about well-established destinations for pleasure travel, like the Hudson valley, Niagara Falls, and Lake George, and they were reissued regularly for tourists seeking easy access to the standards. It was in this spirit that T. Nelson and Sons published a brief overview of popular tourist spots in 1858, chattily titled *Our Summer Retreats*. Its subtitle promised "a handbook to all the chief waterfalls, springs, mountain and sea side resorts, and other places of interest in the United States."[2] The publication of such an ambitious national tourist guidebook was soon interrupted by the Civil War, but during its brief run *Our Summer Retreats* exemplified the antebellum market for tourist print in its most developed form. It described a tourist landscape that was national in scale, thoroughly canonized, easy to understand and to undertake, and available to a national marketplace of consumers.

The content of *Our Summer Retreats* was indelibly shaped by the commodity marketplace of the moment in which it was published. It contained almost no practical information about getting to "the chief waterfalls, springs, mountain and sea side resorts" that filled its pages. By the late 1850s, the anonymous authors of commercial guidebooks could comfortably assume that the details of transportation would be handled by steamboat, railroad, and stagecoach lines, as a part of the ticket price paid by the tourists who perused their pages. They did not organize their popular destinations into fixed tours, like an earlier generation of guidebooks had, because tourists looking to follow a particular route could choose from any number of more specialized print products that packaged the same information along particular rail lines or steamboat routes. Instead, the authors of *Our Summer Retreats* filled their pages with lively descriptions of the kinds of experiences that tourists could expect to have at each of the destinations they described.

Each summer retreat offered a specific, unique kind of experience, designed to appeal to a particular kind of tourist, or a tourist in a particular mood. "Life at [Saratoga] springs is a perpetual festival," the guidebook enthused. "The people dance and drink—drink and dance,—rising early to do the one, and sitting up late to perform the other."[3] If Saratoga was a "perpetual festival," then Lake George was a place where city dwellers threw "themselves into the full enjoyment of the bright pure atmosphere of the country." Niagara left its visitors with "a feeling that they have beheld one of the 'wonders of the world,'" one that had an "effect upon the mind" that was "deeply solemnizing." The White Mountains, on the other hand, was where "enterprising tourists" would "find savage wilds and romantic solitudes enough . . . to occupy all their time." The authors had a harder time with the Virginia springs, due to their number and variety, but tourists could expect to enjoy "the extreme beauty of the scenery in which they are situated, the valuable qualities of their waters, and the excellence of the hotel and lodging accommodation."[4] In each case, *Our Summer Retreats* distilled the kinds of experiences tourists could expect to have at each popular destination, in return for spending their leisure dollars there.

Our Summer Retreats was emblematic of the 1850s because it described the possibilities of tourism as a set of experiences available for purchase in a national marketplace, offered by providers who were discovering how to turn leisure into a commodity. It was the product of a distinct process of commodification that was nevertheless fundamentally connected to the processes of commodification that reshaped the marketplaces for printed geographical knowledge and for transportation during the first half of the nineteenth century. The emerging tourist industry turned consumers of geographical knowledge and consumers of commodified travel into consumers of leisure experiences, a group that increasingly came to be labeled "tourists." A wide range of entrepreneurs, including hotel owners, steamboat and stagecoach operators, printers, and local merchants sought to capture some of the enormous sums that Americans spent on traveling each year by advertising the experiences that travelers could reliably expect at their destinations. They did so using a set of recognizable and desirable cultural categories, offering interchangeable social and aesthetic experiences to anyone with the money to pay for them. Between the 1820s and the 1850s, tourism entrepreneurs gradually constructed a national market for commodified leisure experiences and turned a pleasurable summer's jaunt into a predictable, standardized commodity that holidaymakers could safely buy from strangers.

The commodified experiences offered by tourism entrepreneurs found a large and growing audience among middle-class and wealthy Americans, even if these enthusiastic tourists would not have described them as such. Such tourists recounted moments of pleasure, as well as the cultural and social value that they derived from those moments. The terms in which they did so largely reflected those that tourism entrepreneurs used to sell their wares; they may not have thought of themselves as consuming commodified experiences, but when they recorded their tours, they revealed that such experiences were precisely those that they sought out and most enjoyed. To borrow Pierre Bourdieu's analytical terms, these tourists obtained cultural capital by consuming culturally significant experiences, like perpetual festivals; pure, atmospheric rural recreations; solemnizing natural wonders; and "savage wilds and romantic solitudes." They also sought to augment their social capital by building connections with a national cohort of similarly educated and prosperous people through shared consumption of these significant experiences.[5] But not all travelers wholeheartedly embraced the opportunities offered by the tourist industry to consume experiences with social peers. By the 1830s, a significant and growing number of Americans who undertook journeys began to express skepticism about the value of commodified tourist experiences because they seemed overly fashionable, superficial, and perhaps even dangerously meaningless. The emerging marketplace for commodified leisure gave the term "tourist" its modern, more specific meaning, describing a distinct subset of travelers who followed well-beaten paths in order to have well-understood and fundamentally predictable experiences. The association of such tourists with broadly available market commodities also helped to give the term its profound modern ambivalence.

In the early 1790s, a New York merchant named Nicholas Low made a daring decision to increase the value of his extensive land holdings in Saratoga County by developing a small cluster of springs in a swampy valley into fashionable spa for the traveling elite of his new nation. Elite Europeans had traveled to mineral and hot springs for pleasure and health since the late seventeenth century. The spas that grew out of this practice in the eighteenth century, like Bath and Tunbridge Wells in England, or Baden Baden and Vichy on the continent, quickly turned into venues where a scattered aristocratic class could meet, build relationships, marry off children, and pursue health in a leisurely environment. By all accounts, the rough settlement of Ballston, where Low owned land around the springs, was an unlikely spot to attract the genteel crowd that would make it an American Bath; it was remote, without any unique natural features, and not really on the way to anywhere else. Indeed, Low was willing to entertain a number of unlikely schemes to attract residents, visitors, and investment to his backwoods property, including political maneuvering to attract the county courthouse and an ill-fated steam-powered cotton mill. Comparatively, enticing a relatively tiny and scattered early national elite to pass their summer months in a remote valley was a reasonable idea, as well as a reasonably successful one.[6]

Since Low's target market was members of his own social class, or even his own social circle, Ballston's early growth was largely fueled by word of mouth. Low and other early hotel proprietors did not pursue a strategy of formal advertising; indeed, in the context of late eighteenth-century print advertising, it is hard to imagine how they would have pitched Ballston's ephemeral attractions amid the long columns of dry goods and ships' cargoes.[7] But they did rely on print descriptions of visitors' experiences in order to attract attention and patronage. In 1802, Ballston received favorable coverage in the *Port Folio*, an early literary and political magazine published by prominent Philadelphia Federalists. Summer at Ballston was characterized by a "determination of cheerfulness," which created an atmosphere of "good humor and sociability." The young resort attracted "the gay, the brilliant and the fashionable from every quarter of the union," who passed their days "riding, walking, reading and fishing," and their evenings with "music and dancing."[8] Such brief notices emphasized the playful crowd at Ballston rather than the material details of lodging or transportation. Since there was precious little reason to pass through the town otherwise, suggesting that fun times could be had at the springs was the best way to persuade summer travelers with money to spend to come to such an inconvenient spot.

At the turn of the nineteenth century, the innkeepers of Ballston were unique in receiving this kind of coverage for providing leisure experiences to a far-flung community of summer pleasure-seekers. Somewhat paradoxically, most eighteenth-century travel-related enterprises were local in their orientation. Stagecoach lines and the coasting trade largely served small short-haul markets, and taverns mostly hosted local gatherings, with overnight guests as a sideline business at best.[9] There was no real national market for travel, so long-distance travelers made their way by negotiating a series of disjointed local markets. To the extent that they advertised, eighteenth-century enterprises tended to publicize information about their services. Stagecoach advertisements listed schedules, fares, and where seats could be bought (see figure 3.1).[10] Tavern keepers were even more sparing when seeking business. With a few exceptions, they tended to publish notices only when opening a new tavern or when an existing house changed hands, such as when Christiana Campbell took out a notice in the *Virginia Gazette* in 1771 to "acquaint the Publick that I have opened tavern in the House, behind the Capitol, lately occupied by Mrs. *Vobe*; where those Gentlemen who please to favor me with their Custom may depend upon genteel Accommodations, and the very best Entertainment."[11] Eighteenth-century travel providers sought to impress potential clients with the quality of their services, but they did not advertise experiences. And other nascent summer gathering places for a leisured elite, like the village of Berkeley Springs, Virginia, relied exclusively on informal social networks to draw a crowd.[12] Updates from those springs were more likely to appear in private correspondence than in the pages of distant city newspaper like the *Port Folio.*

By the second quarter of the nineteenth century, however, the emergence of radically improved transportation networks meant that small innkeepers and stagecoach operators could no longer rely on being the default option for a limited number of travelers on the road. At the same time, the small handful of colonial "watering places" like Berkeley Springs, or Bristol Springs in Pennsylvania or Stafford Springs in Connecticut, were joined by new destinations that were established in the early years of the nation, like Ballston. More travelers—especially more leisure travelers—meant more business, but it also meant more competition. Furthermore, the increasing facility of long-distance travel meant that entrepreneurs looking to profit off of leisure travel had to learn to sell their services in distant markets, to strangers unacquainted with the virtues of particular routes and destinations. The informational notices of the eighteenth century offered little to attract travelers who had a

PARKER's

Mail Stage,

From Whiteſtown to Canajoharrie.

THE *Mail leaves Whiteſtown every
Monday and Thurſday, at two o'clock
P. M. and proceeds to Old Fort Schuyler the
ſame evening ; next morning ſtarts at four
o'clock, and arrives at Canajoharrie in the
evening ; exchanges paſſengers with the Al
bany and Cooperſtown ſtages, and the next
day returns to Old Fort Schuyler.*

 *Fare for paſſengers, Two Dollars ; way
paſſengers, Four Pence per mile ; 14lb. baggage gratis ; 150wt. rated the ſame as a
paſſenger.*

 *Seats may be had by applying at the Poſt-
Office, Whiteſtown, at the houſe of the ſub-
criber, Old Fort Schuyler, or at Captain
Roof's, Canajoharrie.*

       JASON PARKER.

Auguſt, 1795.   8ᵒ

FIGURE 3.1. Advertisement for Parker's Mail Stage in central New York State, 1795.

growing range of choices and who were increasingly seeking pleasure, not just utility, in their travel. As a result, these entrepreneurs learned to sell experiences rather than services. In order to do so, they increasingly turned to longer-form descriptions in nationally oriented publications that were aimed specifically at potential travelers, like the early updates on life at the springs that appeared in the *Port Folio*. But three decades into the nineteenth century, the growing number of such destinations and the resulting competition between them meant that entrepreneurs could no longer rely on chatty, informal updates from sympathetic editors to drive visitors to sample the experiences they offered.

That the 1820s was both the decade in which travel entrepreneurs embraced the marketing of leisure experiences and the decade in which Gideon Davison and his early imitators pioneered the genre of the tourist guidebooks—and that both innovations were pursued most aggressively in the same economic landscape of upstate New York—was not a coincidence. Like Nicolas Low in the 1790s, the travel entrepreneurs of the 1820s were attempting a culturally and commercially novel strategy. Selling experiences required explanation; potential leisure travelers had to be taught precisely what was for sale, what they could expect from a summer excursion to one of these new tourist destinations, and why they should find those experiences socially and culturally valuable. Promotional pamphlets and booster guidebooks were extended and extensive forms of advertising that taught these lessons while pitching the specific experiences available at specific destinations. This effort was slow and gradual, and appeared earliest and most intensively in the places where there was the most competition for discretionary—that is to say, recreational—travelers. But the collective effect of this advertising was to create a set of standardized experiences that came to represent recreational travel purchasable in the marketplace; experiences, in other words, began to be turned into commodities.

Entrepreneurs relied on long-form narrative advertising to train consumers of commodified experiences through the 1850s. By midcentury, however, at least some leisure providers felt comfortable enough selling experiences to an educated consumer base that they began to offer social whirlwinds, or the comforts of the old country homestead, or aesthetic immersion into sublime wonders in simple single-column newspaper advertisements. By the eve of the Civil War, potential tourists understood that they were buying fundamentally standardized experiences—and that those experiences were valuable and desirable—which allowed providers to advertise them in a pithy shorthand. Whether in pamphlets, guidebooks, or newsprint, leisure travel entrepreneurs did not sell generic experiences; they sold specific experiences, based on their perception of their locale's desirable features. Facing increasing competition for leisure travelers after 1820, each destination that sought to attract such travelers pursued a strategy of specialization. They focused in on specific experiences that travelers could expect to have on a visit, distinct from those that could be expected at other destinations. In doing so, travel entrepreneurs were forced to carefully identify the quintessential experiences that their guests typically had, and to articulate them in culturally meaningful and appealing terms.

Early innovators like Nicholas Low understood that the appeal of a destination like Ballston was predominantly social; it was the presence of "the gay, the brilliant and the fashionable from every quarter of the union," as the *Port Folio* put it, that would entice leisure travelers to visit Ballston rather than other, perhaps less inconvenient, mineral springs. Even though entrepreneurs in spa towns that had eighteenth-century roots like Ballston and Berkeley Springs had several decades' head start at convening a socially desirable crowd, they were quickly surpassed by a new generation of entrepreneurs willing to aggressively advertise an active social scene, which they called "company" or "society." Hotels that sought a national clientele of leisure travelers emphasized both the entertainment that they offered to their guests and the quality of the crowd that they attracted as a result. As early as 1825, Saratoga Springs booster Gideon Davison advertised the "card parties," the "pleasing recreation at the reading rooms," and "the billiard rooms, which are annexed to most of the boarding establishments." More important was the "ball or promenade" that "usually crowned" the "amusements of the day." He emphasized the size of the "cotillion rooms," which, "when enlivened by the associated beauty and gaiety resorting to the springs, present a scene of novelty and fascination seldom equalled."[13] In this pitch, the recreational establishments of Saratoga Springs were not just advertising their facilities, they were selling a unique experience of beauty, gaiety, novelty, and fascination.

Such descriptions commonly focused more on the crowds that inhabited the hotels than on the rooms that contained them. By focusing on the "company" or "society" present at a destination, these entrepreneurs were selling a particular kind of refined social experience. In the broadest terms, they advertised the social quality of the guests in their rooms, which allowed them to offer other potential guests an experience both free of social embarrassment as well as potentially socially enriching.

For example, Theodore Dwight's 1826 guide to the Fashionable Tour in upstate New York and New England advertised the Pine Orchard, a large hotel built on a plateau in the Catskill Mountains, by promising that "the attractions of its scenery are redoubled by the presence of agreeable and refined society. Individuals of taste and leisure, and still more, parties of travellers, will thus often enjoy a gratification which is rarely to be found in a place naturally so wild and difficult of access."[14] In this guidebook pitch, scenic splendor paired with social "gratification" to produce a leisure experience enticing enough to draw travelers up the steep, rugged, and inconvenient mountain road to the hotel.

By the 1830s, entrepreneurs outside of upstate New York had begun to adopt the strategy of selling exclusive social experiences through long-form guidebooks. William Horner, a doctor in the springs district of western Virginia who penned a guide to the region in 1833–34, found that most of the springs hotels offered "many personal attractions of high polish and cultivated intellect," but that above all White Sulphur Springs was "distinguished by the excellence and polish of the company." Travelers seeking a rarefied social experience could do no better than White Sulphur, where the cream of Virginia society "finds itself represented, and by a proper combination forms a gay and highly finished aggregate." White Sulphur was also the place to meet a broader national elite, because its "model of a courtly and well constituted company, has its interest enhanced by contributions from most other parts of the United States, but more largely from the South and West."[15] These descriptions of the crowd present at the various destinations were similar in their broad outlines while differing in their particulars. This combination was the hallmark of a commodified experience; the social offerings of these resort hotels were sufficiently similar that potential consumers knew what to expect when shopping for them, and also sufficiently different that they could compete against each other in an emerging national market for sociable summer vacations.

Although many destinations advertised the social experiences that they offered to leisure travelers, not all were able to offer a "model of a courtly and well constituted company" as effectively as the large, well-established, and fashionable mineral springs resorts like Saratoga and White Sulphur Springs. Smaller hotels and newer, more obscure destinations that could not command the same social power or social polish sought to offer a distinctly different kind of summer experience, one that nevertheless had enough cultural resonance to be recognizable and desirable in the leisure marketplace. These smaller destinations were more likely to advertise pastoral experiences, and they did so by playing on contemporary cultural associations between rural life, virtue, peacefulness, and wholesomeness. In 1826, Dwight described Suffield Springs, a small place in northern Connecticut, as "pleasant, in the midst of a rich rural scene, with a pretty flower garden, &c. calculated to render it an agreeable resort, which it will, no doubt, in due time become."[16] These small, pastoral resorts multiplied in subsequent decades. An 1855 guide recommended Clifton Springs, a small village along the Erie Canal in upstate New York, as "a desirable retreat . . . for those who, with their families, are disposed to leave the heated walls of a city residence, to enjoy the refreshing breezes and pure atmosphere of the country."[17] Like Lake George in *Our Summer Retreats*, these small destinations advertised "enjoyment of the bright pure atmosphere of the country" to urban consumers who were looking to purchase a pastoral experience. They did so by using terms associated with romanticized country life like "refreshing," "pure," "pleasant," "rich," and "pretty."

This romanticized country life was its own distinct kind of social experience. The company at such rural retreats was advertised as healthy, unpretentious, and virtuous, often in implicit or even explicit opposition to the fashionable, glittering, and cosmopolitan crowd at the big resorts. For example, in an 1851 pamphlet written to promote the "Rural Resort," a small hotel on the edge of Trenton Falls, a scenic gorge in upstate New York, Nathaniel Parker Willis heartily recommended the rural experience that the proprietor offered to potential visitors. "The company of strangers at Trenton is . . . somewhat select," Willis claimed, consisting of hotel guests anchored by "three or four families . . . who form the nucleus of an agreeable society to which any attractive transient visitor easily attaches an acquaintance." The boarders at the hotel were complemented by day visitors from "every village within thirty miles; and from ten in the morning till four in the afternoon, there is gay work with the country-girls and their beaux—swinging under the trees, strolling about in the woods near the house, bowling, singing, and dancing." And if this description of simple, wholesome country leisure with real "country-girls and their beaux" was insufficiently clear, Willis drew an explicit contrast with the "courtly" company at the bigger destinations. The Rural Resort was "for those who love country air and romantic rambles without 'dressing for dinner' or waltzing by a band."[18] Willis was the ideal spokesman for such a marketing campaign built around the pleasures of a comfortable, domestic rural experience. With scores of popular print depictions of his home life at his rural estates at Glenmary and Idlewild, Willis was known as much for being the embodiment of sentimental, respectable, and bourgeois rural life as he was for the literature he produced. Attaching his name to a piece of promotional literature for Trenton Falls meant that potential visitors knew precisely what kind of experience they could expect to have there, and why it would be one of cultural value.[19]

The strategy of selling experiences was pioneered in the East, but it was increasingly adopted by leisure entrepreneurs in the South and West in the 1850s. At the same time, publishers in the increasingly competitive guidebook market were only too glad to hear from "proprietors of Mineral Springs, and those interested in Sea-Bathing Establishments, Water-Falls, and other places of retreat" all around the country, who could "contribute information and patronage" that could sell books and vacations.[20] Given the thinner population of the interior states and territories, a majority of these southern and western destinations advertised a wholesome rural social experience. The proprietors of the "Ohio White Sulphur Springs" near Columbus highlighted its combination of "healthy location, agreeable scenery, suitable provisions for both comfort and recreation, with mineral waters of undoubted virtue."[21] John Disturnell described Mackinac, Michigan, as "so far north, and so surrounded by cool waters, that it always enjoys a pure, bracing air, inviting exercise, and ensuring a good appetite."[22] But interior destinations sometimes sought to sell fashion and social distinction, as well. By the end of the decade, a Virginia slave trader named John Armfield had opened a hotel at Beersheba Springs in Tennessee that offered "society" that was "always select, elegant and cultivated, and this, in connection with the value of the waters, and the salubrious character of the atmosphere, [made] *Beersheba* a very desirable summer retreat."[23] Although places like Ohio White Sulphur, Mackinac, and Beersheba attracted a largely regional crowd, the experiences of rural relaxation or elegant cultivation that they offered were advertised in the same terms and in the same publications as the more established eastern destinations.

Like many successful tourist destinations around the country, Armfield's hotel at Beersheba Springs promoted its unique and significant setting as one of the features that made it worth visiting. In Beersheba's case, the hotel and spring were perched on "the summit of one of the spurs of the Cumberland Mountain," so its proprietors touted the "scenery" as "both beautiful and picturesque, and remarkable alike for its extent of range and its wild and romantic prospects."[24] Embedded in this brief description was a promise that visitors to Beersheba could expect to have a meaningful aesthetic experience as well as a valuable social experience. Proprietors commonly offered such aesthetic experiences, often at greater length than this pithy shorthand. Willis's 1851 pamphlet advertising Trenton Falls spilled considerable ink on the falls themselves, a series of cataracts at the bottom of a deep gorge in an otherwise gentle, pastoral landscape. It described the experience of descending the long staircase into the gorge, where "You have passed into a subterranean world . . . your attention is forthwith attracted to the magnificence, the grandeur, the beauty, and sublimity of the scene. You stand and pause. You behold the operations of incalculable ages. You are thrown back to antediluvian times."[25] He continued in this vein for pages, describing an intense aesthetic experience in an insistent second-person narration designed to pull potential visitors into imagining what it would be like to have such an experience themselves. Willis promised a pleasurable juxtaposition between the gentle grace of the Rural Resort's country surroundings and the awe-inspiring drama of the nearby ravine. Like Beersheba's potential visitors, those considering a trip to Trenton Falls would have instantaneously recognized a description of an experience of the picturesque.

Beginning in the 1820s, and increasingly in the 1830s and 1840s, well-read Americans used the language of the picturesque to evaluate the aesthetic quality of their travel. They borrowed this concept from Britain, where a growing number of tourists had begun canvassing the nation's highways and byways in search of picturesque scenery in the late eighteenth century. These largely middle-class tourists were constructing a cultural form that reflected their growing social refinement and powerful sense of British nationalism, particularly in opposition to the aristocratic practice of Grand Tour on the Continent. They produced countless "delineations in pen and pencil"—meaning written narratives of travel, and sketches and paintings of scenery—as part of a craze that lasted through the early decades of the nineteenth century. American readers were introduced to the hunt for the picturesque by the historical romances of Walter Scott, particularly *Waverly*, first published in the United States in 1815, and by Washington Irving, who integrated picturesque tropes into American stories in his *Sketch-Book of Geoffrey Crayon*, in 1819. They similarly received a visual education in picturesque scenery from the paintings of Thomas Cole and his followers in the Hudson River school, who, beginning in the 1820s, applied the rules of British picturesque landscape painting, practiced by painters like J. M. W. Turner, to American landscapes, particularly in upstate New York and New England. By the 1830s, culturally literate Americans had fully embraced the picturesque as a refined form of landscape appreciation, and they began to seek experiences of the picturesque as a sign of their personal refinement.[26]

The specific qualities of a picturesque landscape remained murky even at the height of the concept's popularity. William Gilpin, the most popular theorist of the picturesque, argued that ideal scenery combined beautiful and sublime elements into a compositional whole as if framed in a painting. The beautiful and the sublime were categories that had been rigorously distinguished in 1757 by Edmund Burke, who analyzed them as opposing aesthetic experiences rooted in the emotions of love and fear. Burke's philosophy was centrally concerned with the relationship between perception and emotion, and as a result, it was too sophisticated to be accessible to casual scenery hunters on either side of the Atlantic. But Gilpin, who was a committed popularizer, leeched much of the complexity out of Burke's thought. For Gilpin, the beautiful described that which was well formed and human-scale; the contemplation of the beautiful was essentially a humanizing and pleasurable experience. By contrast, the sublime was characterized by a combination of astonishment and terror, and necessarily turned the viewer's thoughts to the almighty and the eternal. The picturesque balanced the two in pleasing harmony. Gilpin's definitions were vague and contextual, especially compared to the philosophical rigor of Burke. But the vagueness of Gilpin's tourist picturesque was precisely its power; in its popular usage, its constituent parts could be applied to any appealing landscape, and thus it was a sufficiently capacious concept to hold the cultural ambitions of many diverse tourists on both sides of the Atlantic.[27]

Like Armfield promoting Beersheba or Willis promoting Trenton Falls, travel entrepreneurs of the 1850s commonly used the language of the beautiful, the picturesque, and the sublime to sell aesthetic experiences to tourists looking to join the transatlantic ranks of scenery hunters. Eastern mountain ranges like the White Mountains of New Hampshire and the Blue Ridge of Virginia, which were the earliest mountains to become reasonably accessible to leisure travelers, offered rugged scenery that promised sublime experiences to visitors willing to make the trek. An 1855 guide designed to lure travelers to the White Mountains advertised the summit houses atop Mt. Washington as a "true home" to those who sought "a gratification of curiosity for the wonderful in sublime scenery." Departing from the usual dry tone of guidebooks, the author rhapsodized: "Ye who delight to behold the works of nature in their most

FIGURE 3.2. *View from Fishkill Looking to West Point*, from *The Hudson River Portfolio* (1820). This important early print shaped the later marketing of picturesque experiences in the Hudson River valley. Courtesy of the New York Public Library.

sublime flights, come to these mountains! Ye who have a love for novelty and desire for true pleasure, come and behold God's wisdom displayed in the bold outlines of this gigantic monument of his almighty power! Here the underlying features of grandeur were moulded in imperishable materials by his hand!"[28] This guidebook both promised "sublime scenery" and modeled the kind of rapturous experience tourists could expect to have in the White Mountains. Similarly, an 1851 guide promoted the Natural Bridge in Virginia's Blue Ridge as "one of the greatest natural curiosities in the country, if not in the world. . . . The view from the top is awfully grand; yet one should go to the brow of the precipice that descends to the level of the creek, where the view, equally sublime, will be found far more interesting, being divested in a great measure, of the awe which is sensibly felt on looking from the bridge down into the dreadful gulf."[29] In both cases, these guides used the fashionable language of the picturesque to sell potential tourists a desirable emotional experience of landscape.

The destination that most prominently advertised intense sensory experience was Niagara Falls. Niagara had been regularly described as "the most sublime and tremendous cataract in the known world" in travel narratives, periodical articles, geographies, and textbooks since the eighteenth century.[30] Entrepreneurs capitalized on this frequent and casual use of Niagara Falls to define the ideal sublime scene by selling this experience to a national marketplace of leisure travelers. As early as 1825, a guidebook promoting travel in New York State promised that at Niagara "the mind can feel the real grandeur inspired by this truly magnificent and sublime prospect." Indeed, "the emotions of grandeur that fill the mind, on beholding this greatest of the wonders of nature, can scarcely be felt from any effort of description."[31] The obvious implication of this description was that it was better for tourists to travel to Niagara and purchase this experience for themselves. Guidebooks published in subsequent decades picked up and elaborated on this theme. One author writing in 1836 asserted that tourists would "leave the spot with a true idea of the vast, the grand, the sublime," while another, writing in 1839, suggested that visitors had "been completely infatuated, and seem only to live in beholding this sublime work of nature."[32] An 1852 guide reinforced this point with a reported endorsement from actual tourists. It described the lunar rainbow occasionally visible over the Falls as "indescribably grand, worthy the attention of the tourist, and will amply pay him for a trip to the Island, to behold. 'Thou hast told me right,' said a party of Quakers, from Philadelphia, to the author, 'this sight alone, is sufficient to pay us for a journey to the Falls.' The mind takes a wild and sublime range, but its emotions cannot be expressed."[33]

By the 1840s, local travel entrepreneurs sought to capitalize on Niagara's growing national reputation for sublimity by advertising up-close encounters with the sublime. Cataract House emerged as one of the earliest and most desirable hotels at the Falls under the ownership of General Parkhurst Whitney around 1830.[34] In its first decade of operation, its domination of the market for tourist lodgings at the Falls was relatively uncontested, and guidebooks of this era mentioned its existence without elaborating on its appeal.[35] By the 1840s, however, the Cataract House faced growing competition on both the American and the British sides of the Falls, so guidebook notices of the hotel increasingly promised "a fine view of the American Falls, the Islands, &c.," and "pleasant suites of rooms looking out upon the sublime scene."[36] Indeed, entrepreneurs beyond the hotel trade advertised sublime experiences; the owners of the *New Maid of the Mist*, a steamboat that carried tourists through the gorge, promised that a ride on their craft would "afford[] the tourist sublime and comprehensive views of all the points of interest on the trip" (see figure 3.3).[37] This advertisement could be expected to work in 1856 because its audience understood the cultural significance of the sublime; because they had been exposed to a generation of print that taught them that Niagara was the place to go to experience the sublime; and because the steamboat operators offered that experience for sale, in a discrete, prepackaged unit, easily accessed by omnibus from the hotels.

By midcentury, the entrepreneurs of Niagara Falls had developed a reputation for being efficient fleecers of tourist dollars; as the *Ladies' Repository* put it: "There exists at Niagara every species of contrivance and machinery to make money out of visitors. There are hackmen to drive you to the bridge and over Goat Island at enormous charges—a tollgatherer to extort twenty-five cents for passing over a bridge—a seller of Indian moccasons [*sic*] and gewgaws, and a loafer offering you a miserable glass prism to look through at the Falls."[38] But by the 1850s, they were not alone. Brief notices advertising summer tourist experiences for sale were a routine sight in popular middlebrow print aimed at a middle-class audience with the resources for leisure travel, and they reflected the growing geographical spread of the tourist industry. They took the form of editorial notices in summer editions, like the brief item in *Frank Leslie's Illustrated Newspaper* on July 16, 1859, that listed "Pleasant Summer Resorts." In an issue that also contained a long article on the wonders of Niagara, the editors of the paper recommended a small selection of other destinations, from the Latourette House in New Jersey, which was "just the spot for a New Yorker to luxuriate in"; to the Pavilion Hotel on Long Island, which offered "good fishing, fine driving, good sailing and shady lounging . . . quite sufficient for those who desire ease and repose, or delightful amusement"; to White Sulphur Springs, Ohio, "an enviable retreat for invalids . . . [that] would, no doubt, repay the tourist."[39]

Such notices also took the form of advertising column inches in national circulation periodicals purchased by tourist entrepreneurs directly. For example, the July 3, 1858, edition of *Harper's Weekly* included an advertisement for the Nahant House in Massachusetts, "combining the luxury of sumptuous entertainment with the genuine comforts of a quiet home" for "families desiring a *cool retreat* during the hot season." On the same page, the proprietors of the Columbian Hotel in Saratoga Springs offered "a pleasant and desirable place of sojourn for

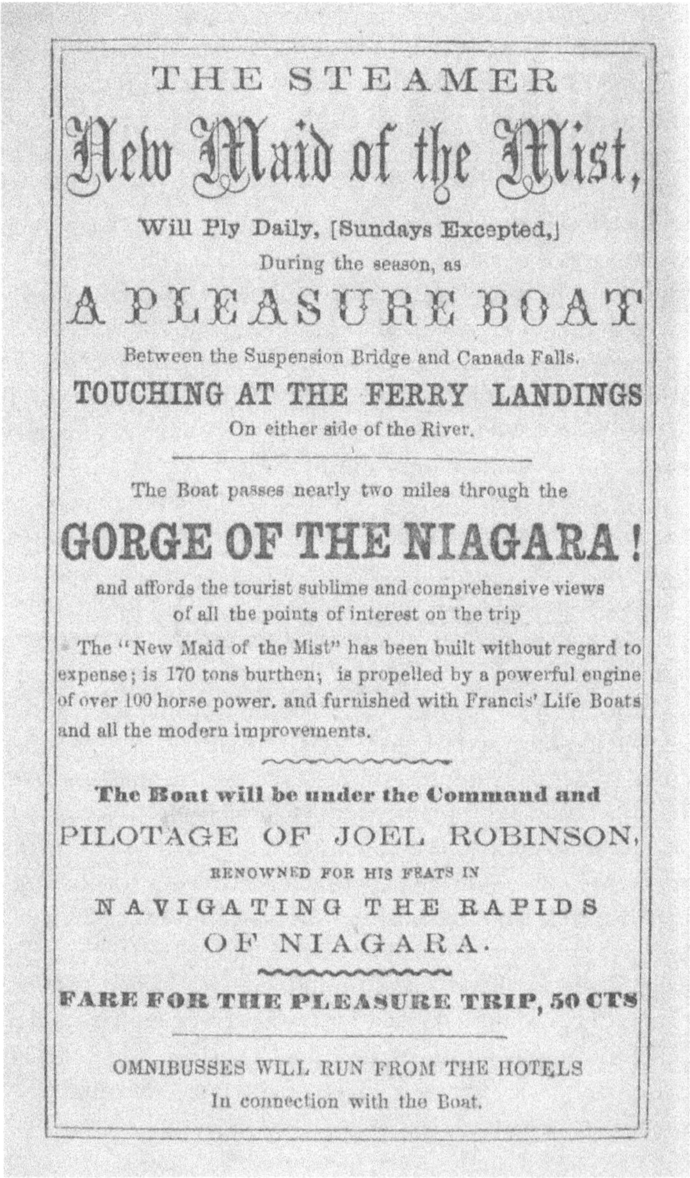

FIGURE 3.3. Advertisement for the *New Maid of the Mist* at Niagara Falls, 1856.

the transient or more permanent guest," especially "all who may wish to avoid the drinking and kindred fashionable follies of other houses."[40] These advertisers all sought to define and differentiate the experiences they offered, by combining luxury, fashion, pastoral peace, picturesque scenery, sobriety, and other desirable and well-established categories of summer pleasure, according to their own unique formulae. Their notices were unremarkable in their context, because by the late 1850s the middle-class consumers who read *Frank Leslie's* and *Harper's* expected to shop for leisure experiences in the back pages of their magazines, and their expectations about the possibilities and cultural value of summer leisure had been shaped by a generation of long-form, narrative advertising in guidebooks and the popular press. The brief advertisements that appeared on the back pages of periodicals in the 1850s catered to those expectations by offering experiences as commodities for sale.

The commodification of experience was most obvious in places like Niagara Falls, Saratoga, and the scattered springs of Virginia, which had built an economy around catering to recreational travelers early in their history. But this economic strategy was not limited to a handful of famous places; travel-related enterprises from Connecticut to Ohio to Tennessee similarly tried to sell local experiences into a national market of potential travelers, with varying levels of success. But even if places like Suffield Springs and the lesser-known White Sulphur Springs of Ohio failed to grow as large Saratoga Springs or the well-known White Sulphur Springs of (West) Virginia, they benefited from the broader process of commodification driven by the big destinations that sought to transform previously unique experiences into standardized and interchangeable ones. The largely urban middle classes who were the main beneficiaries of the development of national markets looked to use their newfound prosperity to enrich their lives experientially through consumption in that same national market. By the middle of the century, a generation of mostly rural and small-town entrepreneurs thrived on selling them those experiences.

These entrepreneurs found success because there was a large and growing number of enthusiastic consumers for the experiences they offered. These consumers sought out commodified experiences of summer leisure for essentially the same reasons that the promotional materials suggested they would, even if they never referred to themselves as "consumers" or thought of their summer vacations as "commodified experiences." Instead, they sometimes called themselves "tourists," occasionally called themselves "pilgrims," and usually settled for the simple and generic term "travellers." The fact that they did not use the analytical language of twenty-first-century historians of capitalism is not a surprise, but it is striking how hesitant they were to adopt the label "tourist," considering that it was a commonly understood actor's category. The problem, for these comfortable consumers of commodified experience, lay in the increasingly negative connotation that the term "tourist" had acquired by the middle decades of the nineteenth century. The specific contours of this negative connotation are the subject of chapter 4, but recall for now how E. L. Blanchard described tourists in his 1847 "physiology . . . of travelling and travellers." He called them "meditative fl[ies] . . . who merely travel[] for the sake of travelling."[41] In the face of such wry condescension, relatively few travelers who went in search of commodified experiences of summer leisure embraced the term.

This reticence creates a research challenge for historians of tourism, because tourists were reluctant to identify themselves as such. As a result, we must apply a subtler analysis of their language to identify those travelers who enthusiastically consumed the experiences of summer leisure offered by this emerging class of entrepreneurs. We can find evidence of this pleasurable consumption in the way they replicated in their own accounts the language that the entrepreneurs used to sell their experiences. These tourists valued the social dimension of their experiences; their participation in social acts of consumption that displayed their status was one of the main attractions of the Fashionable Tours that spidered across the American landscape in the decades after 1820. The proximity of these tourist routes to well-publicized picturesque landscapes demonstrated the wide appeal of scenery hunting. In their accounts of their summer tours, they used the language of the picturesque to display their refinement and cultural knowledge with a conveniently flexible set of terms. If travel entrepreneurs offered social and cultural capital in the form of commodified experience, then a large and growing number of middle-class American tourists showed that they were enthusiastic consumers of that status and refinement by echoing the terms of their offer.

Such acts of consumption were ends in themselves, but their effects were magnified when tourists made them public. They commonly recorded their tours for themselves, for friends and family, and sometimes even for a wider community of print readers. They penned manuscripts that articulated the value of their tours for a smaller audience of family and friends. These narrations were sometimes literally epistolary in that they were contained in letters to family and friends at home. But tourists also frequently kept diaries on the road, intended either for themselves or for a readership of family and friends upon their return. These handwritten accounts were often also epistolary, a format that made sense for a document that was usually added to daily. A small number of wealthy, well-connected, or literarily talented tourists found ways to publish their tours, either as letters to the editor of a hometown newspaper, as books, or occasionally as both. Whatever the format, written accounts of tours allowed tourists to articulate and demonstrate their socially and culturally significant acts of consumption.

One such public tourist was Philip Nicklin, a young Philadelphia lawyer who undertook two summer tours, first to the Virginia springs in 1834, and then to Pittsburgh and back in 1835. He recounted his Virginia tour in letters to the *United States Gazette* in Philadelphia, and then the following year under the pen name Peregrine Prolix in a book entitled *Letters Descriptive of the Virginia Springs*. His Pennsylvania tour was published only in book form, under the title *A Pleasant Peregrination through the Prettiest Parts of Pennsylvania*, and with a correspondingly playful ear for prose that Edgar Allan Poe called his "exceedingly witty-pedantic style."[42] In his guise as Peregrine Prolix, Nicklin recorded the unabashed pleasure he took from the experiences offered by Virginia's and Pennsylvania's nascent tourist industries. As contemporary guidebooks and hotel advertisements suggested he would, Nicklin joyfully consumed the social experience available at mineral springs resorts, which he recounted in lengthy descriptions of his fellow tourists and the fun they had while eating, drinking, walking, talking, and dancing.

In both Virginia and Pennsylvania, Nicklin felt himself to be part of a comfortable, harmonious crowd, and his stays at the various watering places of those states gave him a sense of belonging to a national community of worthy middle-class elites. At each destination, he carefully described the crowd by the kinds of people that were present, a listing of categories that outlined the social experience offered by each destination. At White Sulphur Springs in Virginia, the experience was one of cosmopolitan variety. "The greatest charm of this place, is the delightful society which is drawn together in every agreeable variety," Nicklin reported. "From the east you have consolidationists, tariffites and philanthropists; from the middle, professors, chemical analysts, and letter writers; from the west, orators, and gentlemen who can squat lower, jump higher, dive deeper, and come out drier, than all creation besides; and from the south, nullifiers, union men, political economists, and statesmen; and from all quarters, functionaries of all ranks, ex-candidates for all functions, and the gay, young, agreeable and handsome of both sexes, who come to the White Sulpher [*sic*] to see and be seen, to chat, laugh and dance, and to throw each his pebble on the great heap of the general enjoyment."[43] At Bedford Springs in Pennsylvania, the crowd was smaller and more regional, "an interesting party of ladies and gentlemen from Virginia, Maryland and Pennsylvania, consisting of governors, judges, senators and congressmen *in esse* or *fuisse*, and even presidents and vice-presidents in *posse*; for there is scarce a lad of twenty in the United States who does not aspire to the presidency." This smaller and more homogeneous group "harmonise[s] very pleasantly, and their modus vivendi much resembles that of the eaters and drinkers at Langenschwalbach," a German spa town known for its decorous crowds.[44] Nicklin stressed both the variety among the visitors at the springs as well as the shades of difference between the crowds at the various destinations, but in each case he described them as a collection of solid businessmen, professionals, and politicians, as well as aspirants to the comfortable bourgeoisie. Above all, they were worthy groups, hardworking enough to deserve leisure but wealthy and refined enough to use it well.

At each of his destinations, Nicklin felt instantly included in this enviable company of regional and national elites. As he described the activities that filled each day at the springs, Nicklin made it clear that the company undertook their health and leisure activities together, which produced in him a profound sense of belonging. Entertainments at the Virginia springs, like dining, dancing, riding, and "Pic Nics," were undertaken in groups, such as when Nicklin joined an excursion, "of whom three were from Virginia, three from Louisiana, one from Scotland, two from North Carolina, one from New York, one from Boston, and three from Philadelphia. Such meetings are very agreeable, and tend to render the Union of the States more perfect." Nicklin ascribed political meaning to this party because it was an intimate meeting of previously unacquainted social equals, who were able to "quaff their wine and puff nicotian fumes most delightfully, under the shade of the forest trees" in social solidarity.[45] At the smaller Bedford Springs, the entire company of hotel guests passed the day together, meeting to drink spring water and at mealtimes, and splitting off between times for walking, reading, sewing, and sleeping, according to gender and inclination. At the end of the day, "the company collect in the drawing-room . . . [and h]ere they pass a chatty hour."[46] Despite being a collection of strangers, the crowd at Bedford Springs professed a sense of community that was almost domestic in its rhythms.

Nicklin's authorial pose was as a worldly "full blooded Philadelphia cockney," but even so, the degree of social ease he felt among the people he met on his tour was remarkable. Not only did he join in the common amusement at White Sulphur and Bedford, at Salt Sulphur Springs he "passed eight days very pleasantly in this abode of comfort and abundance," surrounded by "a large and agreeable society." At Gray Sulphur Springs, he found that "Every thing here is conducted after the polished and agreeable manner of South Carolina . . . and a little pleasant circle from that state, may generally be found there."[47] Nicklin felt settled and comfortable wherever he visited, even when surrounded by South Carolinians, people that he otherwise dismissed as "Nullifiers." His experiences showed that the feeling of belonging to extralocal elite of leisured yet worthy individuals and families was one of the most important attractions that the proprietors of both Virginia and Pennsylvania mineral springs resorts offered for sale, and Nicklin sought it out with evident relish.

Nicklin's sense of belonging to a group of attractive strangers was not unique; tourists' accounts regularly marveled at the pleasures of social immersion that tourist entrepreneurs offered, although the exact nature of those experiences varied at different destinations. In the summer of 1838, the *Southern Literary Messenger* published a series of letters recounting a New Englander's tour of Virginia. This tourist reflected that "life . . . at a watering place is dull and monotonous enough . . . without books, [and] without acquaintance. . . . The first, a sensible traveller will always carry with him,—the second such a one can never be at a loss to find."[48] Immersing himself in new acquaintances was easiest amid the whirl at White Sulphur Springs, which hosted "Shoals of valetudinarians, of convalescents, of robust impersonations of ruddy health, and of that numerous class of Spa-visitants who drink the water 'from mere wantonness.'" This crowd spent its time in "intervals of lounging or sleeping, of reading, writing, eating, drinking, and bathing,—until night-fall, when the ball-room is lighted."[49] In an 1856 piece in *Harper's New Monthly Magazine*, another tourist reported a more active and intimate social experience at Avon Springs, a small, rural springs resort in western New York. At Avon, the *Harper's* correspondent found "himself surrounded by persons as sociable as old friends, and he experienced many regrets at parting." Walking, bathing, and "sports for exercise" filled the daytime hours, along with "riding-parties, in chaise or on horseback." "At sunset new-comers were eagerly waited for," the correspondent noted, "for the advent of a fresh guest kept curiosity on tiptoe, until the clerk's register had been scanned by each eye, and the 'position' of the last visitor had become manifest to all."[50] Different destinations offered different kinds of social experiences with different crowds of people, from the leisured and the glamorous to the wholesome and the homey, all of which tourists sought out and took evident pleasure in.

Tourism entrepreneurs who had access to picturesque scenery also advertised intense sensory and aesthetic experiences, and tourists often cited the hunt for picturesque scenery as an important motivation for making a tour. They regularly applied the term "picturesque" to scenery that they found pleasing, and commonly described intense emotional reactions to the picturesque.[51] In doing so, they demonstrated their cultural competence by using language that was fashionable in both the United States and in Britain, which purported to give their tours a higher aesthetic and intellectual meaning. Above all, the language of the picturesque showed the cultural refinement of the tourist who used it. As a result, tourists sought out destinations that offered to sell them picturesque experiences.

This is not to say that most tourists used the language of the picturesque precisely or even particularly carefully. In part, this tendency toward approximation was the genius of the term; because it was never very sharply defined by William Gilpin or any other major popular writer, its very vagueness lent it a flexibility in practical usage that made it easy for tourists to use in their letters and their published accounts. Few tourists engaged directly with Gilpin's theoretical writings—let alone those of Edmund Burke—in letters home to friends or even in published accounts of their "rambles." Instead they used the term as a kind of shorthand, to demonstrate that they understood the cultural significance of the scenery that they saw. It was in this spirit that William Parker Foulke wrote a letter to his aunt from a journey through central Pennsylvania in 1848, in which he described the "wild descent" of Ray's Hill as "winding, precipitous, romantic, picturesque & all that."[52] But even when tourists explored their experiences of the picturesque in greater depth, their musings directly reflected guidebook descriptions of scenery rather than the rigorous categories of the philosophy of aesthetics. In other words, they took pleasure in summer scenery as it was marketed to them by tourism entrepreneurs.

Commercial descriptions of picturesque experience changed between the first generation of booster guidebooks published in the 1820s and later, more comprehensive guides that were the products of an emerging urban culture industry. Significantly, tourists' recorded descriptions of their actual experiences of picturesque scenery evolved more or less in direct parallel. Early guidebook authors were often at a loss for words when they sought to describe picturesque destinations like Niagara Falls. For example, Gideon Davison's 1825 *The Fashionable Tour* described the experience of witnessing the Falls as beyond language. Visitors would find that "the emotions of grandeur that fill the mind, on beholding this greatest of the wonders of nature, can scarcely be felt from any effort of description. You must behold [the Falls] at one view . . . before the mind can feel the real grandeur inspired by this truly magnificent and sublime prospect."[53] Henry Gilpin's *A Northern Tour,* published the same year, similarly demurred. "To describe the scene which then bursts upon our view," Gilpin wrote, "would be hopeless for the pen as it has ever proved for the pencil. . . . A scene like this is not to be described—it is only to be felt."[54] For Davison and Gilpin, this was smart salesmanship; prizing direct aesthetic experience over aesthetic description incentivized leisure travel, sold guidebooks, and developed local tourist economies. It also provided their readers with model language that they could use to articulate their enjoyment of their picturesque experiences.

Early tourists echoed this studied pose of overwhelmed awe and similarly disavowed the possibility of capturing picturesque scenes for friends at home. Charles Stoddard, a Boston merchant who narrated a tour of New York State in 1820, was impressed by Kaaterskill Falls in the Catskills, "the grandest sight I ever beheld." He confided to his diary that he thought that "No adequate idea of this picturesque scene can be given by description."[55] Mary Scollay Bigelow, another Bostonian who kept a diary of her tour to Niagara Falls in 1825, wished that her friends at home could share the intensity of the moment. "With the awful grandeur is mingled a beauty," she wrote, "an exquisite beauty which pen + pencil alike fail to express." Words failed her both in the moment and later in its narration: "my powers sunk so far beneath this scene of magnificence, that I longed for some human sympathy, the sympathy of those I love best, to sustain me in this silent, this awful communion with nature and its Author."[56] Michael Jenks, who visited the Falls in 1829, not only felt personally overwhelmed by the sight but openly doubted that any visitor could feel otherwise. In the face of their "unspeakable grandeur" he "def[ied] all the painters—all the poets—all the tourists—and in fact all mankind, to give to one who has not already seen this awfully magnificent scene, the most faint impression of its sublime and terrible reality."[57] This rapturous inability to express the experience of visiting nature's marvelous creations served to reinforce the distinction between having seen the picturesque in person and having only read about it. These tourists directly repeated guidebook authors' best arguments for the intellectual, social, and cultural value of taking their tours.

This pattern of imitation between guidebooks and tourists' accounts of the Falls continued in the 1830s, as guidebook authors changed their strategy. Later texts increasingly followed the lead of Theodore Dwight, whose *The Northern Traveller* described them aptly if somewhat dryly in scientific and scenic terms, and then recommended that a tourist "visit this place as often as he can, and . . . view it from every neighbouring point; as every change of light exhibits it under a different and interesting aspect."[58] By the late 1830s, Davison's guidebook, now published under the title of *The Traveller's Guide through the Middle and Northern States*, had abandoned its former wonderment in favor of a description nearly matching Dwight's marshaling of data. New guidebooks published in the 1830s and 1840s also conformed to Dwight's pattern. By the time the Appleton firm launched their guidebook series in the mid-1840s, guidebooks routinely recommended that the Falls "should be visited several times, as they increase in interest and beauty at every succeeding visit." Through such repeated viewings tourists would "at last . . . [learn] by degrees to comprehend the wonders of the scene, and to feel its full magnificence." Far from an awed lack of words, the Appleton guidebooks described visitors to the Falls as able to "comprehend" its "full magnificence," but only through repeated viewings.[59]

Tourists in the 1830s and 1840s were similarly precise in describing what the experience of picturesque landscape meant to them. John Alonzo Clark, a Philadelphia minister who visited Niagara as part of an extended tour of the West in the 1830s, described the experience as a kind of conversion. He wrote that "I never understood their full grandeur and majesty till I . . . remembered that the water of all those lakes upon which I had travelled more than a thousand miles, was pouring in one gathered column over that precipice!" The force and volume of the falling water seemed to Clark to be awesome like God's judgment, like "his mighty hand when he poureth out his fury like fire." At the same time, however, the rainbow that formed in the mist above the Falls was like "the mercy of God in Christ"; while witnessing it he was just as suddenly reminded that "it was the bow of promise; and new emotions of gratitude were waked up in my heart."[60] Clark was able to report that he found meaning in his experience of the Falls as a reminder of his evangelical conversion. Similarly, in 1840, Elizabeth Ellet was able to articulate her experience of the Falls succinctly. She began her account with a nod to the earlier sense of awe, asking, "who can adequately paint such a scene?" and answering, "None, surely!" However, she then proceeded to do exactly that, describing the experience in physical, religious, and literary terms. She specifically avoided the "moraliz[ing] on our situation" that Clark found so appealing, but she detailed her "own sensations" at length.[61] Ellet and Clark were typical of their era; later tourists who wrote about the Falls were much less at a loss for words than their predecessors. As the print sources that advertised to tourists changed their assessment of the value of consuming sublime aesthetic experiences, tourists' descriptions of consuming those experiences changed along with them.

Tourists' experiences were shaped by the concepts and values that tourism entrepreneurs used to sell them those experiences, but tourists tended not to acknowledge the debt explicitly. Instead, they often cited sources of information and inspiration that were outside the explicit marketplace for tourist experiences, in the form of literature or art. These references gave heavier cultural weight to their tours, reflected favorably on tourists' cultural literacy, and obscured the cash nexus at the heart of tourism. For example, tourists in Virginia commonly quoted Thomas Jefferson's *Notes on Virginia* to express their awe at Harpers Ferry or the Natural Bridge. Philip Nicklin let Jefferson's description stand in for his own, using the passage that was most popular with nineteenth-century tourists: "The passage of the Patowmac through the blue ridge is perhaps one of the most stupendous scenes in nature. . . . On your right comes up the Shenandoah, having ranged along the foot of the mountain a hundred miles to seek a vent. On your left approaches the Patowmac, in quest of a passage also. In the moment of their junction they rush together against the mountain, rend it asunder, and pass off to the sea."[62] Nicklin was less impressed than Jefferson, though he allowed that perhaps Harpers Ferry was more sublime during the spring flood. Nevertheless, Jefferson's was the standard description to which he turned. Elizabeth Ellet recorded a visit to the Natural Bridge, because "Mr. Jefferson's 'Notes on Virginia' have made [it] an object of primary curiosity . . . which is set down in the note book of every traveller, for special observation; and wo betide him, if he return home, without something wherewithal to answer the inquiries of his untravelled friends."[63] Rather than acknowledging that their tours were shaped by guidebooks or periodical notices, tourists like Nicklin and Ellet instead credited Jefferson's canonical text as their inspiration.

Fiction could also shape tourists' itineraries and sense of the purpose of traveling. While she was traveling through western Massachusetts on the way to Niagara Falls in 1825, Mary Scollay Bigelow noted that her journey replicated the travels of Mr. Lloyd, a character in Catharine Maria Sedgwick's novel *A New-England Tale*. Published in 1822, Sedgwick's novel was regionally popular, so Bigelow's reference would have been culturally meaningful to her, her fellow tourists, and anyone at home who perused her diary.[64] On the road to Lebanon, Bigelow was disappointed in the weather. "The sky, however, continued lowering," she recorded, "and involved the landscape in considerable obscurity." She felt a sense of regret, "as we had here hoped to trace and recognize some of the individual beauties which are so powerfully and feelingly pourtrayed [*sic*] in that interesting little work, The New-England tale."[65] The "beauties" to which she referred were the features of the mountainous landscape around Becket, which had charmed Mr. Lloyd's dying wife and induced him to resettle in Massachusetts in his widowerhood. The landscape was picturesque; in Mr. Lloyd's words, it showed "a more perfect and intimate union of the sublime and beautiful." Sedgwick gave the mountains a moral dimension as well as an aesthetic one; Mrs. Lloyd imagined that "they enclose a sanctuary, a temple, from which the brightness of His presence is never withdrawn."[66] By referring to these "beauties," Bigelow made the landscape and her tour both aesthetically and morally meaningful. Indeed, moments later she got over her disappointment, when the clouds changed shape and "infused into our spirits a deep and reverential contemplation."[67] Sedgwick's description of the landscape of Becket became Bigelow's own, which reminded the readers of her diary that she understood its cultural significance.

Whether written out longhand on summer evenings along the road or published by hometown presses, tourists' accounts recorded the pleasure that they took in consuming the experiences of a tour. Just as tourism entrepreneurs promised, they valued the social dimension of tourism, especially at destinations that purposely catered to a tourist crowd. They moved comfortably in a regulated world of strangers and relished the sense of belonging to an elite and worthy class of leisure travelers. They hunted the emotional thrill of picturesque scenery, and generally found it where their guidebooks and promotional materials said they would. They recorded their finds and their fashionably appropriate emotional responses, in language that both demonstrated their acquaintance with culturally current aesthetic and intellectual categories and reflected the marketing pitches of tourism entrepreneurs. Even if these satisfied customers rarely embraced the term "tourist," the consumption of tourist experiences generally provided the social and cultural benefits that their promoters promised they would. But the very predictability that made tourist experiences such reliable sources of pleasure increasingly made a subset of potential tourists nervous about being perceived as, in Blanchard's terms, a "meditative fly." The standardization of commodified experience caused some travelers to regard them as limited, superficial, and insincere, and perhaps ultimately meaningless. Right from its earliest moments of origins, tourism was a profoundly ambivalent phenomenon.

Tourism entrepreneurs' ability to reliably provide enjoyable leisure experiences required that those experiences be as standardized as possible so that they could be provided at a predictable price and would produce a predictably pleasurable response. This standardization began with the information that potential tourists consumed about the possibilities of leisure travel, continued with the organizations and technologies that provided their transportation, and concluded with the carefully calculated spaces and routines of popular tourist destinations. For a small but growing number of travelers in the 1830s and 1840s, the carefully planned standardization of commodified tourist experiences began to feel constricting. These uncomfortable tourists were still tourists, although they were even less likely to embrace the term than their more enthusiastic counterparts. Indeed, they often used words like "pilgrim" and "pilgrimage" to describe themselves and their journeys. As John F. Sears has argued, the pilgrimage was an important analogy for early national tourists who sought meaning in consumer experiences that "yoked the sacred and the profane, the spiritual and the commercial, the mythic and the trivial, the natural and the artificial, the profound and the superficial, the elite and the popular in a sometimes uneasy combination."[68] But these tourists' care to highlight the value of their tours also coexisted with creeping doubts about whether or not they really were valuable. They pushed back against the services that offered reliable pleasure, on the grounds that they limited travelers' choices; that they produced meaningless or inauthentic encounters with people and nature; and that the mediation of profit-minded entrepreneurs made them insincere. Sometimes these doubts emerged when their carefully calibrated experiences broke down through incompetence or circumstance, and other times they emerged from a deeper uncertainty about the authenticity of commodified experience. In their accounts of their journeys, these conflicted tourists revealed a deepening ambivalence about the entire project of being a tourist.

In 1833 and 1834, New York editor Charles Fenno Hoffman undertook an unusual wintertime tour around the Great Lakes and the upper

Mississippi valley, which he recounted in both the *New-York American* and in a subsequent book. In his account, Hoffman was often content to be a tourist, like when he visited "Jefferson's Natural Bridge" and demurred in describing the road leading up to it on the grounds that the "pretty scenery along the rest of my route is probably familiar to you from the descriptions of the numerous travellers who have resorted to the interesting spot where I now found myself a pilgrim."[69] For at least part of his journey, Hoffman cheerfully tread beaten paths and reported on the famous destinations well known to other "pilgrims." But Hoffman also chafed at the restrictions placed on his movement by the standardization of commodification. In Michigan, he reported that "it was with a feeling of almost boyish pleasure that, after the slight taste I have had of stage-coach travelling from Pittsburgh to Cleveland, and from Detroit to Monroe, I found myself once more in the saddle, with the full privilege of regulating my motions as I choose." He enjoyed the physical exercise of horseback riding, but more importantly, it allowed him to travel where and when he pleased, without being bound to the routes and schedules of a stagecoach company. Even though, mounted on his "stout roan," he no longer had "the luxurious carriage to enhance the gratification and relieve the weariness of travelling, the feeling of independence still remains."[70] Hoffman expressed deep ambivalence about his tourist experiences. He enjoyed his acts of pilgrimage to popular destinations, and he luxuriated in the comfort and convenience afforded by commodified transportation, but he also valued the "feeling of independence" that came from forgoing the pleasures of a tour.

While preparing for a similar "ramble over the Western States" in May 1837, Frederick Hall, a Washington, DC, college professor, had the "intention to travel by public conveyances—the canals and steamboats, the stages and rail-road cars." But like Hoffman, Hall reconsidered, because on second thought the "public conveyances" would prevent him from engaging on his own terms with the territory he passed through. As Hall himself put it: "What could I learn of the out-door affairs of the broad world confined in this straight-jacket mode of journeying? Shut up in a long dark prison, and moved over the land with lightning speed, how could one gain a knowledge of the structure of the ball on which he was running a John Gilpin race?" Charging along in such a prison was a fool's errand, Hall suggested, by comparing it to the subject of a famous 1782 comic poem by William Cowper. In this poem, John Gilpin found himself mounted on a series of uncontrollable steeds and carried at high speed around the countryside outside of London, much to the

amusement of his spectators (see figure 3.4). Comparing his fellow tourists to the subject of Cowper's gentle ridicule emphasized not only their
lack of control over their own movement but also the foolishness of their
haste. Hall preferred to travel more slowly, under his own direction, so
he could "learn of the out-door affairs of the broad world." As a result,
he rejected his initial plan and instead "purchased a strong horse, and
a strong, but light, open wagon, and [I] am accompanied by a pleasant,
able-bodied nephew, who will aid and cheer me in my accidental pilgrimage."[71] Hall's "ramble" may have been a "pilgrimage," but he was
skeptical about whether the mechanisms of commercial travel could
provide the kind of experience he sought.

Among the "out-door affairs" that tourists like Hall sought was picturesque scenery, which led some skeptics to worry that the "long dark
prison" forestalled proper aesthetic appreciation of nature. As Louis
Tasistro, a journalist who published his tours of the South, wondered
in Alabama in the early 1840s, "How much is lost of nature's grandeur
and loveliness to him who catches but a passing view of either as he hur-
ries along in a stagecoach—leaving rail-road cars, from which absolutely
nothing is seen, out of the question." The very technologies that made
pleasure travel possible for many tourists also insulated their passengers
from nature. "The beauties of Nature are to be appreciated only by him
who courts companionship with her," Tasistro declared, and hurrying
along in a stagecoach or a railroad car did not count as courtship. Thus
it was, on that fine spring afternoon in the wilds of Alabama, that he
gladly took advantage of an hour's delay of the stagecoach to walk ahead
along the road, "too happy of an opportunity to escape, even for so short
a time, from the confinement I had hitherto been obliged to undergo."
Self-identified connoisseurs of the picturesque like Tasistro worried that
the "straight-jacket mode of journeying" removed their control over
their own itinerary, and it insulated them from "the out-door affairs of
the broad world."[72] It made their travel easy and predictable but also aesthetically impoverished to the point of meaninglessness.

George Featherstonhaugh was another northerner who published an
account of his tour of the South in the 1830s. He expressed the same
skepticism as Hoffman, Hall, and Tasistro when he observed with wry
understatement, "Travelling in a public vehicle would seem to present
singular impediments to a correct investigation of the geology and natural history of a country."[73] Nevertheless, he and his wife could not resist
the comfort and convenience of commodified travel when they set out
on their journey from Baltimore to the Virginia springs. They purchased

FIGURE 3.4. George Cruikshank's 1828 engraving of John Gilpin on his runaway horse, which illustrated numerous editions of *The Diverting History of John Gilpin* in the nineteenth century. Courtesy of the Yale Center for British Art.

a through ticket to Harpers Ferry, which entitled them to passage on the new Baltimore and Ohio Railroad as far as Frederick, Maryland, at which point they were to be transferred to a stagecoach for the remaining twenty miles. But upon reaching Frederick, the local agent of their ticket seller refused to honor the connection. The agent claimed not to have access to a coach, and so Featherstonhaugh, a sharp bargainer, found another coach that was willing to take him, and demanded that the agent refund him the price of the new conveyance. The agent, "cursing and swearing and vapouring about, and declaring that he never did meet with 'sich a *on*reasonable parson' as myself . . . at length produced a stage-coach and four horses." Luckily, Featherstonhaugh had had the foresight to obtain a paper receipt in Baltimore, for "if I had not taken a receipt, stating that I was to be conducted to Harper's-ferry on that same day, there would have been no remedy for me, and I should have been cheated out of the money."[74] Commodification limited tourists' engagement with the world they traveled though, but its convenience made it worth it, at least when it functioned properly. Featherstonhaugh was wise enough in the dangers of the marketplace to know that distant agents, even of reputable firms, might try to cheat their customers on the road. So he armed himself with a commercial remedy—a receipt—that would ensure that the contract was fulfilled.

Featherstonhaugh also expressed a healthy skepticism about the sincerity of the hospitality they received at tourist destinations. Upon arriving at the Warm Springs in Virginia, Featherstonhaugh and his wife received an enthusiastic welcome at the hotel, but he knew better than to believe that such warmth was genuine. Arriving at the resort over the heights of Warm Springs Mountain, he complained that "we exchanged the tranquil and elevated feelings that are inspired by the simple honest dignity of nature, for the distrust which experienced travellers entertain of the obsequiously cordial reception which in every country graces their arrival at the hotels of watering-places." He explained that "until it is determined that you do not go to the rival hotel, the zeal in your service is overwhelming; the landlord brings out his very best politeness," applying flattery "with an apparent disinterestedness that would induce a novice to suppose that the fable of the Prodigal Son was acting over again."[75] Featherstonhaugh recognized that the elaborate hospitality with which they were greeted was a business strategy, a standardized product designed to convince them to purchase the Warm Springs experience.

These newly arrived tourists were tired and dirty from their stagecoach ride and eager to settle into their accommodations, so they did not pause to enjoy this flattery for long. Upon announcing their intention to stay a few days, "it was a matter that excited our admiration to perceive how suddenly that anxious solicitude, of which we had so lately been the objects, had assumed an abstract position. The landlord had made his bows, the waiters their grimaces, our names had been taken, *in limine in libro*, and being regularly bagged, we were left to provide for ourselves, not a soul coming near us." To a skeptical consumer like Featherstonhaugh, the commercial experience of hospitality offered at Warm Springs was a simulacrum of real hospitality offered outside the marketplace. They did not change their plans as a result, but he and his wife were well girded for the "good deal of trouble" they had in actually getting rooms and were not too badly disappointed by "fashionable society" in which they found themselves, where they would have "to depend upon the tender mercies of landlords, landladies, and dirty, impudent, black *waiters*."[76] The Featherstonhaughs still found a way to enjoy consuming commodified hospitality, even if they were able to recognize it for what it was. Like Hoffman, Hall, and Tasistro, they were deeply ambivalent about tourism because while it provided pleasure, and perhaps even a valuable sense of pilgrimage, it was nonetheless shaped, limited, and ultimately defined by the standardizing effects of commodification.

The entrepreneurs who operated stagecoach lines, hotels, and railroads; who published guidebooks; and who placed advertising notices in metropolitan periodicals built a domestic American tourist industry by identifying socially and culturally meaningful experiences, routinizing and standardizing them into commodities, and selling them into an increasingly national marketplace in which ambitious members of the elite and middle classes bought them as a reflection of their own status and refinement. Many of these newly minted tourists recorded being enthusiastic consumers of these social, emotional, and aesthetic experiences. A smaller but still significant number of travel accounts revealed an emerging uneasiness about the commodified experiences of tourism. Some tourists found the relatively narrow range of experiences available to be limiting, even while they enjoyed the pleasures and their comforts they did purchase. Others were nostalgic for autonomy allowed by older modes of self-produced travel, even while they enjoyed the ease and even luxury of modern means. And the relentless injection of the market for commodified experiences into the social and cultural joys of traveling produced a degree of cynicism about the sincerity and authenticity of those sentiments, even among those who sought them out.

This strain of skepticism evident in some tourist accounts did not emerge in a vacuum, however. The specific qualities of commodified experience that these skeptics noticed—including its predictability, its unoriginality, its superficiality, and its fashionableness—were also remarked upon by a range of cultural observers, many of whom made no claim to be travelers themselves. These undesirable qualities of tourism became grist for the mills of literary satirists on both sides of the Atlantic, who made the figure of the tourist ridiculous in order to lampoon a wide range of targets. These satirists helped to adhere a negative connotation to tourism and to tourists, which in turn engendered an emerging cultural strain of wholesale rejection of commodified experience and of an attempt to identify and encourage purposeful, meaningful travel outside the marketplace of experience. Thus, the market habits of mind that enabled the commodification of experience also contained the seeds of its most enduring critique. The market forces that made tourists' summer leisure widely available could also decrease its value because experience that had been commodified for easy consumption could also be passive and superficial, and as a result it was perhaps not worth the advantages it offered in predictability, comfort, and convenience.

4 / I'll Picturesque It Everywhere: The Archetype of the Tourist in Satire

When modern readers think of the great nineteenth-century American humorist Mark Twain, he is most often remembered for his tales of boyhood adventure on the banks of the Mississippi. But in his own lifetime, his best-known and bestselling book was *The Innocents Abroad*, a satirical tale of the ship *Quaker City*, which carried a party of American tourists to France, the Mediterranean, and the Holy Land in 1867. As both nineteenth-century and modern critics have recognized, *The Innocents Abroad* worked as satire because it aimed its barbs at the ship's tourists more than at its European destinations.[1] The book was funny and popular because by the time it was published in 1869, Twain's audience was already acquainted with the tourist as a social type, and they had been trained to see the absurdity in tourists' behavior. After all, Twain wrote more than two decades after E. L. Blanchard had labeled "The Tourist" as "a class" that "merely travelers for the sake of travelling."[2] It was no coincidence that Twain's most popular satirical protagonists were tourists, who were ambivalent cultural subjects for an author whose humor was rooted in ambivalence at its very core.

While *The Innocents Abroad* survives in the modern canon as part of Twain's celebrated body of work, in its original historical context it relied on a long-standing tradition of tourist satire for its effect. At the beginning of the nineteenth century, authors on both sides of the Atlantic aimed their wit at hapless travelers, and they sold their wares into a transatlantic marketplace for print in which American readers, at least, consumed as much British literature as they did American.[3] The British tourist satire that Americans read was often motivated by the rapid entry of the new middle class into travel practices that had been the province of the elite, and absent their own stock figures, early national American authors borrowed this preoccupation with puncturing the social pretentions of parvenus.[4] But by the 1820s, American satirists had identified a valuable target of their own: a new generation of British tourists in the United States, whose observations most Americans found to be inaccurate, condescending, and mean-spirited. Although they continued to draw inspiration from British writers, American satirists in the 1830s and 1840s increasingly incorporated indigenous forms of humor like the tall tale and broadened their range of targets to include the emerging American bourgeoisie. Since its production was widely spread over time and space, the tourist satire that American readers consumed was extremely diverse, and its authors wrote in response to widely varying provocations. Each author's individual agenda rarely overlapped precisely with that of his or her fellow satirists, but they often borrowed each other's tropes and stock figures in order to drive home their points. As a result, even though tourist satire was not a coherent genre in the first half of the nineteenth century, these texts can be read together to discern the existence of a relatively unified and negative tourist archetype in American culture by the time of Twain's writing in 1869. The process was not intentional, but it was effective.

Although individual authors played up different aspects of the tourist archetype depending on their satirical target, the stock figure of the tourist that they deployed shared broad outlines. Tourists moved quickly and thoughtlessly through the landscape, and satirists lampooned their banal and formulaic accounts of their journeys, which linked trite observations of picturesque scenery with minor quotidian adventures. Lacking meaningful geographical knowledge, tourists displayed profound ignorance about the places they traveled through. This ignorance was frequently teamed with condescension; as Washington Irving put it, if a modern tourist "has ever any doubt on a subject, [he] always decides against the city where he happens to sojourn, and invariably takes *home*, as the standard by which to direct his judgment."[5] This ignorance was often magnified in satirical accounts through an absurdist exaggeration of tourists' tendency to exaggerate. Most satirists also saw tourist practices as frivolous vehicles for social ambition; indeed, it was frequently the tourist's nakedly ambitious motives for traveling that attracted satirical attention. Since these satires usually took the form of published travel narratives, they implicitly mocked tourists for freighting their experiences with more meaning and worth than they could really carry, and their readers for their inability to perceive their fundamental meaninglessness. Critically, these characteristics were unambiguously framed as negative by all satirists who wrote about tourists. The roughness of their treatment of their subjects varied; some authors poked gentle fun at ridiculous but sympathetic characters, while others angrily mocked a social type that they thought was guilty of real social harm. Either way, tourists never appeared as figures worthy of emulation.

Although the negative tourist archetypes used by these authors were similar in their broad outlines, they became richer and more filled out as the century progressed. More importantly, the causes which these satirists identified for tourists' undesirable practices changed significantly between 1800 and 1869. The earliest satires read by nineteenth-century Americans attributed them to unchecked social ambition, while the second generation of texts written in the 1820s and 1830s added a layer of national competition to the existing base of class resentment. Beginning in the 1840s, satirists began to depict tourists' ambition, ignorance, superficiality, and lack of originality as the result of their status as consumers of commodified experience. The processes of commodification that shaped tourists' experiences may have had their roots in the entrepreneurial innovations of the 1810s and 1820s, but the touristic consumption of commodified experience was neither widespread nor noticeable enough to attract satirical attention until the late 1840s. As the widespread delight at the sublime wonders of Niagara showed, many tourists placed great value on their commodified experience. But it was precisely the features that made their experiences commodifiable that the midcentury critics of tourism focused on to delegitimize their travel practices. Considered as a whole, the diverse and transatlantic practice of tourist satire slowly adhered a negative connotation to the term "tourist" in American culture and created the dismal archetype that Twain so expertly deployed in 1869. The consumption of commodified experience increasingly defined the midcentury tourist, and popular satirists creatively adapted existing critiques to ensure that this relationship was broadly considered not to be a good thing.

Travelers became the subject of popularly circulated literary satire in the first decade of the nineteenth century, beginning with one of the best-sellers of early American literature, Washington Irving's 1807 *Salmagundi*. This volume was a collection of self-described "whim-whams and opinions" that launched Irving's career as the new United States' first professional popular author.⁶ Leisure travelers were rare on American roadways in 1807, so this first generation of tourist satire responded to the existing social practices of British picturesque tours and the European "Grand Tour." As a result, the earliest identifiable satires took as their target the tourist's unseemly ambition. They sought to puncture the pretensions of parvenus, who aped established aristocratic practices for social advancement or material profit. As portrayed by the earliest satirists, the ambitious tourist could never truly replicate the refinement and erudition of a real Grand Tour, and so the narratives that they produced ranged from the predictably banal to improbably absurd.

Irving's slim 1807 volume included a series of sketches called "The Stranger in New Jersey; Or, Cockney Travelling," which represented the first clearly recognizable tourist satire by an American author. The eponymous "stranger," a New Yorker named "Jeremy Cockloft, the younger," traveled in search of social status. After graduating from "our university," meaning Columbia College, "Jeremy was seized with a great desire to see, or rather to be seen by the world; and as his father was anxious to give him every possible advantage, it was determined Jeremy should visit foreign parts." In this brief mise-en-scène, Irving captured and satirized the social ambition implied by a young man's tour of the world. The Cockloft family's dynastic desires were encapsulated in his father's desire to "give him every possible advantage"; indeed, "old Cockloft was determined his son should be both a scholar and a gentleman,"⁷ or a member of the social elite—a problematic goal in a self-proclaimed republic. Irving cleverly restated Jeremy's own desire to see the world as a desire "to be seen by the world." Cockloft the younger's travel was ostensibly educational, a capstone to his studies at Columbia, but its actual purpose was to demonstrate his social prominence by parading it in front of the "world," both at home and in "foreign parts."

Even though Cockloft was a native New Yorker, and the New York elite was the target of Irving's satirical pen, the phrasing of his ambition directly echoed that of turn-of-the-century British narratives of the European Grand Tour. Young aristocratic British men had been making extended journeys through France, Italy, and the German states since the beginning of the seventeenth century, a practice that put an experiential polish on their classical educations and began the process of integrating them into national and international networks of social elites. By the end of the eighteenth century, members of the rising British commercial and industrial middle classes had begun to take more modest tours of their own, as a part of their claim to participation in the cultural life of elite Britain.⁸ Their desire to "see the world"—with its implied educational and social benefits—was a primary justification for their extended continental sojourns, even if Irving's rapier reversal of that formulation, the desire "to be seen by the world," was often closer to the truth. The Cocklofts were members of the New York social elite, seeking to cement their social status in the new United States by aping British practices of "seeing the world." That Jeremy's notion of "seeing the world" was limited to an excursion into New Jersey, a neighboring state already derided for its provincialism, only sharpened the satirical attack on his ridiculous pretensions and, by extension, the pretentions of turn-of-the-century elite New Yorkers generally. Thus Irving briefly and efficiently skewered the borrowed transatlantic notion of taking a tour as a means of cementing social status.

For this satirical formula to work, however, the actual cultural value of such a tour had to be less than travelers' imaginations projected it to be. Irving achieved this satirical tension by juxtaposing the loftiness of Cockloft's ambitions against the banality of his destination. He high-lighted this tension by means of a highly stylized formatting choice: in his entire chapter on Cockloft's travels, only his introductory remarks, narrated in the voice of *Salmagundi*'s chatty editor, were written in com-plete prose. The body of the piece, encompassing young Jeremy's account of his journey, was recounted as a series of dense notations for a travel narrative—sentence fragments connected by em-dashes—and supple-mented with a similarly dense set of footnotes referencing a number of published British tourists (see figure 4.1).⁹ Irving's Cockloft did not actually write out a full account; rather, his "travel narrative" consisted of a series of fragmentary notes about what he would write were he to finish his travel narrative, connected to examples of British travelers who had made similar observations. For example, in Princeton, Cockloft noted that he attended "a ball and supper—company from New-York, Philadelphia, and Albany—great contest which spoke the best English—Albanians vociferous in their demand for sturgeon—Philadelphians gave the preference to racoon and splacnuncs [*sic*]."¹⁰ For this assertion, he footnoted British traveler William Priest's 1802 account of *Travels in the United States of America*, in which he claimed while that Americans "dine on what is usual in England, with a variety of American dishes, such as bear, opossum, racoon [*sic*], &c."¹¹ Cockloft's absurd observa-tions of the ball in Princeton, written against the quotidian observations of Priest, satirized the formulaic observations of the narratives that he cited, as well as the thinness of observation necessary for publishing a narrative describing already well-traveled ground. This combination of prose fragments and footnoted asides highlighted both syntactically and visually the superficial nature of the actual tour in which Jeremy placed such high social hopes. Like most of Irving's best satire, "The Stranger in New Jersey" highlighted the absurdity of his target with an elegant simplicity, but his economical scorn would have been less effective had he not been writing in sync with an already emerging world of satirical tourist tropes.

Irving could easily mock social-climbing American parvenus copying British aristocratic practice because British satirists were already attacking their compatriots on the other side of the Atlantic. After all, figures like Jeremy Cockloft were much more common on the highways of Britain than they were in New Jersey at the turn of the nineteenth century. This point was most famously made on both sides of the Atlantic by William Combe's 1809 poem *The Tour of Dr. Syntax, In Search of the Picturesque*, which gently mocked the upwardly mobile traveling middle classes of England. Indeed, one British observer, lecturing in New York in 1860, dismissed these travelers as "gentry [who] regarded their trashy experiences as of so much moment to society at large that they absolutely committed them to print." This observer went on to claim that "the mania for publishing tours subsided after the scourge of the satirist [Combe] had been pretty widely distributed."[12] *The Tour of Dr. Syntax* told the tale of a poverty-stricken schoolmaster who proposed to make his fortune by taking a picturesque tour of England and writing a book about it, which he thought would inevitably sell well. The poem then recounted his journey, a farcical, even slapstick affair propelled by Dr. Syntax's perpetual foolishness. Combe's was a gentle satire; despite his bumbling, Dr. Syntax's mild manner and good nature ultimately brought him the prosperity he desired. And Combe's gentleness brought him similar success as an author. *The Tour of Dr. Syntax* remained in print as an important cultural touchstone in Britain for decades. More significantly, despite its British subject, the poem was reprinted in Philadelphia in 1814, a delay that led one American reviewer to lament that "the best literary productions are often left in the shade of obscurity, while works of inferior merit glitter in the broad sun-shine of popularity."[13] It went through four subsequent American editions in the next two decades, as well as being excerpted in newspapers, and it remained on American booksellers' shelves throughout the first half of the nineteenth century.[14] Dr. Syntax was the best-known satirical embodiment of the tourist before Twain's passengers on the *Quaker City*, and the many of

MEMORANDUMS
For a Tour, to be entitled
" THE STRANGER IN NEW-JERSEY ;
OR, COCKNEY TRAVELLING."

••••••••••••

BY JEREMY COCKLOFT, *the younger.*

CHAPTER I.

THE man in the moon*—preparations for departure—hints to travellers about packing their
trunks†—straps, buckles and bed-cords—case of
pistols *a la cockney*—five trunks—three bandboxes
—a cocked hat,—and a medicine chest, *a la
francaise*—parting advice of my two sisters——
quere, why old maids are so particular in their
cautions against naughty women—Description
of Powles-Hook ferry-boats—might be convert-
ed into gun boats and defend our port equally
well with Albany sloops—BROM, the black ferry-
man—Charon—river Styx—ghosts—major Hunt
—good story—ferryage nine-pence—city of Harsi-
mus—built on the spot where the folk once danced
on their stumps, while the devil fiddled—quere, why
do the Harsimites talk dutch?—story of the Tower
of Babel, and confusion of tongues—get into the
stage—driver a wag—famous fellow for running
stage races—killed three passengers and crippled
nine in the course of his practise—philosophical
reasons why stage drivers love grog—causeway—
ditch on each side for folk to tumble into—famous
place for *skilly-pots ;* philadelphians call 'em tara-

* *vide* Carr's Stranger in Ireland. † *vide* Weld.

A 2

FIGURE 4.1. The stylistically abbreviated text of Irving's "The
Stranger in New Jersey." From *Salmagundi; Or, the Whim-
Whams and Opinions of Launcelot Langstaff, Esq. and Others*
(1808), Albert and Shirley Small Special Collections Library,
University of Virginia.

the tropes of the emerging genre of tourist satire could found in Combe's stanzas.

Like Jeremy Cockloft on his tour of New Jersey, Dr. Syntax undertook his tour around England as an absurd project to cement his social status and reap a financial windfall. Although Oxford-educated, Dr. Syntax was scraping by on the social and financial margins of middling English life as a curate and a schoolteacher. "Of church-preferment he had none"; Combe lamented: "Nay, all his hope of that was gone: / He felt that he content must be / With drudging in a curacy." The promise of a comfortable life as a rector was withheld by his lack of "church-preferment," which was generally acquired through prominent personal connections.[15] Given his lack of preferment, the publication of a travel narrative seemed to Dr. Syntax to be the most expedient means of allaying his poverty:

I'll ride and *write*, and *sketch* and *print*,
And thus create a real mint;
I'll *prose* it here, I'll *verse* it there,
And *picturesque* it ev'ry where:
I'll do what all have done before;
I think I shall—and somewhat more.
At Doctor *Pompous* give a look;
He made his fortune by a book;
And if my volume does not beat it,
When I return, I'll fry and eat it.

This grand scheme of Dr. Syntax's was designed not only to "create a real mint" but was also intended to procure for his wife the social prominence that the lack of "church-preferment" left her without:

New days will come—new times appear,
And teeming plenty crown the year:
We then on dainty bits shall dine,
And change our home-brew'd ale for wine:
On summer days, to take the air,
We'll put our Grizzle to a chair;
While you, in silks and muslins fine,
The grocer's wife shall far outshine,
And neighb'ring folks be forc'd to own,
In this fair town you give the ton[e].[16]

The successful publication of Dr. Syntax's tour promised to translate the cultural capital of his Oxford education and his acquaintance with the tourist tropes into the concrete economic and social capital that the Syntaxes lacked. For both Irving and Combe, the grand and absurd ambitions that tourists harbored were a central part of the satirical formula.

As with Cockloft's grand tour of the banal sights of New Jersey, the satirical force of Combe's work lay in tension between Dr. Syntax's soaring social ambition and the quotidian normalcy of his experiences on the road. Combe achieved this effect by having Dr. Syntax spend his tour, as his title put it, in search of picturesque scenes that he could sketch or narrate for his volume. As we saw in chapter 3, picturesque scenery-hunting was popular among the emerging British middle class at the turn of the nineteenth century, a cultural trend that increasing inspired the American bourgeoisie after 1815. Popularizers of the practice like William Gilpin defined the term "picturesque" very loosely, which only added to its appeal because tourists could locate the picturesque wherever they found it most useful for their purposes. The vogue among the socially ambitious for chasing a vaguely defined version of the picturesque made it a prime target for satirists of tourism. Dr. Syntax made this quest the obsessive focus of his tour; as he explained to a passing member of the nobility:

> With curious eye and active scent,
> I on the Picturesque am bent;
> This is my game; I must pursue it,
> And make it where I cannot view it.

His pursuit led him into the comic misadventures that gave the poem its slapstick humor. Upon learning that lightning had partially destroyed a nearby abandoned castle, Dr. Syntax immediately leapt on the picturesque possibilities of the scene:

> But this new thought I must pursue:
> A castle, and a ruin too!
> I'll hasten there, and take a view.

In his haste to sketch the ruined castle for his account, Dr. Syntax tumbled into a muddy river and lost his hat and wig (see figure 4.2). His hat was caught by an angler, his wig was retrieved by a swimming urchin, and he was forced to "[run] the gauntlet to [his] inn" while "o'erwhelm'd with mud, and stink, and grief." Dr. Syntax's reflexive enthusiasm for moments of picturesque possibility left his pride foolishly exposed and

FIGURE 4.2. *Doctor Syntax Tumbling into the Water* while trying to capture a picturesque scene, from *Poetical Magazine* (1809). Courtesy of the Department of Special Collections, Memorial Library, University of Wisconsin–Madison.

humbled by "the rude insults of the street," until the only thing left for him to do was go to bed.[17]

Dr. Syntax's enthusiasm for the picturesque was so strong that he regularly stretched the definition of the term in order to turn the most mundane details of his trip into picturesque scenes. For example, during a moment in which he had lost his way, he decided to let his horse Grizzle graze in a field with a post in it:

> But, as my time shall not be lost,
> I'll make a drawing of the post;
> And, tho' a flimsy taste may flout it,
> There's something *picturesque* about it.

However, the post was not truly picturesque; in order to make it so, Dr. Syntax moved a pond, then changed it into a stream, and added a bridge and a "shaggy ridge." He defended his invention of a picturesque scene—"What man of taste my right will doubt, / To put things in, or leave them out?"—because the framing of picturesque scenery was one of the central goals of a narrated tour: "Thus I (which few I think can boast) / Have made a Landscape of a Post."[18] Indeed, this willingness of the connoisseurs of the picturesque to shape specific landscapes to fit their taste, rather than the other way around, was a frequent point of criticism of the followers of Gilpin; Gilpin himself wrote in 1784 that "I am so attached to my picturesque rules, that if nature gets it wrong, I cannot help putting her right."[19] The absurdity of Dr. Syntax's silk purse of a "landscape," made out of the sow's ear of an old mossy post, embodied in one efficient anecdote the superficial engagement with aesthetic practice that was the result of tourists' relentless canvassing of scenery in search of predictably picturesque scenes. For both Combe and Irving the satirical force of their work lay in the sharply drawn contrast between their subject's lofty social ambitions for their tours and the insignificance and superficiality of their experiences on the road. Thus even in the first decade of the nineteenth century, when taking tours was still a relatively uncommon practice in the United States, literate Americans were learning to associate both the figure of the tourist and the print accounts that they produced with inappropriate social ambition, and their tours with superficiality, formulaicness, and a general failure to live up to the cultural standards suggested by their social ambitions.

The enduring nineteenth-century popularity of Irving's and Combe's works shows that Americans had already begun to absorb unflattering portrayals of tourists and their tours by the time an identifiable tourist industry began to emerge in the 1820s. Satirists did not immediately fasten onto the commercialization of tourist experiences, at least not as an obvious driver of touristic practices. But they absolutely noticed the increasing number of leisure travelers on the road, which deepened their skepticism about tourists' motivations and their practices. The relatively gentle fun poked at Jeremy Cockloft and Dr. Syntax was supplanted by satire with a sharper edge, whose mockery was more aggressive and more cynical. The satirists of the 1820s and 1830s noticed many of the same tourist characteristics that their predecessors had, but they attributed them to darker impulses and painted their effects as more socially and culturally destructive. Tourists were still ignorant and gullible, but now the shallowness of their knowledge produced arrogant condescension rather than merely simple foolishness. Tourists still chose predictable itineraries along well-beaten paths and produced superficial and formulaic accounts of their travel, but now their reluctance to venture beyond the safe and familiar began to cast doubt on whether they had even traveled at all. In this way, the second-generation satires of the 1820s and 1830s built on the tourist archetypes established at the turn of the century while sharpening them for a world of increasingly visible tourists.

This new cohort of satires was also increasingly written by American authors about British tourists. Americans continued to read British satires penned by British authors, but as more American authors began to try to make writing a career in the 1820s, they expanded the market for specifically American satires aimed at specifically American targets.[20] For most of these authors, this meant mocking British travelers in America. By the 1820s, literarily inclined Americans had been locked in a "paper war" with British travelers and British writers since the beginning of the century over the nature of the new nation and the degree and extent of Anglo-American difference in the postrevolutionary era.[21] American readers were especially alert to snubs, whether explicit or implied, in the accounts of British tourists. Indeed, this sense of national grievance lay behind the sharper tone of these second-generation satires, at least for American authors. But American readers still encountered British satires—including those written by the very travelers whose accounts of the United States they so despised—which reflected a similar hardening. The motivations of these later satirists were complex, as they increasingly layered nationalist resentments on top of the existing class critique. But even as their targets became more diverse, the satirical image of the tourist as superficial, formulaic, prone to exaggeration, and ultimately meaningless became stronger and more coherent.

Appropriately enough, James Paulding, Irving's collaborator on the *Salmagundi* project, was a prominent contributor to this new generation of American tourist satire with his 1825 *John Bull in America; Or, the New Munchausen*. Like many other American writers at the time, Paulding was galvanized into writing by a disagreement with a British commentator on the United States, in this case a reviewer writing in the London edition of the *Quarterly Review* in 1823. This reviewer wrote approvingly of William Faux's *Memorable Days in America* because it revealed "that truth, so long perverted and concealed, [which] may contribute to destroy the illusions of transatlantic speculation, and to diffuse solid, home-bred satisfaction amongst his industrious countrymen." That truth, according to Faux and his reviewer, was that the United States was a violent and uncivilized place, "knavish" at the north and "slavish" at the south.[22] Indeed, the review was so outrageous that it was "suppressed" by the American reprinters of the *Quarterly Review*. They found that it brought "forward wantonly and unnecessarily the names of private individuals, whose feelings must be outraged by being thus dragged before the public"; and, what was worse, was legally libelous.[23] Paulding nonetheless saw the review and responded with a satirical broadside two years later, which was serialized in *Niles' Weekly Register*, published as a monograph, and routinely included in later compilations of Paulding's work.

In order to tear down his British antagonist, Paulding adopted the literary pose of editor of an English traveler's manuscript of a journey from Boston to New Orleans, found abandoned at the Mansion Hotel in Washington. He linked the manuscript to the *Quarterly* reviewer through the satirical claim that "we have the best reasons, as well as the highest circumstantial testimony to warrant us in the assertion, that the author of this work, was, and if living, is still, one of the principal writers of the Quarterly Review—the very person who wrote the masterly review of Faux's Travels in the fifty-eighth number."[24] His decision to make the reviewer the target of his satire, rather than Faux, the original critic of American backwardness, may have been personal, because the *Quarterly Review* had published unflattering reviews of some of his earlier works.[25] Regardless of his motivation, Paulding's attack on the reviewer drew attention to the fact that he had written approvingly of Faux's account without ever having seen the United States. This choice framed the travel narrative that followed as at least suspect, if not completely fabricated, an implication reinforced by Paulding's tone of sarcastic graciousness toward the manuscript's (and thus the review's) author throughout his commentary, flattering him in terms that no reader would mistake for sincere. Paulding's complex satirical stance suggested that in a modern world already filled with travelers' accounts, tourists did not even need to make a tour in order to claim to speak authoritatively; like the *Quarterly*'s reviewer, they traveled in books. That the unknown author of *John Bull in America* had in fact toured the United States suggested that such tours were as meaningless as traveling in books.

The fictional travel narrative that followed worked hard and rather artlessly to reinforce the meaninglessness of the anonymous English reviewer's tour. He spent his entire journey in a state of complete geographical ignorance and confusion. He sailed for Boston because he thought it was the "nearest port" to New Orleans. Once landed in the United States, he consistently got the names of cities, states, rivers, and hotels wrong, often spectacularly so, like when he confused Charlestown, Massachusetts, with Charleston, South Carolina, and described it as "the capital of the state of North Carolina, a city famous for eating negroes." A running joke was his repeated departures for points north when he thought he was traveling south, from accidentally boarding a stagecoach to New Hampshire to accidentally boarding an upriver steamboat on the Mississippi. The observations he made along the way ranged from the ridiculous to the grotesque, from his ongoing obsession with slave cannibalism, to the obscene drunkenness of most Americans he met, to his attribution of all difficulties, from minor rudeness to major mishaps, to "democracy." Although Paulding painted his caricature in broad strokes, he carefully made all of his English tourist's confusions and exaggerations echo contemporary commentary on the United States found in the pages of the British press. He made it just barely plausible that an English armchair reviewer could confuse Charlestown and Charleston, for example, or the real horrors of chattel slavery with his imagined orgies of slave hunting and slave cannibalism. The overall effect was to suggest that his subject's tour held no more meaning than a handful of unreliable travel narratives; or, given the anglophile blinders that his tourist wore, perhaps even less. Paulding could not resist driving home the point by having his narrator return to the *Quarterly* in times of difficulty to, as he put it, "refresh my memory."[26]

The distinction that Paulding sought to collapse between the superficial tours of British visitors and the armchair travels of London reviewers was attacked more directly by Captain Marryat, a British naval novelist and travel writer who toured North America in 1837–38 and whose 1839 *Diary in America*, published upon his return to Britain, gained him a good deal of notoriety in the United States for its unflattering portrayal of the Americans he met. In 1833, he published a short satirical essay in the *Metropolitan Magazine* entitled "How to Write a Book of Travels."[27] This essay took the form of a dialogue between a struggling writer named Arthur Ansard and an experienced writer named Barnstaple. Ansard was frankly ambitious for material success, because he had as yet been unable to support himself in proper style by writing. Barnstaple had previously coached him through the writing of a "fashionable novel," to some financial success, and his publisher was pushing him to produce an account of a tour up the Rhine, with hopes of a similar payoff. The problem was that Ansard had "never been out of England in [his] life" and had neither the time nor the intention to change that fact. Luckily, Barnstaple assured him that it was unnecessary to actually travel to write the narrative of a tour of the Rhine, explaining at length how Ansard could "travel post in [his] old armchair." Ansard was to begin by reading as many tourist accounts as possible, which, along with appropriate reference works like gazetteers, would allow him to speak authoritatively about the geography and scenery of the Rhine. Barnstaple recommended choosing one tourist's account in particular to copy directly, while praising that tourist for "his exactitude and fidelity." When Ansard raised practical, if not moral, objections to such obvious plagiarism, Barnstaple responded, "On the contrary, he is the obliged party—your travels are a puff to his own." He then suggested filling the account full of minor quibbles with other tourists' travels, such as contesting their measurements of important landmarks. Always suggest that they are smaller than earlier travelers had claimed, Barnstaple counseled, because "the public will, in all probability, believe you, because you are the last writer, and because you have *decreased* the dimensions. Travellers are notorious for amplification, and if the public do not believe you, let them go and measure it themselves."[28] Such cynical tactics would make the book-buying public believe Ansard's account long enough for the print run to sell out, which, after all, was his main concern.

When crafting the narrative itself, Barnstaple advised "that there is a certain method required, even in writing travels. In every chapter you should have certain landmarks to guide you." The key to believability was conscientious adherence to a formula. Each chapter must outline the arc of a day, including "Travelling—remarks on country passed through—anecdote—arrival at a town—churches—population—historical remarks—another anecdote—eating and drinking—natural curiosities—egotism—remarks on women (never mind the men)—another anecdote—reflections—an adventure—and go to bed." Like Irving before him, Marryat gestured at the essentially formulaic nature of tourists' accounts by stringing vague phrases together with em-dashes. Ansard proved an adept student at applying this formula and quickly filled two volumes with fabricated days on the road. But then his creativity began to flag, and he turned to Barnstaple for new ideas: "I have remodelled several descriptions of mountains, and such wonders of creation—expressed my contempt and surprise at the fear acknowledged by other travellers, in several instances. I have lost my way twice—met three wolves—been four times benighted—and indebted to lights at a distance for a bed at midnight, after the horses have refused to proceed."[29] Barnstaple inspired fresh efforts by suggesting buying a poodle, commenting on the food, and recommitting to overt plagiarism. The humor in this situation lay in the great strategic lengths to which Ansard went to avoid actually traveling.

This creative back-and-forth between two fake tourists was premised on the notion that Ansard could convince his readers that he had visited the Rhine without ever leaving his armchair, which lampooned the predictable rhythm that commonly characterized tourists' accounts. All Ansard had to do was to copy the formula, and any reader would believe that he had actually made the trip himself. In this short sketch, Marryat sharpened existing critiques of tourists. They were crassly ambitious, taking tours in the hope of simple financial profit. Their tours were so unoriginal as to be meaningless, ranging from the merely formulaic to the outright plagiarized. They were so predictable, in fact, that they could be easily replicated by clever authors from the comfort of their own firesides, and those invented tours would be equally meaningful as countless actual journeys. Marryat's caricature of meaningless tourism relied for its power on a sense of touristic abundance. Tours could be easily fabricated because real tourist experiences were essentially interchangeable and easy for a fraud like Ansard to skim off of a library or a bookseller. And they could be profitable because those frauds could then be sold in the same anonymous marketplace for experiences. No wonder Ansard bestowed Barnstaple with the Barnumesque title "All-powerful and mighty magician, [with a] wand of humbug."[30]

Marryat's target may have been British tourists on the continent, but his work generally found an appreciative audience in the United States. As Dr. Syntax's transatlantic popularity showed, American readers understood the satirical stock figure of the ambitious and pretentious British tourist, an understanding that had been exploited by Knickerbocker authors like Irving and Paulding. Marryat's American contemporaries also took advantage of this familiarity to lampoon the growing number of British tourists who ventured onto American soil in the 1830s. Americans were sensitive to the negative portrayals of their country offered by contemporary British tourists like Mrs. Trollope, Thomas Hamilton, and Captain Marryat himself, and these sensitivities produced bitingly critical satires. For example, the American editor and humorist Asa Greene conjured George Fibbleton, an angry and aggressively foolish British tourist, for just such a purpose in 1833.[31] In Greene's briefly popular but ultimately ephemeral *Travels in America, by George Fibbleton, Esq.*, the tourist was the "ex-barber to His Majesty, the King of Great Britain" whose radical political views cost him his royal position.[32] He sought refuge in the United States, but his disgust at republican institutions and culture soon drove him back to England a "perfect tory." Upon his return, Greene's Fibbleton published his travels "to put down the spirit of reform; to render republicanism odious, and to establish loyalty in the affections of the people . . . (as well as to recruit to my purse, which not being a public reason, I speak it in parenthesis)."[33] Fibbleton's social ambition, in the form of a return to His Majesty's political good graces, as well as his parenthetical economic ambitions, structured Greene's satire in the tradition of ambitious tourists. Indeed, Fibbleton's ambition was so overwhelming that it turned his hyperbolic ignorance into absurd condescension.

Fibbleton's time in the United States was marked by this combination of unflattering traits, which satirists like Greene presented as endemic to all British travelers to America. Frederick Shelton, who penned a distinctly unfunny satire on the subject in 1837 entitled *The Trollopiad, Or, Travelling Gentlemen in America*, took British travelers as a whole, and Frances Trollope in particular, to task for the shallowness of their acquaintance with the United States and the condescension of their opinions. Americans owed them a debt of gratitude, Shelton sarcastically argued, for having "gone vaunting, and sneering and sardonically grinning, through the land, pleased with nothing, and visiting all things with their sovereign contempt . . . [and for having] been pleased, in the excess of their benevolence, to record their opinions and feelings—to throw open to the hallowed gaze of the world the domestic sanctuaries where they have found a refuge, and to make the confidential expressions of private intercourse the theme of public ridicule."[34] Shelton's work was a monument to bitterness, but he articulated a common opinion. Even the *New-England Magazine*'s literary reviewer, who thought that Greene's Fibbleton "failed" his goal of "burlesqu[ing] the publications of some of the late tourists with whose company we have been favored," agreed that the "exaggerated and partial statements of British travelers in the United States are a fair subject of satirical retort." Most American observers thought that British travelers deserved this reputation for exaggeration and for partiality, and for balancing condescension toward American institutions and culture with valorization of their British counterparts. Whatever the weaknesses of Greene's book, this particular critic thought that the goal of his satire was valid. Indeed, he failed by not living up to the potential of his subject: "Considering the capabilities of the subject, it is a matter of surprise that it has not drawn out more wit, more amusing description, and more pointed ridicule." The *New-England Magazine*'s reviewer compared him unfavorably to other great satirists, including, not coincidentally, Washington Irving.[35]

Notwithstanding Greene's failings in the eyes of contemporary literary critics, Fibbleton's tour exemplified the ignorance and exaggeration that satirists attributed to tourists. For example, when the ex-barber arrived in Saratoga Springs, he mistook the derivation of the name of Congress Spring, the most important mineral spring in town. Fibbleton thought that "the reason wherefore it is so called, as I am informed, is, that this water is particularly drank by Congressmen; and is moreover believed to be exceedingly efficacious in fitting a man to fill the honorable station of a member of Congress. This is pretty well proved by the fact, that nearly every Congressman in America may be seen at this spring, during the season; and that all those, who wish to become members of Congress, in like manner resort to the same efficacious fountain." Fibbleton then added a layer of bogus scientific "proofs" on top of his extreme credulity. He related the chemical qualities of the water to its political purposes, claiming that "it runs through the system with very nearly the velocity of quicksilver; all except the fixed air, which often remains stationary for upwards of a year, and is a principal reason of that windy quality, which is apt to distinguish both those who are, and those who wish to be, members of Congress."[36] Fibbleton displayed what critics took to be essential characteristics of tourists: their ignorance and foolishness, and their gullibility in the face of mischievous local informants. To this ignorance, however, Fibbleton added the condescension that American satirists found to be particularly characteristic of British travelers. "I was disgusted with the country, and resolved to abandon it forever," Fibbleton reminded his readers. "But I could not resist so fair an opportunity as I now had, of trying my capacity for becoming a member of the American Congress."[37] Despite his dismissal of Saratoga's charms, and his denigration of its supposed method of choosing congressmen, Fibbleton decided to make a run, and failed to drink enough water to gain office. In Saratoga, Fibbleton's disgust fueled his ignorance, and vice versa, a dynamic that characterized most of his adventures in America.

Fibbleton's ignorance was also complemented by his gullibility and his tendency toward exaggeration. For his trip up the Hudson, he boarded that *De Witt Clinton*, "a boat which I was told by a Yankee, who seemed to be a tolerably intelligent man for an American[,] was five hundred feet long, three hundred wide, and forty-six deep." Fibbleton's character judgment was questionable, because the Yankee's, and thus Fibbleton's, estimate of the *De Witt Clinton*'s size was grossly exaggerated.[38] The next day, and fifteen pages later, the boat ran aground on a mud bank, occasioning Fibbleton to cite the Yankee again, this time claiming the boat was six hundred feet long. A page later, Fibbleton was "credibly informed [that the boat's sides] were six hundred and fifty feet long."[39] Fibbleton's own ignorance, and his gullibility with local informants, led not only to condescension but also to gross mismeasurement of everyday sights. Collectively, these characteristics produced a tourist who was comically disengaged with the world he traveled through. In a satirical thread that stretched back to James Kirk Paulding, tourists were such poor observers and such faulty judges of human nature that they failed to understand anything meaningful about their destinations, which fundamentally undermined the purpose of their tours in the first place.

Greene also echoed Marryat's characterization of tourists as over-reliant on the accounts published by earlier tourists. Fibbleton actually undertook the tour that he wrote about, unlike Ansard, but even on the road he was entirely too inclined to let his impressions be shaped by other tourists' accounts. This reliance was a product of his social ambition, because he routinely referenced those British travelers hostile to "republican" America whom he idolized. These references were intended to include him in that elite company of authors, or, satirically, to bring that elite company down to the level of ignorance and absurdity on which Fibbleton operated. He thought: "Though I am a barber, that is no reason why my name should not be immortalized in the world of letters. There is an Ashe, a Fearon, a Hall, a Trollope, a Fiddler [*sic*]; and though last, perhaps not least, there may also be added a Fibbleton." At Lebanon Spring in New York, he observed the landlord boiling dinner in the spring itself, a sight that Fibbleton thought his readers would find incredible. "All this I am ready to avouch on the word of a traveller," he wrote, "and although it has not been noticed, so far as I can find, either in the books of Captain Hall, Mrs. Trollope, or the Reverend Mr. Fidler, still it is none the less true."[40] It was definitely not true, for the simple reason that Lebanon Spring was a mineral spring, not a hot spring. This curious negative citation—Fibbleton assured his readers that his observations were valid despite other travelers not noticing the same thing—ridiculed both the confabulations of tourists and their desire to have their con-fabulations confirmed by other tourists.

However, such direct citations were relatively rare in Fibbleton's narrative, a point made several times by Greene himself, writing in footnotes as the work's "American Editor." While on board the *De Witt Clinton*, Fibbleton recounted a long story about the "catamountain" of the Hudson Highlands, a creature that ate human flesh and "rather prefer[red that of] the English." It was known to attack steamboats and had recently eaten a Lord Mortimer. Fibbleton's telling of the tale emphasized his own bravery in the face of danger, as usual, but the "American Editor" did not let him take credit unquestioned. The footnote claimed that "A certain ex-reviewer to a magazine, who has been looking over our shoulder while we were reading the proof of the above, assures us that Mr. Fibbleton has filched the entire scene from the author of 'John Bull in America;' and that the catamountain, which carried off Lord Mortimer, is no other than the veritable owl which flew directly in the face of Captain Baltus Van Slingerland, as recorded in the 'Dutchman's Fireside:' in proof of all which he avers, that sundry words used by Mr. Fibbleton—such for instance, as *'the,' 'of,' 'and,'* besides several othere [*sic*]—are precisely the same as those used by Mr. Paulding."[41] The satire in this footnote operated on at least three separate levels. First, it pointed out the lack of originality in travel narratives. Second, it positioned Fibbleton squarely in the tradition of touristic plagiarists like Ansard. Third, the editor's claim is entirely specious—there is no such scene in *John Bull in America*, and no owl attack in *The Dutchman's Fireside*—as any reader could probably guess from the linguistic evidence of plagiarism he presented.[42] Greene's skillful editorial intervention left tourists' overreliance on and misuse of other tourists' accounts thoroughly skewered.

The second-generation tourist satires of the 1820s and 1830s built on tourist caricatures from early in the century, but they sharpened them and increasingly framed them as problems of touristic abundance. Leisure travelers were growing more obvious on American highways, which made their foolish ignorance and banal predictability seem less like charming foibles and more like real threats to the integrity of travel as a cultural project. The growing presence of British tourists—at a moment when American writers were deeply locked in a cultural struggle with their transatlantic counterparts about the meaning of Anglo-American difference—added a layer of national grievance to the darker tone of these satires. Although the earlier, gentler satires of Irving and Combe remained popular, by the 1830s American readers of tourist satire commonly encountered more aggressively negative portrayals of the tourist archetype at the same time that they encountered more leisure travelers on the road.

The hyperbolically foolish and banal tourists conjured by the satirists of the 1820s and 1830s shared another feature in common, even though it was one that went unremarked upon at the time. Their misadventures were increasingly consumer misadventures, brought about by their failure to properly navigate the market for commodified travel. Their slapstick mishaps increasingly involved stagecoaches, steamboats, and railway carriages rather than pedestrianism and the antics of old mares like Dr. Syntax's Grizzle. They missed connections, boarded boats headed in the wrong direction, and were whirled along at improbable speeds by primitive rail cars. While embedded within these new forms of transport, their novel and intimate interpersonal contexts provided ripe settings for satirical treatments of social interactions. They frequently misunderstood the commodified knowledge they purchased in books, and demonstrated endless gullibility in the face of anonymous human informants. They may have shared Jeremy Cockloft's silly superficiality and Dr. Syntax's penchant for physical and cultural pratfalls, but drivers of their ignorance and the causes of their mishaps were increasingly the things they bought: books, tickets, and even entire experiences of politically motivated guzzling of spring water.

None of the authors writing in the 1820s or 1830s drew this connection explicitly. The entrepreneurial innovations that produced commodified experiences of summer leisure were still developing, and their cultural effects were as yet still too unformed, to be a convenient subject of popular satire. By the 1840s, however, the marketplace for commodified experience brought forth a new generation of tourist satires that increasingly revealed an explicit link between consumer practices and tourist archetypes. Their caricatures of tourists built on existing satirical practice, but they heightened their emphasis on those features of commodified experience that skeptics were already noticing: its predictability and interchangeability from one tourist to the next, its preoccupation with existing patterns of travel rather than exploration and discovery, and the growing suspicion that experiences purchased in the marketplace might be meaningless. Midcentury satirical tourists were fundamentally frivolous consumers of commodified experience, and all of their negative characteristics were derived from this relationship to the marketplace for leisure travel.

These midcentury satires also began to lose the intimate connection to their British forebears and to the transatlantic concerns that had characterized their predecessors before 1840. Instead, the ambitious, superficial, gullible, disengaged tourist became an increasingly integrated stock figure within the main currents of American humor. Beginning in the late 1830s, tall talk, an indigenous American form of oral humor, started to appear in print.[43] These tall tales were built around an artful performance of exaggeration and fantasy built on solid base of plausible reality. The humor and pleasure of the tall tale, according to Henry Wonham, came when the audience was "suspended between knowledge of the tale's falsehood and appreciation for the teller's dexterity in stretching the limits of plausibility."[44] Tall talk had thrived as an oral form, particularly on the geographical margins of American life, since the eighteenth century, and in the nineteenth century American authors began to experiment with ways to import the form into literature. By the late antebellum period, tall tales had become a staple of the American popular literary diet, culminating in Mark Twain's skillful literary renditions of backwoods dialogue. By the 1840s, foolish literary tourists had begun to take on the characteristic of tall talkers, and their tours had begun to appear as clever exercises in calculated foolishness and exaggeration. The tourist remained an identifiable and identifiably negative stock figure in American satire, but it was no longer one that appeared in isolation. Instead, the growing ubiquity of both literary and actual tourists allowed satirists to use the figure as a powerful shorthand referent for ambitious, foolish, and superficial modern consumers of travel.

Even before the 1840s, American tourist satires had occasionally incorporated moments inspired by vernacular tall tale telling. In keeping with his double interests in creating an authentically American literature and in satirizing English tourists, James Kirk Paulding wrote a scene into his 1831 play *The Lion of the West* in which the frontiersman protagonist sought to convince an English tourist transparently named Mrs. Wallope that Kentuckians traveled underground through the mud after rainstorms.[45] Asa Greene, the inventor of George Fibbleton, was serving as the editor of the *New York Constellation*, an early humorous newspaper that published tall tales, when he penned the angry barber's tour in the early 1830s.[46] And with his epic feats of water consumption and dinners boiled in hot springs, Fibbleton himself embodied the comic instincts of the tall tale teller. But in the decades after 1840, that connection turned into submersion, as satirists paid less attention to British antecedents and turned their attention instead to American targets. As the perceived slights of British tourists stung American readers less sharply, foolish English barbers were increasingly replaced with exaggerated, and exaggerating, American tourists.

In 1842, a struggling newspaper editor in Augusta, Georgia, named William Tappan Thompson created Major Jones, a fictional small but respectable planter from Pineville, Georgia, whose letters to the editor about his life and adventures were full of artful misspellings and absurdly humorous situations. Although Thompson's newspapers were short-lived, Major Jones's immediate popularity meant that his fictional creation followed him from one publication to the next. The Major's letters gained a broader following as well, appearing in national periodicals like *Spirit of the Times* and the *Western Continent*. Thompson collected these letters and published them in a series of popular epistolary novels that remained in print throughout the 1840s and 1850s. Major Jones occupied an odd position among the archetypes of American literary humor. His diction, spelling, and general sense of wonderment at the modern world marked him as a backwoods southerner, a stock character in humorous literature by the 1840s. But his position as a militia officer and slave-owning planter, along with his Whiggish temperance politics, marked him as a respectable member of Pineville's middle class. This unique combination allowed Thompson to write deadpan commentary on the social and cultural practices of middling Americans, by having Major Jones engage in them with the truth-telling hyperbole of the tall talker. The inadvertent honesty of the awestruck backwoodsman, mixed with the cultural preoccupations of the ambitious middle classes, made Major Jones a well-honed vehicle for biting social satire.[47]

In 1848, Thompson published *Major Jones's Sketches of Travel*, an account of a summer tour along the old northern Fashionable Tour route, taken by Major Jones and his family, and written as usual as a series of letters addressed to Thompson, the Georgia newspaper editor. Although other popular literary tall talkers like Simon Suggs and Artemus Ward published "travels" in this era, Major Jones's uniquely respectable middling profile mean that his "travels" engaged directly with the negative characteristics of the tourist that earlier satirists had shaped.[48] Right from the beginning, he confessed that his tour had no real purpose; "I've made up my mind," as he put it, "to make a tower [*sic*] of travel to the big North this summer, jest for greens, as we say in Georgia, when we hain't got no very pertickeler reason for any thing." His mother, however, saw it differently. According to Major Jones, "She ses it's fashionable to go to the north, and she don't see why I haint as good a right to be like other folks, as sum people she knows, what goes to the Sarrytogy springs every year."[49] In this opening discussion, Thompson neatly skewered tourists for two of their established albeit paradoxical negative qualities: first, their travel was meaningless and without a larger purpose—"jest for greens"—and second, that it served merely as a vehicle for their social ambitions. That his mother picked Saratoga Springs as the destination most likely to reinforce Major Jones's social status was not an accident, since by the 1840s it was widely considered the most fashionable northern tourist destination.

In the letters written home from his tour, Major Jones lost no opportunity to speak the language of the picturesque. Recalling a moment peering out at the vast ocean from the deck of a coastal steamer sailing from Charleston, South Carolina, to Wilmington, North Carolina, he wrote, "I could preached [*sic*] a sermon on the sublimity of creation, and the insignificance of man and his works, but I had no congregation then, and it's too late now." At Niagara Falls, he was similarly awestruck by the Falls' superlative scale. "When my eye tuck in nothing but the mighty river," Jones wrote, "the everlastin battlements of rock, and the terrific cateract, why then they didn't seem to have no partickeler dimensions . . . [but then] I was able to comprehend the stupendous wonders of Niagary, and to feel myself no bigger, standing thar on that rock, than a seed-tick in Scriven county."[50] In these moments, Thompson recreated the satirical formula of Dr. Syntax by having Major Jones seek out hackneyed picturesque sights and describe them using the clichés of picturesque tourism, with an added dose of slapstick for good measure. Although Major Jones never fell in the mud while attempting to view Niagara (despite a close call when seeking a moonlight view), his colorful similes represented the kind of verbal slapstick well recognized by aficionados of backwoods humor. The effect was to portray tourists' mindless scenery-hunting as absurd, which was a defining feature of the transatlantic tourist archetype.

On his tour, Major Jones had some moments of credulity and foolishness, although this feature was less prominent than in the bitter satires of British tourists from the 1820s and 1830s. In Washington, DC, he wandered into the Capitol Building, only to find it empty of inhabitants. He approached a guide lounging nearby and "ax'd him whar the government was." When the guide told him that President Polk was at home at the other end of Pennsylvania Avenue, Major Jones begged his pardon because "I thought the government all lived at the Capitol." Once he got over his disappointment at not finding the government at home, he toured the building itself and contented himself with conducting a phrenological analysis of the Capitol Dome itself. He found prominent "bumps" indicating an overdeveloped "organ of secretiveness," "combattiveness," and "excess of veneration." "I ain't much of a frenologist myself," Major Jones declared, "or I'd go on and give you a full description of Uncle Sam's knowledge-box."[51] Major Jones was not as aggressively gullible as the British tourists who populated the pages of earlier American satires, but he still approached the sights and destinations of his tour with foolish notions that led him to outlandish conclusions.

Acts of touristic consumption figured prominently in Major Jones's tour. Throughout his tour, he took advantage of all the latest forms of

" I drapped the glass and spirted the rest out of my mouth quicker'n lightnin, but before I could git breth to speak to the chap, he ax'd me if I wasn't well."

Letter ix. p. 73.

FIGURE 4.3. Major Jones drinking soda water for the first time while on his tour (1848).

ticketed travel, including steamboats and especially the "railrode." In Weldon, North Carolina, an important transfer point between the North Carolina and Virginia railroad networks, Major Jones described a scene of chaos as the agents of two different Virginia lines competed for his patronage on his journey north. When they were purchasing their tickets, "a big fat feller" approached Major Jones's party, trying to sell them on taking "the Bay route," which ticketed them through on the Portsmouth and Roanoke Railroad to Hampton Roads, and then on a Chesapeake Bay steamer to the head of the bay. Major Jones told him he'd be "very glad to commodate him, only [he] wanted to go by Washington; [and the agent] sed, he'd be dad fetched if he didn't have the seat of government moved down on the Bay, jest for the commodation of the public what travels on his line. He's a monstrous good agent, and ought to be well paid for his trouble."[52] This parodic version of the market negotiations required to purchase travel tickets exaggerated the extent to which railroad ticket agents were selling packaged experiences to ignorant tourists. In classic tall tale fashion, the ticket agent's claims straddled the line between believable and unbelievable, and Major Jones's congratulatory response left open the question of the extent to which he believed what the agent was selling.

Either way, Major Jones chose to board the Petersburg Railroad instead, opting for the overland route across Virginia to Washington. Once on board, he began to articulate a common tourist complaint about travel purchased from railroads, that "these railrodes play the mischief with a man's observations." Major Jones complained that he failed to get a sense of Virginia, a state he was looking forward to touring, because the train moved so quickly that he got "a kind of flyin panorama of trees and houses, and fenses and bridges, all mixed up together—one runnin into tother, and another beginnin before the last one's left off—so he can't make hed nor tail to 'em." And when the train did stop, he was "so pestered with hack-drivers and porters, and he hain't hardly got time to buy his ticket or eat his breckfust, let alone doin any thing else." He felt the same way about his train journey across New York, which he called "a Empire State, shore enuff—a empire of cities and towns, standin so thick that, in the railrode cars, it jest seems to be one everlasting Broadway. . . . I tried to keep a run of the towns, but they stood so thick together and the cars went so fast, that when I ax'd anybody the name of a place, before I could make him understand what I wanted, in the bominable racket, we was in the middle of another town."[53] Major Jones's artful exaggeration of the experience of riding the railroad heightened the sense that his tour was ultimately a superficial exercise.

Both Major Jones and the other tourists he encountered on his journey used guidebooks to understand the conventional significance of the sights they saw. At the "fortress of Quebeck," Major Jones visited the Plains of Abraham and the monument to General Wolf, a routine stop on the northern "Grand Tour" since the 1820s. The French Canadians disliked their British rulers, he noted, and "Every countryman that crosses over the Plains with a basket of eggs for the market, gives [Wolf's Monument] a pelt with a stone, til the whole side of the monument is almost nocked off." Indeed, it was so disfigured "that if it wasn't for the gide-book nobody could tell what was on it." An English tourist that he encountered on the way to Niagara Falls was similarly equipped with a print product that shaped his experience of his tour. "He was runnin about all the time with his gide-book and pencil in hand," Major Jones recorded, "axin evrybody questions, and gabblin and talkin on 'bout evry thing, like he was half out of his senses." This English tourist was no George Fibbleton; Major Jones called him "a man of excellent good sense" because of his appreciation for Niagara.[54] Nevertheless, he cut a ridiculous figure in his touristic frenzy, armed with the consumer products that made him a tourist.

Major Jones was ultimately impressed by the extent to which the "Yankees" had figured out how to make money from selling experiences to tourists like himself, especially at Niagara, which was the most highly developed tourist destination that he visited. He described "Northerners" as "strivin on for wealth and power like all the rest of the world," and he found their methods for doing so to be impressively creative. The industrial waterpower harnessed from the Falls was striking enough, but Major Jones was most taken with the "old Curiosity Shop," a store for tourists that sold souvenirs and featured a mechanical model of the Falls. "What upon yeath could possess a man to try to run opposition to sich a wonder, rite in hearin and in sight of the real cataract itself, is what stumps me," Major Jones queried. "Nobody but a jennewine Yankee would ever undertake such a thing. He don't charge nothing to see his Niagary, but makes a heap of money by selling Yankee made Ingin fixins." He also saw unrealized opportunities for profit-making in this "Yankee" vein. On his trip behind the Falls to "Termination Rock," he wondered "that among all the ways they have of making money here, out of strangers, they never have hit upon a order of brotherhood, the initiation ceremony of which to take place upon the Termination Rock."[55]

The "Yankee" ingenuity that Major Jones encountered at Niagara was the emergence of a marketplace for commodified experiences—of nature's wonders, of Native American life, and, in his excited proposals, of mystical brotherhood. In classic tall tale fashion, Major Jones's account of this marketplace at Niagara toyed with the limits of believable exaggeration, and in doing so drove a satirical dagger straight into the heart of the negative archetype of the tourist in the late 1840s. The ambition, superficiality, and ultimate disengagement from the world he traveled through were all products of the commodification of experience at the hands of tourism entrepreneurs.

In many important ways, Thompson and the other literary craftsmen of tall tales in the 1840s and 1850s laid the groundwork for the spectacular career of Mark Twain. Like Thompson, Twain transposed elements of the tall tale into middle-class cultural settings and published them in mainstream venues where they were broadly popular. The most popular application of this formula during his lifetime was *The Innocents Abroad*, which, like *Major Jones's Sketches of Travel*, built upon the existing archetypes of tourist satire by merging them into a literary tall tale. In this case, Twain's subjects were a party of Americans who chartered a steamship for a Mediterranean cruise in 1867. Twain facetiously apologized that his book did not have the "gravity" and "profundity" of "a record of a solemn scientific expedition." "Yet notwithstanding it is only a record of a pic-nic, it has a purpose, which is, to suggest to the reader how *he* would likely see Europe and the East with his own eyes instead of the eyes of those who travelled in those countries before him."[56] *The Innocents Abroad* framed itself as a universal account of authentic touristic experience.

Twain's narrator decided to join the party on board *The Quaker City* as a result of a "seductive programme" for the expedition published in a newspaper. This prospectus offered an ideal experience. The extensive itinerary touched on many of the most popular cultural and historic sites of western Europe and the Mediterranean. The majority of these destinations were to be visited directly from the ship, completely lifting the problem of transportation from the tourists' shoulders; and the remainder were easily accessible by rail from the nearest port of call. The chartered ship promised that the tour could be made with a minimum of danger; not only did it have an "experienced physician" on board, the prospectus promised that it would avoid all ports with "contagious sickness," even if they were on the itinerary. This sense of security from exposure to unknown environments would be emotional as much as medical;

the advertisement envisioned that the "ship will at all times be home, where the excursionists, if sick, will be surrounded by kind friends, and have all possible comfort and sympathy." This entire experience could be purchased as part of a single ticket, "fixed at $1,250," which covered food, lodging, transportation, and even "all boating" to and from the ship in port.[57] Even though the price was substantial—more than twenty thousand dollars in 2015 dollars—it was a highly simplified market interaction, an entire European experience purchasable in a single transaction.

The price and duration of the tour and the relative isolation of the community of "excursionists" made *The Quaker City* an ideal setting for the cultivation of elite social contacts. The organizers of the tour understood the social possibilities of such an elite and intimate experience, and they created a "Committee on Applications" charged with curating a "select company" for the voyage. In other words, wealth was an insufficient qualifier for joining the tour; potential tourists had to bring social capital as well. Twain trained his acerbic wit on the manifest social ambition of a "company to be rigidly selected by a pitiless 'Committee on Applications'"; after paying his deposit, his narrator sought to "avoid a critical personal examination into my character, by that bowelless committee, [so] I referred to all the people of high standing I could think of in the community who would be least likely to know any thing about me." The infrastructure designed to produce social exclusivity produced a group including "three ministers of the gospel, eight doctors, sixteen or eighteen ladies, several military and naval chieftains with sounding titles, an ample crop of 'Professors' of various kinds, and a gentleman who had 'Commissioner of the United States of America to Europe, Asia, and Africa' thundering after his name in one awful blast!" The tour fit the narrator's social ambition to be part of a company of "uncommonly select material," even if the "Commissioner" whose prominence so impressed him was merely charged with "the collecting of seeds, and uncommon yams and extraordinary cabbages and peculiar bullfrogs for that poor, useless, innocent, mildewed old fossil, the Smithsonian Institution."[58] Thus Twain both noted and mocked the ambitions of *The Quaker City*'s tourists.

Twain deployed many of the markers of touristic superficiality that earlier satirists had honed in their work, but like E. L. Blanchard, he distinguished among different types of ignorance; his text was, to borrow Blanchard's terms, a "physiology" of touristic foolishness. The company included a cast of credulous fools, including "the Oracle"; a "poet"; and "a good-natured enterprising idiot" who was "known about the ship as

THE ORACLE.

"INTERROGATION POINT."

"POET LARIAT."

THE OLD TRAVELER.

FIGURE 4.4: Four typical characters from *The Quaker City*, from the first edition of *The Innocents Abroad* (1869). These vignettes originally appeared on different pages, next to Twain's description of each type; they appear together here to reveal Twain's "physiology." Courtesy of the Beinecke Rare Book and Manuscript Library, Yale University.

the 'Interrogation Point,' and this by constant use has been shortened to 'Interrogation.'" Like Fibbleton, Interrogation had no sense of the scale of the sights he visited, and readily believed the most absurd and impossible dimensions suggested by his fellow tourists. Twain also delineated the foolish pretentions of "Old Travelers," who "prate, and drivel and lie." The "Old Travelers" encountered by the narrator sought out those who had never traveled before, and "then they open their throttle-valves, and how they do brag, and sneer, and swell, and blaspheme the sacred name of Truth! Their central idea . . . is to subjugate you, keep you down, make you feel insignificant and humble in the blaze of their cosmopolitan glory!" In keeping with his literary heritage, Twain's narrator himself was the type of tourist to engage in the winking exaggerations of the tall tale. In the Moroccan city of Tetouan, he discussed a recent territorial conflict between Spain and Morocco, during which he claimed that the Spanish had refused to give up Tetouan "until the Spanish soldiers had eaten up all the cats."[59] This claim played humorously on both Western ideas about Islamic reverence for cats and on a well-known recipe for "roast cat" from a fifteenth-century Spanish cookbook.[60] Twain's narrator spun this fanciful story into tales of French ministers who made patterned carpets of multicolor cat hides, a familiar pattern of plausible exaggeration that marked the cultural link between tourists and tall tale tellers. The resulting tale broke down the more general tourist archetype into a catalogue of discrete tourist types.

The fundamentally superficial nature of tourism was further marked by the ways in which the members of the company—Twain's narrator aside—recorded their experiences. Many of *The Quaker City*'s tourists showed an initial "ambition . . . to keep a faithful record of [their] performances in a book," for their own memory, for friends at home, or even for sale "for more than a thousand dollars." But "Alas! that journals so voluminously begun should come to so lame and impotent a conclusion as most of them did!" Even those tourists who still had a spark of ambition to publish their tours resorted to "copy[ing] France out of a guidebook, like old Badger in the for'rard cabin who's writing a book." Even though Twain's tourists were actually touring, they resorted to strategies of plagiarism like Barnstaple and Ansard, suggesting that the tour itself was less meaningful in shaping their experiences than were the products of commercial print culture that they brought with them. Even when tourists did not directly plagiarize from guidebooks, they sublimated their lived experience to the products of the print marketplace. "The people who go into ecstasies over St. Sophia" in Constantinople, the narrator claimed, "must surely get them out of the guide-book (where every church is spoken of as being 'considered by good judges to be the most marvelous structure . . . that the world has ever seen')."[61] Ultimately, for Twain, the superficiality of tourism emerged from its fundamentally consumer nature. The passengers on board *The Quaker City* were purchasing an experience of Europe, bought from steamship owners and guidebook publishers, and they expected that experience to meet their social and cultural expectations precisely. For Twain, the humor in the expedition lay in the moments when his tourist-consumers unexpectedly got either more or less than they paid for.

The satirizing of tourists in the nineteenth century was such a broad and diverse practice that tourist satire can hardly be called a coherent genre. These satirists all wrote in different moments, and they sought to skewer different groups for different reasons. In Britain, William Combe was after the upwardly mobile acolytes of William Gilpin, while Captain Marryat sought to deflate the pretensions of continental tourists who portrayed their tours as novel and meaningful. In the United States, Washington Irving mocked the aristocratic ambitions of New York's early republican elite, James Kirk Paulding and Asa Greene defended their country from the attacks of real British tourists, and William Tappan Thompson and Mark Twain gently ridiculed the social and cultural practices of the emerging American bourgeoisie. But notwithstanding this great diversity of satirical aims and techniques, these authors' portrayals of tourists had significant overlap: they tended to see tourists as ambitious yet ignorant purveyors of tired clichés, who were equally given to condescension and exaggeration. The specific contours of this archetype, as well as the relative emphases of its different features, varied depending on the historical context and the satirical target. But over time, the deeper cultural causes of touristic unoriginality and superficiality came more sharply into focus. Turn-of-the-century satirists had located the roots of tourists' behavior in their idiosyncratic individual ambition. By the 1820s and 1830s, satirists had begun to notice that a considerable portion of tourists' foolishness was set in the commercialized spaces of stagecoaches, steamboats, and hotels. By the 1840s, satirists had begun to make this connection more explicit and to give it the status of causal explanation. The midcentury tourist was the subject of satire because he or she was an absurd and laughable consumer of trite experiences.

Throughout this period, the connotations that adhered to this tourist archetype were decidedly negative. The cynicism of the satirists' condemnation varied; the satires written early in the century and again at midcentury were notably gentler than the angry portrayals of the 1820s and 1830s. But the tourist was never an admirable figure and was never held up as a model worthy of emulation. Thus, the coalescing nineteenth-century genre of tourist satire helped give the figure of the tourist its negative connotation, a value judgement that was increasingly rooted in the tourist's identity as superficial consumer of commodified experience. This denigration of tourists and touristic practices also inescapably shaped discussions of travel and tourism by midcentury. As Major Jones put it on departing his plantation in Georgia, "bein as I'm a literary carater I ought to see something of the world."[62] Being a tourist could lead a traveler in just such thickets of absurdity.

5 / Traveling to Good Purpose:
The Invention of the True Traveler

In February 1860, a peripatetic Englishman of Portuguese descent named Joachim Stocqueler mounted the stage at Clinton Hall in New York City. Formerly the Astor Opera House, Clinton Hall was owned by the New York Mercantile Library and was a well-established venue for middle-class New Yorkers to gather for lectures by leading cultural figures of the day. Stocqueler was less well known than many Clinton Hall lecturers, but he was a man who knew about travel and travel writing. He had roamed widely across the British Empire and the United States, often only one step ahead of his creditors. He wrote guidebooks, travel narratives, and historical texts based on his journeys, and he had even run "a general enquiry office" for travelers in London in the 1840s.[1] By the 1860s, he was living in New York, working as a lecturer and a journalist under the name of Joachim Siddons. On that February evening, Stocqueler's subject was one he knew well: "Travel, Its Pleasures, Advantages, and Requirements."

Like his contemporary E. L. Blanchard, Stocqueler thought that the modern era was potentially a golden age of global travel. Thanks to steam-powered transportation and an increasingly peaceful Europe, he thought, "all persons travel who can afford to do so." But all this modern travel was not necessarily meaningful or useful. "The grand secret of travel is but partially known," he complained, and "the *art* of traveling to a purpose is very imperfectly developed." Looking back, he dismissed the formulaic tours of the eighteenth century, popularized by "gentry [who] regarded their trashy experiences as of so much moment to society

at large that they absolutely committed them to print." Luckily, Stocqueler thought that nineteenth-century satire had struck a grievous blow
to frivolous accounts of routine pleasure tours. He especially credited
William Combe's 1809 *The Tour of Dr. Syntax* with shaming such superficial tourists into silence: "The mania for publishing tours subsided after
the scourge of the satirist had been pretty widely distributed," Stocqueler
claimed. But even if Combe had dissuaded tourists from attempting
to publish their experiences, he could not mock them into traveling
meaningfully. Stocqueler thought that most contemporary travelers
"idly surmised that nothing further is necessary than to pack up trunks
and carpet-bags, fill a purse with money, procure a passport, engage a
passage, and depart. Vain notion!"[2] Such travelers were mere tourists,
engaged with the surface of things. Luckily Stocqueler stood before the
crowd, ready to instruct them in "the *art* of traveling to a purpose."

At the podium in February 1860, Stocqueler could draw upon several
decades' worth of transatlantic print discussions about the difference
between superficial tourism and useful travel, and about the qualities
that a traveler needed to cultivate to make him- or herself more than a
tourist. Reactions to the emergence of a new class of tourists were shaped
by both British and American observers, who perceived similar phenomena in their different cultural contexts. As we have seen, critics on
both sides of the Atlantic increasingly questioned the value of commodified experience with a drumbeat of satire directed in overlapping ways
at both British and American tourists. It was out of this context of growing concern about the lack of value in touristic experiences that a transatlantic literature aimed at teaching "the *art* of traveling to a purpose"
emerged. A few eighteenth-century British commentators had sought to
train "intellectually curious traveller[s]," most notably Count Leopold
Berchtold, who published *An Essay to Direct and Extend the Inquiries of
Patriotic Travellers* in London in 1789.[3] More popular prescriptions for
traveling to a purpose began to appear on American shelves around 1830,
and by the end of the decade London-based scholarly organizations were
producing book-length treatises on the subject, which quickly joined
domestic observers' works in the catalogues of American booksellers. By
the time Stocqueler summarized this literature for his New York audience in 1860, librarians on both sides of the Atlantic were grouping these
works together as an identifiable genre under headings like "Treatises
on Travelling—Instructions for Travel."[4] By the century's midpoint,
middle-class potential travelers like those in Stocqueler's audience could
easily study "the *art* of traveling to a purpose." And as his framing of the

problem showed, the growth of this genre was a direct reaction to the emergence of tourism, a form of travel he perceived to be purposeless.

For Stocqueler and his contemporaries, "travel to a purpose" was synonymous with "useful" travel. Another product of the dichotomous thinking about the uselessness of tourism, a growing number of observers argued that even pleasure travel could be valuable and meaningful if it served some higher cultural or intellectual purpose—if it produced new geographical knowledge or contributed meaningfully to its diffusion. Useful travel generally required substantial, original observation and a real contribution to the larger good, unlike tourism, which was superficial and served only the tourist's pleasure. Indeed, the body of Stocqueler's Clinton Hall lecture was an elaborate list of the categories of inquiry pursued by any traveler "professing to describe a country or countries minutely," because the production of just such a minute description could make even pleasure travel useful, unlike the "trashy" experiences of the tourist.[5] This definition of utility was shaped by evolving intellectual and institutional structures of nineteenth-century science and education, as useful travel was defined in opposition to increasingly aestheticized tourism. The figure of the tourist and the figure of the useful traveler emerged in conjunction with and in opposition to each other and became the fundamental governing dichotomy shaping perceptions of the value of travel in the modern era.

This dichotomy had a special and distinct resonance for nineteenth-century Americans, however. Nineteenth-century Americans were deeply suspicious of the consumption of luxuries, which they associated with British aristocratic decadence and found incompatible with sober, self-sufficient republicanism. They expressed this suspicion by embracing a culture of "refinement," which was a form of enlightened gentility that seemed more compatible with a political culture that celebrated egalitarianism.[6] They also celebrated hard work and the production of useful goods, which they associated with sturdy American yeoman independence. The cultural and political value system that celebrated producers over consumers was overdetermined; it had roots in seventeenth-century radical Protestantism, in eighteenth-century opposition politics, in the national identity forged during and after the American Revolution, and in the rhetorical struggles of nineteenth-century partisan politics.[7] Indeed, in many ways, the story of American culture in the early republic is the story of this value system coming into conflict with the realities of emergent market capitalism.[8] As tourism increasingly became associated with ease, superficiality, unoriginality, and consumption, it began to tap into these deep cultural preoccupations and value structures. Consuming leisure experiences was pleasurable and offered social cachet, but at the same time it smacked of aristocratic decadence. Alternatively, seeking recognition as a traveler to good purpose helped a traveler remain a producer, even when the means and mechanisms were purchased in the market for leisure travel. A traveler to good purpose produced something useful even if he or she also consumed. As a result, the useful traveler claimed a specifically nineteenth-century form of social and cultural worth that was unavailable to tourists.

The model of the useful traveler, as outlined by Stocqueler and other commentators, was even more appealing precisely because it did not require rejection of the comforts of commodified travel or the conveniences of commercially packaged geographical knowledge. After all, Stocqueler celebrated "every new invention for facilitating locomotion" that had shaped the age, and regarding guidebooks, he declared, "It would be absurd to deny that a great deal is to be learned from these compilations."[9] But following the protocols of the useful traveler translated acts of consumption like the purchase of a railroad ticket or guidebook into acts that conveyed cultural and intellectual status. Even if the means of travel were commodities, the experience of travel itself was not a standard commodity purchased in the marketplace. For those who sought to acquire the status of usefulness and to avoid the opprobrium of tourism, the model of useful travel held an obvious appeal.

This strategy of traveling to a purpose was a fundamentally gendered strategy. Male travelers could comfortably claim the mantle of producers of geographical knowledge, because the literature of traveling to a purpose almost uniformly imagined its subjects to have masculine bodies, and because men's increasingly gendered domination of knowledge-producing institutions like learned societies, colleges, and the military gave them an authoritative outlet for that knowledge. However, the gendered monolith of traveling to a purpose had significant cracks through which female travelers could drive their horses and carriages. As male travelers lay claim to the institutions of knowledge production and an increasingly gendered conception of "rationality" in the second quarter of the nineteenth century, female travelers responded with an emphasis on the value of cultivating sympathy and schooling the nation in morality, both of which were increasingly held to be the province of women.

It is apt that Theodore Dwight was the first American author to explicitly prescribe "travelling to good purpose." The scion of a prominent family of New England writers and theologians, Dwight's first literary endeavor was editing and publishing his uncle Timothy Dwight's manuscript accounts of his travels around New England and New York between 1796 and 1815. The elder Dwight, longtime president of Yale College, made annual journeys to collect information about his native region, which he hoped to publish as a corrective to the flawed accounts of European travelers in America. He considered himself a "curious" traveler, and unlike the "incurious" travelers who slid through their journeys content with a general notice of the surface of things, Dwight claimed an "intention to give you a view of my proposed subject, at once comprehensive and minute." Curious travelers such as himself were "eager in the pursuit of knowledge, both from the pleasure and profit which it affords."[10] He made good on his intentions by taking rich and detailed notes on the flora, fauna, agriculture, and the "morals and manners" of New England's people. His nephew Theodore published these notes in four volumes as *Travels in New-England and New-York*, first in New Haven in 1821–22 and then in London the following year. At the same time, Theodore moved to New York to build a career in the city's burgeoning literary marketplace. He quickly carved a niche for himself as an author and editor of popular geographical texts, including travel narratives, a gazetteer, and, in 1825, one of the earliest tourist guidebooks for the northern Fashionable Tour through upstate New York and New England, the very territory his uncle had covered several decades before.[11] Dwight published this guidebook, *The Northern Traveller*, with A. T. Goodrich, one of the early geographical publishing specialists whose shops clustered on Broadway above Trinity Church. Both Dwights demonstrated personal and professional commitments to the print culture of geographical knowledge, as it was understood by their respective generations.

Four years after his guidebook helped to open the northern interior to commercial tourism, Theodore Dwight published his *Sketches of Scenery and Manners in the United States*, a collection of short essays designed to further the family project of "excit[ing] . . . new interest in the beauties of our scenery, and in the traits of our manners." Goodrich saw enough of a link with the earlier guidebook to advertise the later miscellany as being "by the author of 'Northern traveller,'" despite the fact that the two books had very little in common. Unlike the guidebooks that were emerging as a distinct genre in the late 1820s, *Sketches of Scenery and Manners* contained no information about routes or destinations and offered no advice about practical preparations for a journey. Instead, in an essay entitled "Travelling to Good Purpose," Dwight proposed to instruct his readers how to travel as his uncle had traveled, in pursuit of the "plea-sure and profit" of real, useful knowledge. Drawing on his experience as his uncle's editor and as a geographical author in his own right, Dwight outlined the intellectual and philosophical preparation necessary for "discriminating with readiness and clearness between the useful and the useless" when traveling.[12]

Notwithstanding that he was himself a pioneering author of Ameri-can tourist guidebooks, Dwight framed his call for "travelling to good purpose" in terms of a dichotomy between superficial, aimless travelers and those who sought to make their travel culturally and intellectually useful. He lamented that the majority of travelers were capricious seek-ers of present gratification: "This is to abuse travelling," he thundered. Presumably some of these superficial travelers were also readers of his guidebook, but nevertheless, Dwight advised that "the annual excur-sions and tours made by so many families in the northern parts of this country might be rendered much more agreeable, and much more useful than they usually are, by a little forethought and method."[13] This call for "forethought and method," a more conscious, rigorous, and creative approach to travel than the mere reading of a guidebook, became a ker-nel of Dwight's and other authors' prescriptions for "travelling to good purpose" in the subsequent decades.

Substantive intellectual preparation was essential for traveling to good purpose, and for Dwight, this prescription meant that travelers should read. "The great features of our country, the leading events of its history, and the details of its natural productions; our arts of life, our condition and habits, are now so easily accessible in popular publications," Dwight claimed, "that foreigners themselves are ashamed to travel without some preparation by reading; and our own citizens have sometimes been hushed into silence while listening to the intelligent remarks of those who have a right to seek of them instruction." The most appropriate of the "popular publications" with which to prepare were "such books as contain necessary information in a compact and convenient form"—a description that sounded very much like *The Northern Traveller*. Dwight thought that this kind of preparation was not nearly common enough among the domestic travelers of 1829; American tourists had "too much given in to the fashion of carrying foreign novels and poems with them to read on their journies [*sic*]—a habit, which, as far as it prevails, has its origin in taste at least ill-timed, if not in pedantry of a very mistaken kind."[14] The substantive preparation that Dwight recommended was fairly limited compared to what his successors would recommend, which may have been the result of his financial interest in a "compact and convenient" guidebook. Nevertheless, Dwight argued that it was important to be acquainted with the geography, history, economy, and society of the United States in order to travel to good purpose.

Dwight's admonition to avoid "foreign novels and poems" on the road was more than just an advertisement for *The Northern Traveller*, however. It was also a gendered warning about the epistemological preparation necessary for traveling to good purpose. "Instead of wishing to see the world through a fancied medium," Dwight wrote, "the rational traveller wishes to view it as it is." Traveling to good purpose required the traveler to shed the imaginative and sentimental constructs of novels and poems and take up instead the objectivity of scientific observation. The rational traveler "endeavours to divest his mind of all prejudice, as well as to prepare his feelings to slide easily over the little trials he must expect, determined neither to fail of the enjoyments which lie before him by extravagant anticipations, nor to diminish them unnecessarily by unfortunate comparisons."[15] Objectivity required not only avoiding prejudgment of the territory traveled through, but also an ability to control "extravagant anticipations" and "unfortunate comparisons." In Dwight's didactic dichotomy, the "fancied media" of "foreign novels and poems" were associated with prejudice, anticipation, and spurious comparison, which were the same adjectives he used to describe the meaningless, superficial pleasure tours that he implored his readers to avoid.

The gendered nature of this dichotomy would have been transparent to Dwight's readers in the late 1820s. Novels in particular had become associated with female readers in the eighteenth century, especially those that used the rhetoric of sympathy for their emotional power.[16] Women, and especially young women, were thought to be the largest group of novel readers, and, by the time Dwight was writing, women were increasingly authoring novels as well.[17] This gendering of fiction was laden with moral danger; as Mary Kelley has argued, persistent stereotypes "that ranked women's reasoning and analytical capabilities lesser than men's" meant that "women who indulged in fiction might become captive to the novel's flights of fancy."[18] Traveling to good purpose, Dwight argued, required a disavowal of the novel's claims to knowledge, which were dangerously associated with women readers and the implicitly female tourists who carried novels with them on their journeys. Purposeful travel required instead an implicitly masculine commitment to nonfiction reading and to rational observation. In drawing this distinction, Dwight was part of a broader movement to associate traveling to good purpose with the emerging scientific values of objective, inductive observation and the systematic recording and reporting of those observations. The distinction between rigorous masculine observation and the feminized fancy of novelistic travel was clearly gendered in Dwight's exhortative essay, and the emphasis on the rational created a fraught landscape for women who sought to avoid being dismissed as superficial, useless tourists. As traveling to good purpose became increasingly framed as a scientific endeavor, women travelers had to become more vigilant and creative in carving out a space of sympathetic, educational observation as their own mode of traveling to good purpose.

In the decade after the publication of Dwight's musings on traveling to good purpose, a broader range of commentators took up the theme at greater length. The new literature on scientific traveling to good purpose came largely out of Britain, where a social and institutional nexus of scientific pursuit thrived in London in the early nineteenth century. The British capital hosted an increasing number of experimentalists, writers, publishers, and institutions that produced a flood of texts on medicine, technology, and the natural and social sciences, all of which supported and were supported by Britain's growing colonial ambitions. Much of this imperial science took the form of "exploration," which meant that the London scientific community was deeply invested in making travel serve useful ends.[19] No American city had an equivalent concentration of learned societies and scholarly publishers, although the growing number of both amateur and professional scientific investigators created a significant American market for imported and reprinted British texts.[20] Furthermore, the cosmopolitan appeal of institutional and intellectual connections to the metropolitan scientific community encouraged Americans interested in such inquiries to build and maintain transatlantic links as much as possible. While Dwight's *Sketches of Scenery and Manners in the United States* called for travel to good purpose in the informal tone of an essayist, his British counterparts undertook the call as a question of scientific precision.

Thus, it was largely to British sources that Joachim Stocqueler turned when crafting his 1860 address, specifically to Colonel J. R. Jackson's 1841 *What to Observe; Or, the Traveller's Remembrancer.*[21] Stocqueler and Jackson moved in the same circles in London in the 1840s, when Jackson was secretary of the Royal Geographical Society and Stocqueler ran a "general inquiry office" on Indian affairs, but the similarity in their prescriptions for traveling to good purpose was explained less by any personal acquaintance than by the canonical status that Jackson's text had achieved by 1860.[22] Jackson's lengthy work was reprinted in London multiple times over the intervening decades, and it provided the model for a shorter pamphlet-length work entitled *Hints to Travellers*, first published in the *Journal of the Royal Geographical Society* in 1854 and regularly printed as its own pamphlet starting in 1865.[23] This essential Royal Geographical Society handbook ran to some seven editions by the end of the nineteenth century, with each edition being expanded and revised to incorporate the latest technologies for observation.[24] *What to Observe* also formed the basis of the British Admiralty's *Manual of Scientific Enquiry*, an abridged guide that was frequently reprinted between 1849 and the 1880s, intended for "the Use of Officers in Her Majesty's Navy; and Travellers in General."[25] Jackson's work quickly circulated to the United States; new editions of *What to Observe* were widely noticed by American periodicals, and it routinely graced the shelves of American libraries.[26] In the wake of its initial London publication in 1841, the Philadelphia firm of Carey and Hart announced an American edition, which was never actually realized.[27] Even without a domestic edition, the geographically oriented American firm of D. Appleton and Company included *What to Observe* in their ideal library of "the most important works in every department of knowledge, in all modern languages" in 1847.[28] Jackson's work, which appeared in multiple versions across several decades and enjoyed wide transatlantic circulation, was the most influential guide for scientifically useful travel in middle decades of the nineteenth century.

Above all, Jackson advocated proper observation and the proper recording of those observations, so that travel could make useful contributions to scientific knowledge. A staff military officer by training, Jackson was a founding member of the Royal Geographical Society (RGS) in the 1840s. He was himself relatively well traveled, but he "envisaged that a major role of the RGS should be to arrange, classify, and evaluate geographical information." Jackson thought a geographer's "labours of the cabinet" were just as important as travel and exploration and needed to be taken just as seriously. *What to Observe* was an attempt to correct the "wrong aims and inadequate achievements" of thoughtless travel by articulating "the sorts of questions which should be examined by an explorer or traveller."[29] Jackson's guide to traveling to good purpose was explicitly intended to make travel more productive of geographical knowledge; in other words, to make it useful rather than useless.

As the long-running abridged versions of the late 1840s and 1850s showed, Jackson and the RGS did not intend their "remembrancer" to be used only by members of the institution itself. Rather, Jackson "intended [it] for general use," and he hoped that "it will prove acceptable alike to those who travel luxuriously over civilized Europe, and to those adventurous and ardent spirits who wander undaunted among hostile tribes, braving every obstacle and enduring every hardship in search of knowledge." Jackson hoped to place his book in as many traveling hands as possible, because the proper acquisition and arrangement of geographical knowledge was a task that scaled up well—the more travelers to good purpose, the better. "Indeed," Jackson lamented, "when we consider the total absence of anything like solid information given to us by the legion of those who quit their native country to roam for a while over the various parts of the globe, we cannot but think that some good must result from pointing out how their peregrinations may be turned to better account than they have hitherto been."[30] In this imperial vision, metropolitan geographical knowledge would grow exponentially not only because the members of the RGS would travel to better purpose, but because otherwise useless tourists would also do their share to add to the collective stock of knowledge.[31]

Jackson paid little attention to the intellectual preparations necessary for travel; indeed, he hoped that travelers would "be encouraged to exertion by the assurance that, without being what is termed a philosopher, he may not only do much to enlarge the sphere of his own ideas, but acquire the means of communicating to others a great mass of valuable or interesting information." In short, Jackson taught technique, not knowledge. His useful traveler did not need to be a "philosopher" because the scope and content of geographical knowledge was to be determined centrally rather than individually; the useful traveler was a collector of data more than a "philosopher." Thus, preparation for traveling to good purpose was largely an affair of packing the right instruments, listing the proper questions to be answered through travel, and receiving the proper inspiration. He "endeavoured to excite a desire for useful knowledge by awakening curiosity" and hoped that the "intending traveller . . . will, from a perusal of the present work see what an immense field of physical and moral research lies open to his investigation."[32] The instruments and techniques he recommended were largely those of the physical sciences, enabling precise measurement of geographical features and atmospheric conditions, and the proper preparation of specimens to bring home.

Beyond Jackson's technical advice for taking accurate measurements, the bulk of the work was taken up with listing the categories of observation and recording that would serve the needs of the RGS and other

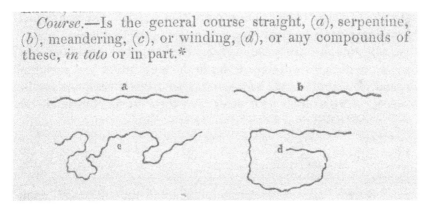

Course.—Is the general course straight, (*a*), serpentine, (*b*), meandering, (*c*), or winding, (*d*), or any compounds of these, *in toto* or in part.*

FIGURE 5.1. A small illustration from J. R. Jackson's *What to Observe; Or, the Traveller's Remembrancer* (1841), which taught travelers to precisely describe river courses by giving technical definitions to commonly used terms. Courtesy of the Yale University Library.

systematizers of geographical knowledge. Jackson went so far as to list questions to be answered and topics to be addressed on any tour, whether in "civilized Europe" or among "hostile tribes." He divided the universe of geographical knowledge into ten categories, each of which was subdivided into sections that contained a range of topics to be addressed and specific questions to be answered. He sought to discipline both observation and the recording of observations in as many situations as possible. The degree of detail reflected Jackson's professional interest in thorough observation and classification and his broader agenda of building the RGS's knowledge of the world through grooming large numbers of travelers to good purpose rather than relying on a small number individual scientific super-travelers. Since these travelers were not necessarily "what is termed a philosopher," Jackson did not explicitly train them to develop creative avenues of inquiry on the fly; instead, he offered them the discipline to be thorough observers and systematic classifiers.

This emphasis on a disciplined, thorough, and systematic approach to observation and recording was neither accidental nor unusual because this rigor was fundamental to the claim to empirical knowledge made by professionalizing scientific organizations like the RGS. This emphasis on objective and accurate observation dated back to the English philosopher Francis Bacon at the turn of the seventeenth century but had become even more important by Jackson's day because it distinguished the RGS's authority from that of older, more impressionistic claims to geographical knowledge.[33] Male scientists began to argue in the seventeenth century that achieving this discipline of observation required intellectual mastery of the passions and weaknesses of the body, which was a triumph of gender. As Jan Golinski has argued, scientific self-discipline was "an ideology of masculinity that denigrated those mental attributes that were gendered female and denied women the capacity to free themselves from them." The rigors of reliable observation were precisely such a form of masculine self-control, "a way of subduing the feminine aspect of the individual man of science."[34] The structured habits of observation and recording required by Jackson's method of traveling to good purpose, along with the strict mental and physical discipline needed to fill in lengthy lists of questions at every stop along the road, constructed an implicitly masculine traveler to good purpose. Jackson's traveler was thus comfortably established at the masculine end of Dwight's gendered binary of "fancied media" and objective observation.

As deep and powerful as this gendered binary was, it remained implicit rather than explicit for advocates like Dwight, Jackson, and Stocqueler. When Stocqueler popularized Jackson's work in his Clinton Hall address, he captured this agnosticism about the gender of objective observation when he admonished all the potential travelers seated before him "to observe an exactitude in relation to facts. . . . Men and women write too much in a hurry," he warned, "and too often give way to first or last impressions."[35] This agnosticism was at least in part driven by Jackson's reliance on scale; his vision, after all, involved training as many travelers as possible to be disciplined observers in order to assist the RGS with data collection. Indeed, the masculine ideal of the lone scientific genius was largely a myth, especially by the late eighteenth and early nineteenth centuries, when professionalizing science was largely a collaborative endeavor. For many scientists, collaboration meant harnessing (and therefore legitimating) the observational powers of female assistants.[36] Since Jackson saw all travelers as potential foot soldiers in a broadly coordinated project to compile useful geographical knowledge, he wrote his manual to appeal to as broad an audience as possible, including "those who travel luxuriously," "adventurous and ardent spirits," and those who were not "what is termed a philosopher"—all categories that contained women as well as men. Jackson remained open to the supporting contributions of both male and female travelers, and in doing so, he was right in step with the leading scientists of his day. While neither Jackson nor his scientific collaborators would have necessarily called their female assistants "scientists," they did not doubt their reasoning ability. It was in this spirit that *What to Observe* opened a small space for women travelers to good purpose, if not for female membership in the RGS.

Dwight, Jackson, Stocqueler, and other promoters of objective observation may have imagined only a highly circumscribed role for women travelers to good purpose, but theirs were not the only guides to traveling to good purpose published in the years after Dwight. In the mid-1830s, "an association of philanthropic geniuses of both sexes" associated with the Society for the Diffusion of Useful Knowledge (SDUK) in London undertook the ambitious project of producing a series of books for useful travelers under the title of *How to Observe*.[37] This series was intended to be popular in the broadest sense, since the SDUK was "devoted to the cause of adult education and the Utilitarian ideal of 'Knowledge is Power,'" with the "aim of providing a mass readership with cheap but authoritative printed material."[38] As its editor explained, "it was originally intended to produce, in one or two volumes, a series of hints for travellers and students, calling their attention to the points necessary for inquiry or observation in . . . Geology, Natural History, Agriculture, the Fine Arts, General Statistics, and Social Manners." However, a single volume seemed too cumbersome, so the original volume was "separate[d into] the great divisions of the field of observation." This plan was carried out for two volumes, one on geology and the other on morals and manners. Noted British geologist Sir Henry Thomas De la Beche's *How to Observe—Geology* was printed only once, by Charles Knight, the Society's publisher, in London in 1835. Transatlantic publishers evidently had higher hopes for an American market for the second volume. *How to Observe—Morals and Manners*, by British traveler, journalist, and philosopher Harriet Martineau, was released by Knight in 1838 and reprinted in the same year by the New York firm of Harper & Brothers and the Philadelphia firm of Lea & Blanchard. Of the two, Martineau's volume received far more press and a larger circulation, especially in the United States.

These extended treatises of expert instruction were intended for at least two audiences: first, "the scientific traveller and student," and second, "the listless idler" who might otherwise "be changed into an inquiring and useful observer." But given the involvement of the SDUK, the "philanthropic geniuses" behind the *How to Observe* series prioritized the latter group. Rather than being a scientific text written to be legible to a popular audience, like Jackson's, the books in the SDUK's series were intended to be popular texts of such high standards that they would also be useful to "the scientific traveller and student." The SDUK sought not only to transform tourists into travelers to good purpose but also to give them "the power of converting a dull and dreary road into a district teeming with interest and pleasure." Such "habits of observation" would also make travelers' writings more interesting, because they would bestow "charm upon the descriptions of the commonest things." These accounts would stand in contrast to common tourist narratives, "abounding with eloquence and picturesque descriptions, [which] are now nearly forgotten, because they are wanting in that accuracy and minute observation which alone can command a lasting interest."[39] As we have seen, intense aesthetic experiences of picturesque scenery were among those most commonly sought by tourists and were also among those most commonly marketed to them by travel entrepreneurs. As a result, the production of trite accounts of predictably picturesque scenes was one of the most frequently satirized practices of tourists, dating from the transatlantic success of *The Tour of Dr. Syntax* in the first decades of the century. It was this cliché of forgettable picturesque description that the SDUK sought to eradicate, by teaching properly disciplined, scientifically inspired "habits of observation" that would make the difference between being a tourist and traveling to good purpose.

De la Beche's guide to making geological observations focused on the diffusion of substantive knowledge of geology. One reviewer found that De la Beche "labours under the disadvantage of knowing a good deal of the matter he writes about, which makes his book rather perplexing to the uninformed, for whose use the society professes to publish."[40] De la Beche's book was fundamentally a treatise on geology rather than one on traveling because he apparently assumed that his reader understood the choice of routes, the mode of travel, and the habits of mind that characterized a journey of geological observation. For De la Beche, teaching his readers "how to observe" meant teaching them how to interpret the geological evidence that they came across in their travels, as well as how to understand the present state of geology so that he or she "may be induced to observe and record facts that may advance the science, and which might otherwise pass unnoticed."[41] In a sense, De la Beche's text performed the same function as Dwight's guidebooks, albeit for a more specialized audience: it provided substantive knowledge of the spaces and places its readers might pass through, so that their travel could be informed. The habits of mind necessary to make empirical geological observations went largely unexplained. This disjunction between the intended purpose of the SDUK series and the specialized geological content of De la Beche's volume led to its critical and commercial failure.

The second and more widely printed of the series, Martineau's *How to Observe—Morals and Manners*, took a different approach. It was a clarion call for traveling to good purpose, which both advocated informed, useful travel and also offered concrete advice for individual travelers who aspired to her ideal. "We should by this time have been rich in the knowledge of nations if each intelligent traveller had endeavoured to report of any one department of moral inquiry, however narrow," she lamented, "but instead of this, the observations offered to us are almost purely desultory."[42] Martineau included very little information about the "morals and manners" of any particular location or group, and she seemed not to share De la Beche's concern that her readers not duplicate observations that had already been made by other travelers. Instead, she explained how to prepare oneself for making useful observations, as well as what categories of observation were important in order to make a complete accounting of morals and manners. The same reviewer who found De la Beche's guide to observation too specialized thought that Martineau's was ignorant. Since she had never traveled to the European continent, her guide "must produce a fortunate sympathy between the teacher and the pupil, however ignorant and inexperienced the latter may be"; in other words, Martineau's relative ignorance on the subject made her a better teacher of observation than De la Beche. Although the reviewer did not intend this observation to be a compliment, it inadvertently highlighted Martineau's interpretation of the "how to observe" genre, which was that the habits of mind necessary to be a good observer were independent of the substance being observed.[43] The critique was also unfair, since Martineau had undertaken extensive travels in North America and published her observations as *Society in America* in 1837.[44]

The habits of mind espoused by Martineau were intended to create precisely the objectivity of observation called for by Dwight almost a decade earlier. Where Dwight issued a vague plea for objectivity, Martineau laid out at length a series of philosophical and moral "requisites for observation." The "philosophical requisites" that she listed read like a primer in the scientific method. The traveler to good purpose, Martineau argued, should possess first "a certainty of what it is that he wants to know," and second, "principles which may serve as a rallying point and test of his observations"—in other words, such a traveler must have both a clearly defined question and a working hypothesis. However, since the topic under consideration was morals and manners, not geology, such traveler must also be acquainted with humanistic philosophy in order to test the hypothesis. He or she must have both "a philosophical and definite, instead of a popular and vague, notion about the origin of human feelings of right and wrong" as well as "a settled conviction that prevalent virtues and vices are the result of gigantic general influences." Following such a method of systematized observation would lend the traveler the patience to make accurate, unbiased judgments.[45]

Martineau agreed with Dwight that the key to proper observation was objectivity, which she thought was produced through the proper moral requisites. All human travelers were fundamentally imperfect observers, she argued, but "by clearly ascertaining what it is that the most commonly, or the most grossly vitiates foreign observation, we may put a check upon our spirit of prejudice, and carry with us restoratives of temper and spirits which may be of essential service to us in this task." The key moral requisite for objective traveling was sympathy, and this "sympathy must be untrammelled and unreserved." Sympathy was defined as an openness to and identification with the diversity and variety of human cultures, and it would allow a traveler insight into their inner workings rather than their superficial features. "If he be full of sympathy," Martineau promised, "everything will be instructive, and the most important matters will be the most clearly revealed. If he be unsympathizing, the most important things will be hidden from him, and symbols (in which every society abounds) will be only absurd or trivial forms." Thus, only through sympathetic observation could a traveler begin to approach the objective truth of morals and manners. Sympathy and objective observation, or affection and reason, had long been understood by Anglo-American philosophers and educators as "equally important sources of insight" for morally educated citizens.[46] Thus Martineau was on firm philosophical ground when she warned that travelers' tendency to judge the morals and manners of the lands they passed through as "absurd and trivial" most likely represented their own failure of understanding rather than actual absurdity or triviality. A traveler to good purpose "will be wise to conclude, when he sees anything seriously done which appears to him insignificant or ludicrous, that there is more in it than he perceives, from some deficiency of knowledge or feeling of his own."[47]

Martineau's instructions for traveling to good purpose diverged from those of her contemporaries by stressing the importance of proper practical arrangements. After all, no "philosophical or moral fitness will qualify a traveller to observe a people if he does not select a mode of travelling which will enable to him to see and converse with a great number and variety of persons." Martineau's recommendations in this regard were the closest any of these prescriptive guides came to denying the legitimacy of commodified travel. She thought travelers should choose means of travel that put them in contact with local people and places, which meant avoiding private conveyances. "A good deal may be learned on board steamboats, and in such vehicles as the American stages," she asserted, but "the wisest and happiest traveller is the pedestrian." Pedestrian travel had many advantages; while contemplating them, Martineau let slip for a moment her scientific veneer when she acknowledged, "One peculiar advantage of pedestrian travelling is the pleasure of a gradual approach to celebrated or beautiful places." Martineau, not usually one to value the appreciation of scenery, nonetheless thought that the scenic benefits of a pedestrian tour might help convince her audience that it represented the best mode of travel. However, what "is most to our present purpose . . . is the consideration of the facilities afforded by pedestrian travelling for obtaining a knowledge of the people."[48] Going on foot gave the traveler to good purpose freedom to explore places and peoples unconstrained by stagecoach and steamboat schedules. Furthermore, it would subject the traveler to the rhythms of the weather, allowing more time for exploration and conversation. Martineau acknowledged that pedestrian traveling was arduous, slow, and thus relatively expensive, but she thought producing one's own travel, rather than purchasing it in the marketplace, best served the traveler who aspired to utility.

In explaining the philosophical, moral, and mechanical requisites for traveling to good purpose, Martineau outlined her ideal traveler. "If the wealthy scholar and philosopher," she wrote, "could make himself a citizen of the world for the time, and go forth on foot, careless of luxury, patient of fatigue, and fearless of solitude, he would be not only of the highest order of tourists, but a benefactor to the highest kind of science; and he would become familiarized with what few are acquainted with, the best pleasures, transient and permanent, of travel."[49] Such a traveler would not only rise to the top among tourists, "he" would transcend the very category by making useful contributions to "the highest kind of science." But even if her ideal traveler to good purpose seemed to inhabit a male body, his intellectual and emotional characteristics were not necessarily strictly gendered male.[50] Although on the surface Jackson and Martineau were engaged in similar projects of training useful travelers, they were actually deploying fundamentally different ideas about the nature of scientific endeavor. Jackson, the RGS, and his American correspondents like the American Philosophical Society and the American Association for the Advancement of Science conceived of scientific endeavor as a practice of "Enlightenment rationalism ... which celebrated diligent observation and notebook recording of external phenomena as the foundation of natural knowledge." Martineau, on the other hand, focused on enhancing the perceptual skills of individual travelers, which situated her in the tradition that Marina Benjamin has labeled "romantic science." Writers in this tradition pursued the questions of natural philosophy with a romantic emphasis on "an individual and an individual's sensory perceptions, the valuing of the natural over the artificial, and the search through self-knowledge for universal truths about the social or natural world." Although romantic science was not exclusively a feminine discipline—male scientists also pursued the perfection of their own individual sensory perceptions—women writers used this mode of natural philosophical knowledge more frequently than the Enlightenment alternative.[51]

The gender ambiguity of Martineau's romantic conception of scientific pursuit was reinforced by her repeated emphasis on importance of sympathy. Martineau and her readers on both sides of the Atlantic in the late 1830s associated sympathy with femininity. In elite Anglo-American thought, women had long been associated with superior "sensibility," a term that denoted acute perception of both interior and exterior emotional signals. Most theorists believed that men could cultivate sensibility, and indeed they were urged to do so, but they thought women embodied it innately—a double-edged sword that called into question women's capacity for rationality as much as it celebrated women's superior emotional and perceptual abilities. But by the early nineteenth century, middle-class women in the United States had fused sensibility with rational discernment and moral strength to create a distinctly female claim to authority, manifested most commonly in movements for women's education and in evangelical reform organizations.[52] This fusion, articulated as the power of sympathy, also carved out a place for women in scientific fields in the United States, first and most significantly in medicine, and later in the nascent social sciences that undergirded the Progressive movement.[53] Martineau's call for sympathy in observation when traveling to good purpose required sensibility, a trait that she thought female travelers possessed innately.

The collection of meteorological and geological data for the RGS may have required masculine self-discipline, but the observation of morals and manners required more subtle skill. "If a traveller be a geological inquirer," Martineau wrote, "he may have a heart as hard as the rocks he shivers, and yet succeed in his immediate objects; if he be a student of the fine arts, he may be as silent as a picture, and yet gain his ends; if he be a statistical investigator, he may be as abstract as a column of figures, and yet learn what he wants to know: but an observer of morals and manners will be liable to deception at every turn if he does not find his way to hearts and minds."[54] Hard-hearted observation, silent contemplation, and mathematical abstraction were all comfortably masculine emotional registers, but the ability to burrow into another's heart and mind was a skill widely associated with women. This is not to say that Martineau thought that women were uniquely suited to observe morals and manners; indeed, men could cultivate sensibility with less danger to their authority, a reality that Martineau recognized when she used the masculine pronoun even when describing the power of sympathy. Nonetheless, even if her ideal traveler to good purpose had a male body, he had also to cultivate feminine-gendered qualities in order to properly observe morals and manners.

When taken together, the prevailing discourses about traveling to good purpose circulating in the United States in the 1830s and 1840s created an ambiguous but real opportunity for women travelers to transcend the status of mere tourists. Jackson's emphasis on rigorous observation and recording, conducted on a large scale and collected in metropolitan centers of knowledge, resonated with the emerging model of professionalized science that required masculine self-discipline to create knowledge. However, both Jackson's work and those of his popularizers were issued in a world in which much of the practical footwork of scientific observation was conducted by women, whose rational observational skills were both valid and valuable. Martineau's dicta for observing morals and manners championed a kind of romantic science that valued the subjective observations of an individual traveler, and they emphasized above all the importance of the observer's capacity for sympathy, a trait that was gendered female. However, laying too heavy a claim to the authority of sympathy was potentially hazardous for female travelers to good purpose, since it also could imply an incapacity for rationality. In both cases, opportunities for traveling to good purpose were structured for male travelers but accessible to female travelers.

There was one role in which women appeared regularly and unambiguously as travelers to good purpose in the nineteenth century: that of educator of children. As early as 1829, Theodore Dwight suggested that "the annual excursions and tours made by so many families in the northern parts of this country might . . . [offer] opportunities for administering to the instruction as well as enjoyment of the younger [members of the party]." Dwight gave instructions to "judicious parent[s]" concerning how best to capitalize upon family travel for the education of their children. They were to prepare their children, like they prepared themselves, by learning "the nature of some of the principal objects they are to observe" and establishing "the foundation on which their future observations are to be built." Both parents and children would be well served by keeping diaries, both to encourage systematic observation and to provide "subjects on which to enlarge by the winter fire-side, to the little listeners of the family circle." Dwight particularly liked to see mothers engaged in such educational work; he found "an affectionate mother directing the attention of her little family to scenes through which they pass" to be a heartening sight on the road. He even suggested judging mothers based on their ability to turn a journey into an educational opportunity, since "an acute observer would hardly wish a better opportunity to form an opinion of the intelligence and judgment of a parent."[55]

Dwight's concern for the role of parents in harnessing travel to their children's education remained a theme in his writings on travel. In his 1834 *Things as They Are; Or, Notes of a Traveller through the Middle and Northern States*, he lamented, "Oh, had I been taught, in my childhood, what I so much desired to know, the names, nature, and uses of the trees and plants by which we passed that day, or the composition of the soils which produce them, or a little of the principles of engineering to understand the constructions and excavations of the railroad, or been informed of the history, products, or inhabitants of that part of the country in such a manner as to feel an interest in them." The deficiency he felt could be best remedied by parents; "How easy would it be for parents to teach their children," he mused, "as one of my fellow-travellers taught me."[56] Travel was an ideal opportunity for education, especially in childhood, and educational travel could be pleasurable for children, as well as instructive. Instructing children, in turn, gave their parents' travel a good purpose.

Dwight's advice was mirrored by the writers of children's books, especially books for girls, which emphasized the educational value of travel to good purpose and the opportunities for usefulness that it offered to women travelers. In 1833, prominent educator and textbook author Almira Hart Lincoln Phelps penned *Caroline Westerley; Or, The*

Young Traveller from Ohio, which laid down a didactic template for how women could travel to good purpose, and, in the process, advocated for the value of such travel.[57] *Caroline Westerley* took the form of a series of letters from a young woman traveling with her father from Ohio to Connecticut, written to her younger sister at home. Phelps intended her protagonist to set an example "in describing the events of her journey, and the various objects which she saw" in order to "induce some other young persons to set about acquiring the same habit." Part of Caroline's exemplary conduct was her desire to educate her little sister: "Remember, my dear Louisa," Caroline wrote, "that I, as your *senior*, am bound to instruct as well as amuse you . . . during my journey."[58] An educational agenda made travel useful, not just amusing.

Caroline recorded four main categories of information for the edification of her younger sister. She provided lengthy historical accounts of the areas they passed through, especially when their route passed battlefields or forts from the Revolution or the War of 1812, along with "remarks" about "Indians." Her narrative was interrupted by lessons on geology, including both passing comments about the soil and rocks of various locations as well as more lengthy expositions on geological anomalies like Niagara Falls. Caroline's interest in natural science was no accident, because as an educator Phelps was deeply invested in scientific training for girls. Caroline also described scenery in relatively precise aesthetic language, out of her refined love for "waterfalls, and all kinds of beautiful and sublime scenery." Finally, Caroline derived moral lessons from her observations. Her moral observations were not the philosophically sophisticated insight of a Martineau; rather, they were calls for substantial over fashionable traveling. On a tour of the salt works at Salina, New York, Caroline bemoaned the "fine ladies who accompanied us on this little tour, as they went rather to *be seen* than to *see*, did not go to the salt-works, or to the Indian settlement." The gendered superficiality of the tourists with whom she traveled seemed "a great misfortune, since the minds of these young ladies have been so wholly sacrificed to gentility, that they possess so little of it."[59] Their superficial pursuit of refinement prevented them from learning history or science, or from having a proper aesthetic reaction to fine scenery.

For Phelps, then, traveling to good purpose meant making the proper historical, scientific, and moral observations, and recording them in an educationally useful fashion. But more importantly, these observations and recordings had to be harnessed for instructing youth. This translational role in the process of turning travel into learning was linked not only to Caroline's gender but also to Phelps's. Sarah Josepha Hale, the widely read editor of the *Ladies' Magazine*, observed in 1833 that *Caroline Westerley* was "a lovely picture to place before the young," and she linked the education it contained directly to motherhood. "Every Mother," Hale wrote, "who presents this volume to her daughters cannot choose, but feels a glow of gratitude and love for the excellent mother who wrote it."[60] Despite the fact that Phelps was already a widely respected educator who was building a long and distinguished career, Hale linked the power of *Caroline Westerley*'s example to her motherhood, to the mothers who would buy the volume for their children, and ultimately, to the useful women who turned travel into knowledge for children.

The literature of traveling to good purpose that emerged in the 1830s and 1840s offered a complex and ambiguously gendered cultural script for transcending the status of mere tourist. A growing number of actual travelers, both men and women, sought to make and to record travels that could be seen as "useful," and they took advantage of these guidelines and their gender ambiguities in order to do so. This strategy played out in travelers' accounts of their own journeys, both published and manuscript, intended both for broad audiences and for friends at home. It was most immediately apparent in published accounts of travels; by the 1840s, the overwhelming majority who bothered to publish their travels did so as travelers to good purpose. Stocqueler was right in 1860; the "mania" for publishing "tours" that were no more than the "trashy experiences" of the "gentry" died down after "the scourge of the satirist had been pretty widely distributed." But travelers did not restrict their ambitions for utility to the printed page. Increasingly, manuscript travel journals and letters home included the kinds of observation and record keeping that aspired to utility. Even when these travelers harbored no illusions that their accounts would serve the purposes of organized scientific knowledge production, they adopted the rhythms and vocabularies of those who did. In this way, they sought to avoid, in Dwight's words, "abusing travelling," and to avoid the stigma of mere tourism by claiming the mantle of utility instead. In a moment in which travel—and especially leisure travel—was increasingly an act of consumption, mid-century travelers sought to show that they were nevertheless still producers of useful observations and new knowledge, which kept them on the positive side of the cultural divide that nineteenth-century Americans characteristically drew between producers and consumers.

A handful of early nineteenth-century Americans published accounts of their travels that provided models of utility to the aspiring midcentury travelers to good purpose. The majority of these travelers recounted journeys in the western territories, especially in the upper Great Lakes and the Trans-Mississippi West. The model for these useful travels was Meriwether Lewis and William Clark's government-sponsored expedition to the Missouri and Columbia Rivers from 1804 to 1806, which gathered information about geography, geology, plants, animals, and Native American populations. Several accounts of their journey were published over the subsequent decade, both by members of the party and by later editors, although the versions that stressed adventure narrative over scientific information were always more popular, much to the disappointment of Thomas Jefferson, the expedition's sponsor and a determined scientific rationalizer.[61] The following decades brought a host of imitators, including Zebulon Pike, William Darby, Henry Schoolcraft, and Ross Cox, all of whom imagined their published travel to be useful, often citing Lewis and Clark by name as examples.[62]

But relatively few Americans published accounts of travel around the settled states in the first half of the nineteenth century. This field was largely left to the European tourists who sparked so much animosity among American commentators, a fact bemoaned by the *United States Magazine and Democratic Review* in 1851. "We never could account for the taste or desire of the American people that leads them into other countries before they have become even superficially acquainted with their own," the editors complained, because it meant that "Most of the books on America have been written by foreigners. . . . The greater portion of them have been written by hasty tourists, who have traveled by rapid stages, from one place to another, without pausing on the road to observe, or wandering out of their way to discover beauties."[63] Not only were such authors "foreigners," but they were also "tourists" who consumed fast travel over fixed routes and failed to make meaningful observations. Emphasizing as they did modern dichotomous thinking about tourists and travelers, such observers made it clear that tourists were poor models for aspiring travelers to good purpose, even without relying on "the scourge of the satirist." But notwithstanding the predominance of "foreigners" and "tourists" among travelers in the settled states, a handful of early national American travelers sought to publish useful accounts of their eastern journeys, which provided a model that subsequent travelers sought to follow.

Timothy Dwight's magisterial *Travels in New-England and New-York*, as edited by an experienced geographical publishing hand like Theodore Dwight, might have provided just such a model when it was finally published in 1821, but the elder man's sensibilities were entirely too Congregationalist and Federalist—in other words, too provincially New England—for his work to have much national impact before the Civil War.[64] But another shorter account of the same territory, written by a younger friend and protégé of Timothy Dwight and first published in 1820, became a more important cultural touchstone. Benjamin Silliman, the first professor of chemistry at Yale College, compiled his hasty notes taken "in public houses, and in steamboats" and published them as *Remarks Made on a Short Tour between Hartford and Quebec, in the Autumn of 1819*.[65] Like his mentor, Silliman was motivated by patriotic concerns, in that his *Remarks* were part of his lifelong interest in encouraging the practice of rigorous, rational science in the United States.[66] But even though Silliman's route took him over relatively well-trodden ground, at least compared to contemporaries like William Darby and Henry Schoolcraft, his travel was still useful because he had "an impression, that less has been said by travellers in America, than might have been expected, of scenes and events, which, to Americans, I conceive, must ever be subjects of the deepest interest."[67] Silliman thought his "short tour" was to good purpose because earlier travelers over the same territory had failed to make their tours so, and because the national imperatives of the early republic required scientific knowledge of American land.

For Silliman, this knowledge was largely geological. As Sally Gregory Kohlstedt has argued, geology was the first "national science" in the United States because its shallow learning curve allowed widespread amateur participation, and because its local specificity enabled networks of popular scientific societies to form.[68] Silliman too thought geology was foundational, because "the geological features of a country, being permanent—being intimately connected with its scenery, with its leading interests, and even with the very character of its population, have a fair claim to delineation in the observations of a traveller."[69] Rigorous national geological knowledge was useful because it had the potential to produce new understandings of the economy, scenery, and morals and manners of New England, New York, and Quebec. In this, Silliman followed European example, because "this course [of observing geology], however unusual with us, is now common in Europe. I regret that my limited time did not admit of more extended and complete observations of this nature."[70] Silliman traveled to good purpose even over familiar ground because he introduced new foundational geographical knowledge that earlier travelers had neglected, and because he claimed to bring the rigors of scientific discipline to bear.

Silliman's useful account of New England, reported without Timothy Dwight's parochial Connecticut preoccupations, quickly proved a popular model for travelers who aspired to good purpose. It warranted a quick reprinting in London, as well as an expanded and revised second American edition, in which Silliman "interspersed various additional remarks, observations, and notices of historical facts" that he hoped "may be found to add to the value of the work, as *a pocket companion of travellers*."[71] Both editions of his work were widely quoted in the following decades by scientists, historians, and other travelers through the region. As Henry Dilworth Gilpin put it in his 1825 guidebook *A Northern Tour*, "Mr. Silliman's Tour from Hartford to Quebec is in the hands of every one; equally delightful from its profound science, its glowing descriptions, and its liberal sentiments."[72] With this kind of endorsement in the emerging market for geographical print commodified for tourists, Silliman's *Remarks* were well positioned both intellectually and commercially to serve as a model for other less prominent American travelers who sought similar utility and good purpose.

Travelers used Silliman's strategy of deploying a specific scientific discourse when recording their useful travels in both manuscript and print forms. Such travelers sought to duck the stigma of superficial travel through rigorous record keeping, whether they found their audience in a bookseller's shop or around the home fireside. In 1847 and 1848, Philadelphia lawyer and prison reformer William Parker Foulke set out on a trip around Pennsylvania, in order to conduct business and to observe conditions in the state's prisons. During this tour, he regularly wrote letters to his aunt Eleanor to share his experiences. He wrote little about the prisons that he visited, but he diligently recorded the geography of the central and western parts of the state. He included observations on geology, surveying, Iroquois history, agriculture, the landscape, and the morals and manners of the inhabitants. The breadth and depth of his coverage of the geography of Pennsylvania was not accidental; in the middle of his travels, he wrote from Harrisburg of the "hugeous epistle" he had previously "despatched," in which he "had gone through the principal heads of the geography-books except the 'manners & customs of the inhabitants.'" He then went on to describe the "three modes" of local discourse, the "ludicrous, querulous, and philosophical." The towns and valleys of central and western Pennsylvania must have been familiar territory for Foulke in the late 1840s. He and his family also had extensive real estate dealings throughout the territory that he covered, and his letters showed familiarity with works like Charles Trego's *A Geography of Pennsylvania*.[73] Nevertheless, he exhaustively described his travels with a thorough and rigorous accounting divided into categories that echoed both J. R. Jackson's and Trego's. Foulke turned routine correspondence with his aunt into an opportunity to collect, categorize, and share geographical knowledge, giving his journey over the familiar territory of Pennsylvania an air of usefulness.

Frederick Hall, a professor of chemistry and natural sciences at Columbian College in Washington, DC, tried a strategy that combined aspects of both Foulke's and Silliman's useful travel.[74] In the late 1830s, Hall embarked on several journeys, which took him from New England to Ohio and Kentucky, during which he wrote letters home. Some of the letters were originally written to his wife, "to cheer her loneliness," though he confessed that he had written them with an eye to their eventual publication. Others were written to the Washington *National Intelligencer* as a series of updates from "our scientific fellow-townsmen," which "compris[ed] his observations on the mineralogy of various localities visited during his journey."[75] Hall used letters to demonstrate the usefulness of his travel to his family and his neighbors, and then eventually, in 1840, to a broader national community when he collected them into a book entitled *Letters from the East and from the West*. Hall tried unsuccessfully to sell his letters "to three or four publishers," but because "the world is full of books; none sell, except novels; the taste of the age is so dainty, it will accept of nothing, which is not strongly peppered; times are hard; money is scarce, and [the publishers could not] run the hazard of buying a work of travels."[76] Despite the setback, he eventually found a publisher, but the sting of rejection shone through, which he expressed in aggressively gendered terms. He clearly considered himself a masculine serious producer of knowledge, in contrast to the feminized "dainty" and "peppered" literary taste of his time. His publishing difficulties led him to draw a heightened dichotomy between the serious and the superficial, between producers and consumers, and between masculine and feminine.

Hall framed the seriousness and utility of his travel in different ways when traveling east than when traveling west. When traveling through the familiar territory of New England, he followed Silliman's model by writing letters that were almost entirely geological in content. Hall included information about the structures that underlay the land he traveled across, as well as their mineral content and the actual and potential commercial uses of those minerals. His travel was to good purpose and worth publishing because of the new geological information it contained, which Hall intended to be useful both to those with geological interests and to those with business interests. For example, in discussing an ore newly discovered in Connecticut called Columbite, he discussed the potential utility of the metal: "No use has, I believe, as yet, been made of the new metal, columbium, in either the arts or sciences, owing, perhaps, till recently, to the scarcity of the article." This lack represented an opportunity and a challenge for inventors and businessmen; "Human ingenuity will, without doubt, devise, ere long, some useful purpose, to which it may be advantageously applied."[77] When covering familiar ground, Hall kept his travel to good purpose by maintaining a tight focus on geological information that was not otherwise readily available and that would be useful to a narrow but important group of readers.

When traveling west, Hall allowed himself a much freer rein while still remaining convinced of the seriousness of his travel, of its avoidance of things "dainty" and "peppered." As he reminded his wife upon departure, "to study the geological features of the country, and investigate its mineral resources, is, you well know, one of the leading objects of the tour," much like his journey to New England. However, he devoted comparatively little space to geological information, especially as he traveled westward out of Pennsylvania. In the place of his previous single-minded focus, he promised his wife an account of "the most interesting objects and incidents I encounter in those boundless regions." The difference lay in Hall's relative unfamiliarity with the Ohio valley, and his presumption that his wife and his broader print audience were equally unfamiliar. Even though Ohio had been a state for more than thirty years by the time he visited it, he still referred to its "native wilderness," its "wilderness state," or "the western wilderness," phrases that he never used in New England. He was also inclined to narrate his modes of travel as similarly pioneering; "No human habitation caught our roving gaze," he wrote as he was nearing Marietta, "not a trace of man's work was visible, except the zig-zag horse-path, which we were threading."[78] As the oldest city in Ohio, Marietta was hardly the edge of civilization, but Hall's recounting of his journey as an information-gathering expedition into unknown territory rendered it as such.

The variety of information that Hall included in his letters from "the western wilderness" resembled the kind of exhaustive coverage advocated by advisors like Jackson and reflected in the letters of travelers like William Foulke. He recorded the topography, politics, economy, and internal improvements of Ohio and Kentucky. He wrote extensively on the design and construction of western cities and on the state of scholarly institutions. He also included more information about the practicalities of traveling that brought him from place to place, which made his letters from the West a more readable travel narrative than his letters from the East. He even included some information on morals and manners, although it was not a central focus for him. He claimed objectivity with a striking assertiveness, although with less sympathy than Martineau recommended; "I do not design to flatter any man. Were I to do it, I could not help despising myself. To commend worth is no flattery," he declared, presumably to his print audience rather than to his wife.[79] Hall's letters from the West represented a catalogue of geographical knowledge about an unknown land rather than a focused scientific account of a known one. For Hall, though, both supported his claim to useful travel for audiences that expanded outward from his wife to his neighbors to the broader national world of print.

These male travelers to good purpose over known territory observed, recorded, and commented on a range of natural and social phenomena, according to their professional commitments and personal interests. The diversity of their efforts at knowledge production on the road was a reflection of their privilege as male travelers. As professors, Silliman and Hall had access to both institutional and rhetorical positions of scientific authority, which they used to produce new knowledge about geology, climate, history, and social practices. Foulke was less connected to the emerging institutional structures of scientific knowledge production, but as a middle-class professional man, he claimed the authority to collect useful information while traveling. The gendered nature of their strategies for travel to good purpose was more apparent when compared to that of contemporary women travelers who likewise sought to avoid aspersions of superficial tourism. For these women, the observation and articulation of sociogeographical knowledge—morals and manners— was the only form of knowledge production that was reliably considered useful. For female travelers with limited access to formal institutional credentials as knowledge producers, the production of new knowledge about morals and manners could defend their travels from accusations of superficiality.

Women travelers thus often wrote analyses of morals and manners, even before Harriet Martineau systematized this strategy in the late

1830s.[80] The most widely published American woman traveler of the 1820s, Mrs. Anne Royall, commented on the morals and manners of her countrymen in nine volumes of travels published between 1826 and 1831. She set out, she remarked, to "note every thing during my journey, worthy of remark, and commit it to writing, and to draw amusement and instruction from every source." These notes would be more useful than an account of a mere tour, because she would "not imitate most journalists, in such remarks as 'cloudy, or fair morning,' and where we stop, dates, &c." Throughout her extensive travels, which took her all across the settled parts of the United States and into its borderlands, she kept her promise to shun touristic superficialities, filling her accounts instead with sharp social observation and critique. So confident was she of the worth of her goals, and of her ability to fulfill them, that she declared these sentences "all the preface I deem necessary."[81]

The things "worthy of remark" on Royall's journey included "a description of the public institutions, manners and appearance of the inhabitants, and the history of the principal places visited by the author, with sketches of the principal characters, physical remarks on the country, &c." She made a clear effort to treat her subjects systematically, to the extent that her written account generally followed the contours of this formula with some precision. While in Philadelphia, for example, she described the layout and history of the city in considerable detail, and she recorded the encounters she had with the city's "principal characters," as promised. She summarized and evaluated the residents' "manners and appearance" in a brief section, in which she found them tall and handsome, and their city more tasteful than splendid, although she castigated them for "their want of charity and hospitality to strangers, one of the brightest of Christian virtues." She found this lack particularly galling considering the "thousands of dollars [that] are spent here annually by strangers." She dedicated the bulk of her entry on Philadelphia to the "public institutions" of the city, which she found to "nearly . . . resemble" each other, "so far as benevolence and the most exalted charity is concerned," which seemed to contradict her castigation of Philadelphians' "charity and hospitality to strangers."[82] Royall's opinions were not always consistent, but her judgments on morals and manners were strongly stated and her elaboration on them was the central feature of her narrative of her own travel. She promised her readers instruction and amusement, and she fulfilled this promise with a catalogue of properly arranged, classified, and evaluated sociogeographical knowledge.

Royall's experience suggests that outside the world of travel advice books, sharp observation of morals and manners could be a double-edged strategy for actual women travelers. On the one hand, she found significant commercial success in publishing her own travel books, which reliably found an audience of subscribers willing to pay for the geographical knowledge she supplied. Contemporary sources spoke of her popularity, and especially in areas whose morals and manners she judged approvingly, "Mrs. Royall's books were sold 'faster than the binder could cover them.'"[83] But where her assessments of morals and manners were less positive, she faced considerable gendered criticism. For example, she thought that "ignorance, impudence and pride, are decided traits in the bulk of the citizens of Washington," a judgment that was so controversial that she was indicted as "a common scold" in that city in 1829. This archaic charge had historically been leveled against women who challenged existing patriarchal structures of social authority by disrupting the peace. Royall was convicted, and although there was an outcry in Washington for her to be ducked in the Potomac, which was the equally archaic traditional punishment for common scolds, she got off with a ten-dollar fine.[84] Royall's 1829 conviction showed the limits of rigorous observation of morals and manners as a gendered strategy for traveling to good purpose. When women's observations were culturally palatable, they could be socially and economically rewarded, but when they overstepped gendered boundaries of appropriate behavior, they could evoke ancient strategies of gender policing.

Of course, a large part of Martineau's purpose in writing her 1838 *How to Observe* was to train travelers to make judicious judgments about morals and manners. Indeed, she sought to systematize what Anne Royall had grasped instinctively, that travelers who made useful, original contributions to geographical knowledge would be taken more seriously than the pleasure travelers who purchased ready-made experiences. Martineau's emphasis on systematic, useful observations that aspired to sympathy and objectivity was designed to help travelers avoid the perceived excesses of Royall's work, and these tools were especially useful for women travelers, given the gendered backlash that Royall's books provoked. Foremost among these travelers was Margaret Fuller, who traveled to the Great Lakes in the summer of 1843 and recounted her journey the following year in the short but remarkable *Summer on the Lakes, in 1843*. That Fuller used Martineau's system for traveling to good purpose was no accident; they were well acquainted with each other, and Fuller had even at points in her life considered Martineau her "intellectual guide."[85] The influence was evident in the evolution of Fuller's thinking over the course of her journey, in the ways in which she recorded it, and in the eventual reception of her book of travels.

Fuller sailed from Buffalo hoping for "Long summer days of dear-bought pleasure" and for a few examples of Anglo-American cultural decline in the western wilderness to illustrate what she called a "Trollopian record." "I come to the west prepared for the distaste I must experience at its mushroom growth," Fuller wrote, in full self-awareness of the reverence for her native New England that peppered her pages. However, she quickly realized that the natural, social, and cultural world that she encountered in the West was not explicable by a simple narrative of western crudeness and ambition. "While I will not be so obliging as to confound ugliness with beauty, discord with harmony, and laud and be contented with all I meet," Fuller stressed, "when it conflicts with my best desires and tastes, I trust by reverent faith to woo the mighty meaning of the scene, perhaps to foresee the law by which a new order, a new poetry is to be evoked from this chaos."[86] She differentiated her travels in the West from those of her predecessors because her description of morals and manners sought explanations rather than characterizations, meanings rather than judgments, and an analysis of its potential future rather than a judgment on the present. Her travels would produce real and original sociogeographical knowledge about the West, not merely another "Trollopian record."

Fuller shared Martineau's goals of traveling to good purpose, and she also aimed to achieve that goal by using Martineau's methodology of philosophically and morally disciplined sympathetic observation. Upon leaving Illinois, she felt the need to defend the state from the "reproach" offered by easterners who thought its "careless, prodigal course" embodied civilization's decline in the West. She argued instead that the natural abundance of the open landscape of Illinois was in the process of forming "free and independent citizens" into "a pleasant society," where friendliness and cooperation predominated over exclusion and competition. This "pleasant society" was built of families "from various parts of the world." Despite difficulties with communication, they had "in common the interests of a new country and a new life" and would thus of necessity come together to form a community. "They must traverse some space to get at one another," Fuller wrote, and they "must bear inconveniences to stay in one another's houses; but these, to the well-disposed, are only a source of amusement and adventure." The physical realities of the spaciousness landscape would produce a new society where "whole families might live together, if they would."[87] Rather than simply describing the morals and manners of the settlers of the Illinois prairie, Fuller sought to explain the formation of those morals and manners by reference to the diversity of the settlers and the characteristics of the landscape. And her willingness to contemplate the virtues of Illinois's unique social arrangements showed a conscious use of sympathy in her observations of morals and manners. As a result, Fuller's travels helped her to arrive at explanatory truth rather than merely compiling a catalogue of judgments, and thus she traveled to good purpose.

Fuller was more explicit than Martineau had been that this strategy of sympathy was gendered. Fuller was particularly sensitive to the gendering of intellectual life and considered herself to have a "hybrid nature—'a man's ambition with a woman's heart.'"[88] This self-conscious hybridity shaped her sympathetic interest in the Native American women she encountered around the lakes. In her observations of them, she was generally careful to follow Martineau's advice not to judge them by arbitrary standards of morality simply because those standards were familiar. At Sault Ste. Marie, she saw women "coming home from the woods, stooping under great loads of cedar boughs, that were strapped upon their backs." Suspecting that her readers would rush to the common judgment that Native American men treated their women like drudges, she hastened to add: "But in many European countries women carry great loads, even of wood, upon their backs. I used to hear the girls singing and laughing as they were cutting down boughs at Mackinaw; this part of their employment, though laborious, gives them the pleasure of being a great deal in the free woods." Fuller suggested with her examples that women might derive pleasure from heavy lifting and cautioned her readers against judging the morality of such practices according to their own preconceived notions of gender. She sought to put this observation into dialogue with other travelers who had written about Native Americans; while stopped in Chicago, she read "all the books about the Indians" she could find, "a paltry collection, truly, yet which furnished material for many thoughts." However, when it came to Native American women, she found that "the observation of women upon the position of woman are always more valuable than those of men."[89] Fuller's interest in Native American women was a gendered strategy for traveling to good purpose. Female travelers were better able to sympathetically observe women than were male travelers, and thus observing and recording their lives represented a uniquely feminine opportunity for making her "summer days of dear-bought pleasure" serve a useful purpose.

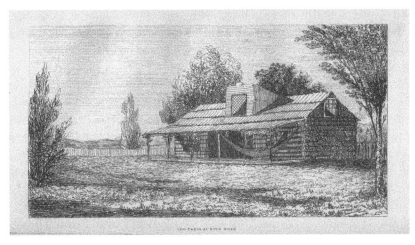

FIGURE 5.2a and Figure 5.2b. *Log Cabin at Rock River* and *Mackinaw Beach* from Margaret Fuller's *Summer on the Lakes, in* 1843. Courtesy of the University of Michigan Library.

Despite her rigorous application of philosophical sympathy, Fuller's travels were published to mixed reviews in 1844. As with Royall, public reactions to Fuller's work were shaped by gendered ideas about travel to good purpose. The conservative Catholic *Brownson's Quarterly Review* admitted that "Miss Fuller is a woman of more than ordinary abilities, and, we are told, of rare attainments," but nonetheless they "dislike[d her writings] exceedingly." They criticized her travel for being superficial and fundamentally meaningless, using strongly gendered language. "They are sent out in a slipshod style," the reviewer lamented, "and have a certain toss of the head about them which offends us. Miss Fuller seems to us to be wholly deficient in a pure, correct taste, and especially in that tidiness we always look for in woman."[90] On the other hand, the Unitarian *Christian Examiner and Religious Miscellany,* which was sympathetic to Fuller and her Transcendental preoccupations, called it "an uncommon book, not at all like an ordinary journal of travel . . . a work of varied interest, rich in fine observation, profound reflection and striking anecdote."[91] In both cases, the success or failure of Fuller's travels was linked to the quality of her observation on the road. Her attempts to explicate the West were either a gendered failure of "tidiness" or uncommonly "rich" and "profound." Although Fuller was spared Royall's brush with the ducking stool, public evaluations of the usefulness of her travel were shaped by the possibilities and pitfalls of women's travel to good purpose.

Notwithstanding these pockets of resistance to the idea of a useful female traveler, *Summer on the Lakes* sold well enough that even its critics acknowledged that the "book has had a very respectable sale."[92] Copies appeared quickly in the catalogues of American libraries, especially in the more popularly oriented mercantile libraries in large coastal cities.[93] Along with the rest of her work, *Summer on the Lakes* received renewed attention less than a decade later, after Fuller died prematurely along with the rest of her family in a dramatic shipwreck off of Long Island in 1850. Her posthumous literary reputation became almost uniformly positive in light of what *Harper's New Monthly Magazine* called "the interest in the genius and character of Margaret Fuller, which has been constantly on the increase since her disastrous end."[94] *Summer on the Lakes* was a key text in cementing her reputation; in 1852, Philadelphia educator John Seely Hart deemed it "one of the best works in its department ever issued from the American press."[95] In the same year, her memoirists recalled that Horace Greeley thought it to be "one of the clearest and most graphic delineations, ever given, of the Great Lakes, of the Prairies, and of the receding barbarism, and the rapidly advancing, but rude, repulsive semi-civilization, which were contending with most unequal forces for the possession of those rich lands."[96] A reviewer writing in 1857 in Charleston-based *Russell's Magazine* called it "a prose poem of a lofty order of merit—the vigorous, hearty, exultant and beautiful utterance of a strong, but sweet and sensitive mind, to whom nature is a muse and an inspiration."[97] In retrospect, the "pleasing narrative" of her travel to the Great Lakes in the summer of 1843 was an important building block of her considerable posthumous literary fame.[98] Fuller effectively took advantage of the opportunity Martineau had opened for women travelers to make useful and authoritative observation of morals and manners, and parlayed it into a lasting reputation, as Hart put it, as "one of the most remarkable women of the present century."[99]

In 1856, Margaret Fuller's brother Arthur wrote the introduction for *At Home and Abroad*, a volume that collected *Summer on the Lakes* and Fuller's European correspondence from the later 1840s. This new collection filled a posthumous demand for Fuller's writing, which "for some time [had] been out of print and inaccessible to the general public."[100] Fuller's many admirers kept the book in frequent print in new editions through the end of the nineteenth century.[101] In his introduction, Arthur Fuller argued that his sister's travel to good purpose warranted republication because of its enduring utility, unlike the accounts of predictable tours undertaken by less serious and insightful tourists. In doing so, he used cultural distinctions that had been drawn with increasing frequency since the 1830s. By the mid-1850s, Fuller could confidently assert that "There are at least three classes of persons who travel in our own land and abroad." The most numerous were "those who, 'having eyes, see not, and ears, hear not,' anything which is profitable to be remembered." This group, the ultimate tourists, "gaze heedlessly, and when they return home can but tell us what they ate and drank, and where slept,—no more; for this and matters of like import are all for which they have cared in their wanderings." They were mindless consumers of commodified experiences, whose tours offered nothing of value to themselves or anyone else. The second group of travelers "travel[ed] more intelligently," making sure to visit all the important sites along their road and taking time to record their observations in detail. "Writers belonging to this class of travellers are not to be undervalued," Fuller declared, because "returning home, they can give much useful information, and tell much which all wish to hear and know."[102] This second category of traveler, to whom Fuller was careful to pay his respects, traveled to good purpose according to the advice offered by Dwight, Jackson, and all those who sought to harness their collective powers of observation. Such travelers produced valuable geographical knowledge and deserved respect and even esteem from a broader American audience.

The problem with such "intelligent" travelers to good purpose was that "as their narratives are chiefly circumstantial, and every year circumstances change, such recitals lessen constantly in value." Systematic observation and classification of geographical knowledge was fine as far as it went, but it went out of date quickly. This failing led Fuller to his third category of travelers, who not only "see indeed the outward, and observe it well" but also "do much *more* than this." Prophetically, "they see the destinies which nations are all unconsciously shaping for themselves, and note the deep meaning of passing events which only make others wonder." They not only accurately observed the surface of things, "their eyes discern the character of those whom they meet, and, refusing to accept popular judgment in place of truth, they see often the real relation which men bear to their race and age, and observe the facts by which to determine whether such men are great only because of circumstances, or by the irresistible power of their own minds." In the narratives produced by this analytical class of travelers, "we have what is valuable not for a few years only, but, because of its philosophic and suggestive spirit, what must always be useful."[103] This third class of traveler used philosophical preparation combined with a sympathetic and analytical mode of observation to reach a deeper, more explanatory, and ultimately more durable form of geographical knowledge about the people and places they visited. They were producers of lasting value.

Fuller, of course, placed his sister in this third and most exalted category, even though her journey had remained well within the boundaries of known territory.[104] *Summer on the Lakes* was worthy of continued interest, even twelve years after its initial release, because "it rather gives an idea of Western scenery and character, than enters into guidebook statements which would be all erroneous now." He thought her "knowledge of Indian character" would be among the most enduring features of the book, and that it gave "additional proof of her sympathy with all the oppressed, no matter whether that oppression find embodiment in the Indian or the African, the American or the European."[105] Margaret Fuller's literary reputation, and her larger cultural worth, were constructed on a firm foundation of travel to good purpose, following a model of acute observation, philosophical inquiry into root causes, and ultimately sympathetic understanding.[106] Her posthumous success at translating travel into cultural status depended on the dichotomy between superficial, meaningless tourism and true travel to good purpose that shaped all discussions of travel and its worth by the 1850s. This dichotomy was produced by, on the one hand, the emerging national markets for commodified knowledge, travel, and experience; and on the other hand, the growing cottage industry of philosophical and scientific advisors who sought to train travelers to avoid or transcend this market for commodi-fied experience. By midcentury, this dichotomy had become the most powerful intellectual framework for evaluating travelers and tourists, and its mutually constituted opposites came to provide the templates according to which all subsequent restless Americans were evaluated.

Epilogue: Not For Tourists

In the early winter of 2008, I was living in New York, trying to wrap my mind around the endlessly "mutable humanity" of the early American republic. I spent most of my days comfortably ensconced in the Wertheim Study at the New York Public Library on Forty-Second Street, but when the library got too solemn, I would venture out to explore the coffee shops of the city, looking for a livelier corner with a working outlet for my laptop. On one of these excursions downtown, the coffee shop I found had a small black sticker on the window, reading "NFT," or "Not For Tourists." With a world of tourists and not-tourists on the brain, it jumped out at me and begged for investigation. The sticker was quickly revealed to be a sign that the coffee shop was recommended in a guidebook with the intriguingly paradoxical name Not For Tourists. How could a guidebook deny that its intended audience was tourists, when my research was revealing that the very invention of the genre by ambitious local boosters in the 1820s and 1830s was critical to the creation of the figure of the tourist in American culture? A deeper investigation of the Not For Tourists series of guidebooks laid bare the cultural mechanics of tourism in the early twenty-first century and, more revealingly, the ways in which those mechanics were rooted in the cultural and economic conditions of the early American republic. The distinction between tourists and travelers was rooted in the market processes of commodification in the nineteenth century, and the perpetuation and growth of national and increasingly global markets for travel experiences in the twentieth and twenty-first centuries means that the same organizing dichotomy continues to shape the way we talk about traveling and about the value of travel experiences.

When Not For Tourists was launched in 2000, its unique and explicit selling proposition was that it was a city guide for locals, directing them to the destinations that locals would frequent and away from the tourist hordes. It did so by combining the practical information of daily life, like FedEx pickup locations and times, with lists of bars, restaurants, and entertainment venues whose appeal lay in their cool and in being off the beaten track. By their very inclusion in the guide, the editors attested to their superiority over the more mainstream choices filling average tourist guidebooks. The promise of insider information embodied by these lists was made explicit by company's slogan, "for you, not them." Like the nineteenth-century handbooks for "travelling to good purpose," the editors of Not For Tourists assumed a fundamental dichotomy between tourism and true, authentic travel. Similarly, they assumed a self-evident value hierarchy between the two; the city that "you," the not-tourist, consume is morally and aesthetically superior to the one consumed by "them," the tourists. Not For Tourists carved out a place for itself in the competitive marketplace for guidebooks to major American cities by making explicit the value judgments that were already implicit in its audience's opinions about visitors in a strange city.

Of course, the actual consumption of Not For Tourists was not nearly as neat as its marketing slogan promised. Right from the beginning, journalists who wrote about Not For Tourists acknowledged that it really was for tourists, too. In November 2001, the *New York Press* suggested that its readers should "give *NFT* to tourists. People don't like to think of themselves as tourists, they like to regard themselves as worldly and savvy. . . . By giving out-of-towners the *NFT 2002*, you'll butter up that part of them that wants to look at home everywhere."[1] In October 2006, the *Toronto Star* published a review of the series entitled "Guides Help Real Travellers Rush in Where 'Tourists' Fear to Tread." Reviewer Ariel Teplitsky celebrated Not For Tourists because it helped him feel like just such a worldly and savvy real traveler: "In the world of travel, it is often said there are two kinds of people: tourists and travellers. Most of us are the former but wish we were the latter. Wherever tourists roam there is a well-beaten path of landmarks, sanitized cultural experiences and inflated prices. . . . This is not meant as a slight to tourists—for I was once one myself." Luckily, an "alternative shop owner" tipped him off about "the anti-guidebook [that] empowers visitors—and locals—to make all their own decisions."² Not For Tourists had hit upon a culturally and commercially powerful formula: a guidebook that tourists would go out of their way to purchase specifically because it was not intended for tourists, because it made them feel like they were "real travellers," not tourists.

Walking into that coffee shop in 2008, I thought I was encountering a deeply paradoxical artifact: a cultural commodity promising an uncommodified experience. Reading journalists' accounts of people actually using Not For Tourists only heightened this sense of paradox. But as the winter wore on and the cultural and economic mechanics of the nineteenth-century origins of tourism became increasingly clear to me, I realized that essentially the same dynamics explained the existence and the appeal of Not For Tourists. Despite its title, it was a guidebook. The publisher, Happy Mazza Media, had figured out how to repackage geographical knowledge for a distinct audience in order to create a new market. Happy Mazza Media sold its product with the implicit promise that it would give its buyers a unique experience of belonging to the city. They expected this experience to find a market because it played on a constellation of ideas about tourists, tourism, and their cultural value. Tourists were those who unthinkingly bought what the market sold them, at artificially inflated prices, and who had superficial and ultimately meaningless visits to the big city as a result. Meaningful experiences, on the other hand, came from avoiding tourists and trying to learn something "real" about the places a traveler visited. These ideas were so foundational to any discussion of travel that they could be easily summed up with a breezy "it is often said." Not For Tourists was not the paradox it first appeared to be; it merely marketed the tourist-traveler dichotomy in a new way for a new audience in a new moment, as its authors figured out a new formula for commodifying authenticity and making a market.

Like its nineteenth-century forebears, Not For Tourists is one product in a world of interrelated products that offer a variety of commodified experiences to their purchasers and thus work to both produce and undermine the figure of the tourist in American culture. As Teplitsky pointed out in the *Toronto Star*, "Populating [the tourist's well-beaten] path are the thousands who carry the usual array of guidebooks: Fodor's, Frommer's, Let's Go. . . . Even Lonely Planet, which encourages adventure and discovery, has its own trail of followers who devotedly adhere to its picks and avoid its pans."³ As in the nineteenth century, these texts embody a range of attitudes about the practices of tourism and their value. The longest-running modern guidebooks, Fodor's and Frommer's, promise to "strive to live up to your discerning approach to travel by delivering the most candid and reliable information," and to offer "the assurance of our expertise, the guarantee of selectivity, and the choice details that truly define a destination."[4] While these august guidebooks promise ease and exclusivity, the Let's Go series is edited by a staff of college students, and aims to help its readers "realiz[e] the dream of accessible budget travel."[5] The Lonely Planet guides grew out of their founders' experiences of backpacking around Asia in the 1970s, which, as Teplitsky noted, gives them a reputation for guiding their readers off the beaten track and toward "independent travel," even while creating a new beaten path of their own.[6] Individual tourists' choice of guide to purchase and carry marks them as enthusiastic consumers of touristic luxury, as seekers of adventure travel, or even, as in the case of Not For Tourists, as visitors hoping the blend in with the locals. These guidebooks all enable the consumption of experience, but in doing so they allow their buyers to position themselves differently in relation to the dichotomy between traveler and tourists.

Although the material and cultural context was profoundly different, this modern constellation of foundational ideas about tourism and tourists was already largely in place by the eve of the Civil War. Trends that were emergent in the 1820s and 1830s—the commodification of geographical knowledge and transportation services, the selling of social and aesthetic experiences by a largely rural class of leisure entrepreneurs, the stock use of the figure of the tourist in a wide range of social satires, and growing concerns about the value of so much market-enabled travel—had become consolidated by the 1850s. By then, travelers along the most developed corridors in the United States routinely thought about their journeys in terms of service schedules and through tickets. They could carry with them, according to their taste, T. Nelson and Sons' *Our Summer Retreats*, any of D. Appleton & Company's many national or regional handbooks, or indeed the Royal Geographical Society's *Hints to Travellers*, if the others seemed too frivolous. Their tickets and their books could carry them to bustling health resorts like White Sulphur or Saratoga Springs if they wanted a social experience; to restful, rural retreats like Avon Springs or Trenton Falls if they wanted to bask in idealized pastoral summer days; or to spectacular landscape features like Niagara Falls or the White Mountains if they wanted to feel the rush of the sublime. Such experiences offered myriad pleasures to the consumers who could afford them, but they also carried social and cultural risks.

Tourists were already being dismissed as ignorant, superficial, unoriginal, and meaningless by skeptics and satirists alike, in the pages of scientific journals and the popular press. For those for whom those risks were too much to bear, a range of gendered strategies had emerged to avoid the opprobrium of tourism, from stressing travel's educational value to treating it as a form of scientific method. The essential features of the modern landscape of cultural meanings around travel and tourism were all in place by the 1850s.

Like it did for much of American life, the Civil War disrupted the emerging tourist industry in the United States. The Virginia springs were the most directly affected. Early in the war, visitors reported hearing cannon fire, and the brand-new main building at White Sulphur Springs served as a Confederate barracks and military hospital. Northern destinations were less affected but still experienced a decrease in traffic. Despite this temporary disruption, the roots of the domestic tourist industry had been planted deeply enough before the war that it quickly flourished once peace returned. Both northern and southern resorts entered a period of rapid popularization and expansion, as prewar crowds were swelled by a booming middle class with the time and money for a resort stay.[7] The number and variety of potential destinations also increased rapidly after the war. Small rural entrepreneurs continued to enter the market for pastoral summertime experiences by opening small boardinghouses and renting out rooms in farmhouses on the outskirts of growing cities. Antebellum leisure-seekers had never shown much interest in visiting the seaside, but after the war beach destinations blossomed, beginning in New England and the Middle Atlantic states, and spreading south along the Atlantic seaboard and ultimately to Florida and the Gulf Coast.[8] Urban entrepreneurs, who had only just started to experiment with selling city experiences to passing tourists before the war, developed a whole new set of businesses, institutions, and conventions for leisure travel to cities beginning in the 1870s.[9] The growth of and competition between transcontinental railroad networks in the 1870s and 1880s drove them to invest in and promote pleasure destinations in the West, within the new national parks and ultimately on the Pacific coast.[10] Amid all this growth, Mark Twain's 1869 blockbuster *The Innocents Abroad* showed that the figure of the tourist that had emerged in antebellum popular culture survived the war intact, ready to inspire a new generation of skeptics and satirists. The rapid expansion of the postwar tourist industry in both scope and scale was driven by its commodification of a wide range of new leisure experiences for a growing middle-class marketplace. It grew in tandem with American capitalism, and as a result the cultural meanings of consuming those commodified experiences remained largely consistent with their antebellum precursors.

As the American culture of capitalism developed in the twentieth century, the meanings of tourism and travel evolved in parallel. The state at all levels became more directly involved in markets during the first half of the century, including the market for experiences. In the World War I era, the federal government took over many of the promotional activities pioneered by the railroads in the late nineteenth century to entice tourists to "See America First" on explicitly nationalist grounds. During the Depression, local governments turned to tourism promotion as a strategy of economic development because it seemed to encourage increased consumption of experiences rather than increased production of goods that no one wanted.[11] This growing comfort with—and even celebration of—capitalist consumption as an economically necessary and patriotic act underlay the rapid expansion of family vacations in the postwar period. The growth in paid time off and automobile ownership, along with a broader cultural valorization of family togetherness and the consumption of the fruits of mass production, combined to make the family summer road trip into a mark of membership in the broad middle class.[12] Although the midcentury national, class, and familial meanings of tourism were different from those of the nineteenth century, they were similarly rooted the period's culture of capitalism. In both cases, tourism was defined by the consumption of commodified experiences produced for a market of leisure-seekers, and tourism drew its cultural meanings from those acts of consumption.

Even though postwar Americans had largely shed their suspicion of consumption and their preoccupation with being a "producer," they did not necessarily embrace tourism as an unproblematic good. In this period, the broader embrace of consumer culture sparked a growing concern about "authenticity," as commercially produced experiences came to seem to some critics to be fundamentally unreal. The language of the twentieth-century critique of tourism was different than that of the nineteenth-century critique—it found tourists to be inauthentic rather than useless—but both critiques were rooted in their century's dominant formulation of the failures and dangers of commodified experience. Where nineteenth-century advisors like Theodore Dwight or Harriet Martineau offered tourists tools to make their otherwise useless tours produce something useful, twentieth- and twenty-first-century advisors like the authors of the Lonely Planet or Not For Tourists series offer tourists a guide to true, authentic experiences.

It was in this cultural moment that Daniel Boorstin drew his acidic but influential distinction between active, adventurous travelers and passive, consumeristic tourists. Writing in 1961, Boorstin thought the commercially produced and intellectually meaningless tourist experience was a new phenomenon. "There is no better illustration of our newly exaggerated expectations than our changed attitude towards travel," Boorstin wrote, because the "modern American tourist now fills his experience with pseudo-events."[13] Trapped as he was in his midcentury moment, Boorstin thought tourism was a degraded, inauthentic form of true travel that was taking over American culture, and that this world in which everything was "sordid, shoddy, thin as pasteboard" was a recently fallen one.[14] This assumption infuses much contemporary discourse about tourism, but it is profoundly wrong. What Boorstin and other modern critics of tourism miss is that tourism and travel are inextricably linked because they are defined in opposition to each other, as they have been ever since the social practices of tourism and the cultural figure of the tourist emerged out of the spread of market capitalism in the first half of the nineteenth century. Boorstin thought that tourists' consumption of commercial experiences was new, but in fact it was rooted in the processes of commodification that underlay the creation of the modern capitalist order in the nineteenth century. Thus, the return to a world of "authentic" travel before or outside of tourism that Boorstin so yearned for is impossible, a historical fact that he probably would have found disappointing. But as satisfied tourists have found, from Trenton Falls in the 1850s to the readers of Not For Tourists in the 2000s, tourism is an inherent part of modern travel, and it provides as many opportunities as it forecloses.

Acknowledgments

This project has germinated over many years, so my true intellectual and material debts are too many to list. My research began at the University of Michigan, under the generous direction of Mary Kelley. At Michigan, both the History Department and the Rackham School of Graduate Studies provided financial and institutional support without which I would not have had the time and space to read and write. Supportive faculty and a close and clever cohort of colleagues, including Jay Cook, Susan Juster, Alisse Portnoy, Allison Abra, Katie Cangany, Victoria Castillo, Nathan Connolly, James Dator, Sara Babcox First, Laura Hymson, Jeff Kaja, Robert Kruckeberg, and Tara Zahra, provided critical early input and ensured that my research came to fruition.

This book took its final shape while I was an assistant professor at the University of Mary Washington. UMW generously supported my scholarly work with a series of Supplemental Faculty Development Grants, a Summer Faculty Research Grant, and a Jepson Fellowship. I was also lucky to be immersed in a group of smart and generous colleagues in the Department of History and American Studies and beyond, who fielded brainstorms and read drafts even during the flurry of a busy semester. I would particularly like to thank Jason Sellers and Nora Kim for their time, and Carla Bailey and Angie White at UMW's Simpson Library for all their assistance. I also valued all the opportunities I had to discuss this work with my students; in research methods classes; first-year and senior seminars; and in department colloquia. These conversations were always helpful with refining both my ideas and their presentation.

My research has benefited from the support of a wide array of archives and archivists. It has received generous financial support in the form of the Isaac Comly Martindale Fund Library Resident Fellowship from the American Philosophical Society; the Andrew W. Mellon Fellowship from the Massachusetts Historical Society; the Gilder Lehrman Fellowship from the Gilder Lehrman Institute of American History; the Albert M. Greenfield Foundation Fellowship from the Library Company of Philadelphia; and the Helen and John S. Best Fellowship from the American Geographical Society Library. I also benefited from the amazing collections of the New-York Historical Society, the New York Public Library, the Library of Congress, and the Lilly Library at Indiana University. At each of these institutions, I received the priceless support of their knowledgeable staff and fellow residents. I am especially grateful to Dan Richter, who gave me an extended appointment as a Research Associate at the McNeil Center for Early American Studies; David A. Smith, who gave me a place to write in the Wertheim Study at the New York Public Library; and Jim Green and all the rest of the great staff at the Library Company of Philadelphia, who provided a welcoming home for me for almost three years.

The arguments and the rhetoric deployed in the preceding pages have been crafted over the years in conference presentations. The audiences and my copanelists have provided valuable feedback at events sponsored by the Society for Historians of the Early American Republic; the Omohundro Institute of American History and Culture; the American Association of Geographers; the University of Michigan; the University of Mary Washington; and the University of Lincoln, Sheffield Hallam University, and Bangor University in the United Kingdom. These countless conference participants are an abstract illustration of the generosity of the historical profession. More concrete is the vital feedback offered by the anonymous peer reviewers of the *Journal of the Early Republic* and New York University Press, and especially my editor at NYU Press, Clara Platter. My work has benefited beyond words from this generosity, especially embodied by inspirational professional friends like Ken Cohen, Bruce Dorsey, Courtney Fullilove, Robb Haberman, Martha Hodes, Cathy Kelly, Brian Luskey, Rodney Mader, Lucia McMahon, Peter Reed, Joe Rezek, Honor Sachs, Nick Syrett, and Wendy Woloson. The intellectual imprint of my old friend Kevin Schlottmann, an accomplished archivist who has read untold millions of my words in draft form, is indelible on this book.

The unwavering support of my relatives has been most important in keeping me moving. They have been enthusiastic champions and cheerleaders who always wanted to know how the project was going, even when I didn't really want to answer. My parents, Steve and Carol, my sister Hollis and her family, and my many Lam in-laws have kept me suspended in a web of love and encouragement. Most of all, I could not have done it without my husband, Brian Lam, and our daughter, Hazel, my magical little family to whom this book cheerfully dedicated.

NOTES

Introduction

1. Edward L. Blanchard, *Heads and Tales of Travellers & Travelling: A Book for Everybody, Going Anywhere* (New York: D. Appleton & Co., 1847), 8. The book was initially published by the London firm of Willoughby & Co. in 1847, and reprinted by the related New York firm of D. Appleton & Co. and Philadelphia firm of G. S. Appleton in the same year. Despite the fact that the earliest London edition has been given the date of 1846 by its cataloguers, it is likely that in fact the three editions were published relatively simultaneously in 1847, because according to his diary, Blanchard did not finish his manuscript until June 20, 1847. For more on Blanchard's writing of *Heads and Tales* in the summer of 1847, and on his relationship with Delamotte, see E. L. Blanchard et al., *The Life and Reminiscences of E. L. Blanchard* (London: Hutchinson & Co., 1891), 49, 56–59. The *Sunday Times* quotation comes from Willoughy & Co. advertising material in the back of *Heathen Mythology, Illustrated by Extracts from the Most Celebrated Writers, Both Ancient and Modern, on the Gods of Greece, Rome, India, Scandinavia* (London: Willoughby & Co., n.d.), 299.

2. Blanchard, *Heads and Tales*, 9.

3. See Judith Wechsler, *A Human Comedy: Physiognomy and Caricature in 19th Century Paris* (Chicago: University of Chicago Press, 1982), 34.

4. Blanchard, *Heads and Tales*, 16.

5. *The Oxford English Dictionary: Being a Corrected Re-issue with an Introduction, Supplement, and Bibliography of a New English Dictionary on Historical Principles, Founded Mainly on the Materials Collected by the Philological Society*, vol. 11 (Oxford: Clarendon, 1978), 189–90.

6. Samuel Pegge, *Anecdotes of the English Language; Chiefly Regarding the Local Dialect of London and Its Environs; Whence It Will Appear That the Natives of the Metropolis and Its Vicinities Have Not Corrupted the Language of Their Ancestors* (London: J. Nichols, Son, and Bentley, 1814), 313.

7. John Davis, *The Original Letters of Ferdinand and Elisabeth* (New York: H. Caritat, 1798), 54. For more on Davis's career, see Scott Ellis, "'Reviewers Reviewed': John Davis and the Early American Literary Field," *Early American Literature* 42, no. 1 (2007): 157–88.

8. Karl Marx, *Das Kapital: A Critique of Political Economy* (Chicago: H. Regnery, 1959): 1–63. See also Susan Strasser, introduction to *Commodifying Everything: Relationships of the Market*, ed. Strasser (New York: Routledge, 2003), 3–9.

9. Cronon has pursed this analysis in two different historical contexts: seventeenth-century New England and nineteenth-century Chicago (see William Cronon, *Changes in the Land: Indians, Colonists, and the Ecology of New England* [New York: Hill and Wang, 1983]; and William Cronon, *Nature's Metropolis: Chicago and the Great West* [New York: Norton, 1991]).

10. Ann Blair, *Too Much to Know: Managing Scholarly Information before the Modern Age* (New Haven: Yale University Press, 2011), 12.

11. David Watkin points out that the British Grand Tour was part of a larger interest in travel as education in late-Renaissance Europe. He argues that "the international nature of the Enlightenment meant that the Grand Tour became by definition something fundamentally pan-European, involving, for example, the French, the Dutch, and the Germans, who established a famous colony in Rome" (Watkin, "The Architectural Context of the Grand Tour," in *The Impact of Italy: The Grand Tour and Beyond*, ed. Clare Hornsby [London: British School of Rome, London, 2000], 56).

12. Michael G. Brennan, *The Origins of the Grand Tour: The Travels of Robert Montagu, Lord Mandeville (1649–1654), William Hammond, (1655–1658), and Banaster Maynard (1660–1663)* (London: Hakluyt Society, 2005), 19.

13. For more on Lassels and the origin of the Grand Tour, see Edward Chaney, *The Grand Tour and the Great Rebellion: Richard Lassels and "The Voyage of Italy" in the Seventeenth Century* (Geneva: Slatkine, 1985).

14. For more on the cultural uses of the Grand Tour, see James Buzard, "The Grand Tour and After (1660–1840)," in *The Cambridge Companion to Travel Writing*, ed. Peter Hulme and Tim Youngs (Cambridge: Cambridge University Press, 2002).

15. James Buzard, *The Beaten Track: European Tourism, Literature, and the Ways to Culture, 1800–1918* (New York: Oxford University Press, 1993), 6.

16. Daniel Kilbride, *Being American in Europe: 1750–1860* (Baltimore: Johns Hopkins University Press, 2013), 2–5. See also Christof Wegelin, "The Rise of the International Novel," *PMLA* 77, no. 3 (June 1962): 305–10, 307.

17. See *A Catalogue of the Books, Belonging to the Library Company of Philadelphia* (Philadelphia: Zachariah Poulson, 1789), iv; and Daniel Kilbride "Travel, Ritual, and National Identity: Planters on the European Tour, 1820–1860," *Journal of Southern History* 69, no. 3 (August 2003): 549–84, 556n18.

18. Jeffrey Alan Melton, *Mark Twain, Travel Books, and Tourism: The Tide of a Great Popular Movement* (Tuscaloosa: University of Alabama Press, 2002), 22. For more on Irving's effect on the structure of the travel narrative genre, see William W. Stowe, "Conventions and Voices in Margaret Fuller's Travel Writing," *American Literature* 63, no. 2 (June, 1991): 242–62, 243–44.

19. Bibliographers have been assiduous in cataloging the prodigious output of American travel writers. See, for example, Thomas D. Clark, ed., *Travels in the Old South: A Bibliography* (Norman: University of Oklahoma Press, 1956); Garold L.

Cole, *Travels in America: From the Voyages of Discovery to the Present: An Anno-
tated Bibliography of Travel Articles in Periodicals, 1955–1980* (Norman: University of Oklahoma Press, 1984); William Stanton, *American Scientific Exploration,
1803–1860: Manuscripts in Four Philadelphia Libraries* (Philadelphia: American
Philosophical Society, 1991); and Harold F. Smith: *American Travellers Abroad: A
Bibliography of Accounts Published before 1900*, 2nd ed. (Lanham, MD: Scarecrow,
1999). Perhaps most useful is Edward Cox's magisterial *Reference Guide to the
Literature of Travel*, published in three volumes between 1935 and 1949 by the
University of Washington Press, which covers the Old World, the New World, and
England.

20. Larzer Ziff, *Return Passages: Great American Travel Writing, 1780–1910* (New
Haven: Yale University Press, 2001), 59; Melton, *Mark Twain*, 16.

21. Alexis de Tocqueville, *Democracy in America* (Cambridge: Sever and Francis,
1863), 164.

22. W. W. P., "Travel," *Yale Literary Magazine* 25, no. 5 (March 1860): 203–9, 203.

23. Charlene Boyer Lewis, *Ladies and Gentlemen on Display: Planter Society at the
Virginia Springs, 1790–1860* (Charlottesville: University Press of Virginia, 2001), 17–
18; Richard H. Gassan, *The Birth of American Tourism: New York, the Hudson Valley,
and American Culture, 1790–1830* (Amherst: University of Massachusetts Press, 2008),
9–33; Theodore Corbett, *The Making of American Resorts: Saratoga Springs, Ballston
Spa, Lake George* (New Brunswick: Rutgers University Press, 2001), 27–39.

24. Boyer Lewis, *Ladies and Gentlemen*, 18–20; Gassan, *Birth of American Tourism*,
34–51; John F. Sears, *Sacred Places: American Tourist Attractions in the Nineteenth
Century* (New York: Oxford University Press, 1989), 12–30, 72–86; Thomas A. Cham-
bers, *Memories of War: Visiting Battlegrounds and Bonefields in the Early American
Republic* (Ithaca: Cornell University Press, 2012), 36–64; Dona Brown, *Inventing New
England: Regional Tourism in the Nineteenth Century* (Washington, DC: Smithsonian
Institution Press, 1995), 15–74.

25. For an overview of the historiography of domestic tourism in early America, see
Jon Sterngass, *First Resorts: Pursuing Pleasure at Saratoga Springs, Newport, & Coney
Island* (Baltimore: Johns Hopkins University Press, 2001), 349–58.

26. Scholars who explore the links between tourism and national and regional identity include Brown, *Inventing New England*; Marguerite S. Shaffer, *See America First:
Tourism and National Identity, 1880–1940* (Washington, DC: Smithsonian Institution
Press, 2001); Boyer Lewis, *Ladies and Gentlemen*; Gassan, *Birth of American Tourism*;
and Chambers, *Memories of War*. Daniel Kilbride has pursued a related analysis of
national identity formation among American tourists to Europe between 1750 and
1860 (see Kilbride, *Being American in Europe*).

27. Scholars who explore the links between tourism and formation of middle-class
or bourgeois identities in the United States include Cindy Sondik Aron, *Working at
Play: A History of Vacations in the United States* (New York: Oxford University Press,
1999); Sterngass, *First Resorts*; Thomas A. Chambers, *Drinking the Waters: Creating
an American Leisure Class at Nineteenth-Century Mineral Springs* (Washington, DC:
Smithsonian Institution Press, 2002); and Catherine Cocks, *Doing the Town: The Rise
of Urban Tourism in the United States, 1850–1915* (Berkeley: University of California
Press, 2001).

28. Sterngass, *First Resorts*, 4.

29. Importantly, James Buzard has arrived at a similar conclusion about tourism's emergence in opposition to "authentic" travel in British culture during the same years (see Buzard, *The Beaten Track*, 6).

30. Dean MacCannell, *The Tourist: A New Theory of the Leisure Class* (Berkeley: University of California Press, 1999), 2–3.

31. John Urry, *The Tourist Gaze: Leisure and Travel in Contemporary Societies* (London: Sage, 1990)

32. The paradigm-setting works on the market revolution are Charles Sellers, *The Market Revolution: Jacksonian America, 1815–1846* (New York: Oxford University Press, 1991); Melvyn Stokes and Stephen Conway, eds., *The Market Revolution in America: Social, Political, and Religious Expressions, 1800–1880* (Charlottesville: University Press of Virginia, 1996); Majewski, *House Dividing*; and John Lauritz Larson, *The Market Revolution in America: Liberty, Ambition, and the Eclipse of the Common Good* (New York: Cambridge University Press, 2010).

33. Joanna Cohen, *Luxurious Citizens: The Politics of Consumption in Nineteenth-Century America* (Philadelphia: University of Pennsylvania Press, 2017), 11.

34. Cronon, *Nature's Metropolis*; Walter Johnson, *Soul by Soul: Life inside the Antebellum Slave Market* (Cambridge: Harvard University Press, 1999); Jonathan Levy, *Freaks of Fortune: The Emerging World of Capitalism and Risk in America* (Cambridge: Harvard University Press, 2012).

35. James W. Cook, "The Return of the Culture Industry," in *The Cultural Turn in U.S. History Past, Present, and Future*, ed. Cook et al. (Chicago: University of Chicago Press, 2008): 291–317, 299. See also James W. Cook, *The Colossal P. T. Barnum Reader* (Urbana: University of Illinois Press, 2005); and Eric Lott, *Love and Theft: Blackface Minstrelsy and the American Working Class* (New York: Oxford University Press, 1993).

36. Barbara Carson gestured to just such an integration of tourism into a larger discussion of culture industries in a 1994 essay in which she argued that "the history of travel in early America" was an "aspect of the larger subjects of the consumer revolution and the commercialization of leisure" (see Barbara G. Carson, "Early American Tourists and the Commercialization of Leisure," in *Of Consuming Interests: The Style of Life in the Eighteenth Century*, ed. Cary Carson, Ronald Hoffman, and Peter J. Albert [Charlottesville: University Press of Virginia, 1994], 373–405, 374).

37. This is far from an exhaustive list, but see, for example, John F. Kasson, *Amusing the Million: Coney Island at the Turn of the Century* (New York: Hill and Wang, 1978); Kathy Bottom of FormPeiss, *Cheap Amusements: Working Women and Leisure in Turn-of-the-Century New York* (Philadelphia: Temple University Press, 1986); Michael Denning, *Mechanic Accents: Dime Novels and Working-Class Culture in America* (London: Verso, 1987); Robert W. Snyder, *The Voice of the City: Vaudeville and Popular Culture in New York* (New York: Oxford University Press, 1989); Richard Butsch, ed., *For Fun and Profit: The Transformation of Leisure into Consumption* (Philadelphia: Temple University Press, 1990); Bruce A. McConachie, *Melodramatic Formations American Theatre and Society, 1820–1870* (Iowa City: University of Iowa Press, 1992); David Top of FormTop of FormNasaw, *Going Out: The Rise and Fall of Public Amusements* (New York: Basic, 1993); William Leach, *Land of Desire: Merchants, Power, and the Rise of a New American Culture* (New York: Pantheon, 1993); Janet M. Davis, *The Circus Age: Culture and Society under the American Big Top* (Chapel Hill: University

of North Carolina Press, 2002); Strasser, *Commodifying Everything*; Benjamin G. Top of FormTop of FormRader, *American Sports: From the Age of Folk Games to the Age of Televised Sports* (Upper Saddle River, NJ: Prentice Hall, 2004); and Trish Loughran, *The Republic in Print: Print Culture in the Age of U.S. Nation Building, 1770–1870* (New York: Columbia University Press, 2007).

38. Indeed, for MacCannell, "modernity" is defined by commodified experience: "Increasingly, pure experience, which leaves no material trace, is manufactured and sold like a commodity" (MacCannell, *The Tourist*, 21). This book is a history of modernity in that it shows how this relationship between capitalism, commodified experience, and modernity was produced over time.

39. Following George Rogers Taylor, *The Transportation Revolution, 1815–1860* (New York: Rinehart, 1951).

40. Blanchard, *Heads and Tales*, 18, 15–16.

41. Daniel Boorstin, "From Traveler to Tourist: The Lost Art of Travel," in *The Image: A Guide to Pseudo-Events in America* (New York: Harper and Row, 1961), 85.

1 / Describing the Terraqueous Globe

1. Matthew H. Edney, "Cartographic Culture and Nationalism in the Early United States: Benjamin Vaughan and the Choice for a Prime Meridian, 1811," *Journal of Historical Geography* 20, no. 4 (October 1994): 384–95, 386–87. Foucault also commented on the conceptual similarity between the Enlightenment archival project and cartography (see Barbara Belyea, "Images of Power: Derrida/Foucault/Harley," *Cartographica* 29, no. 2 [1992]: 1–9).

2. See, for example, Michael Denning, *Mechanic Accents: Dime Novels and Working-Class Culture in America* (London: Verso, 1987); Ronald J. Zboray, *A Fictive People: Antebellum Economic Development and the American Reading Public* (New York: Oxford University Press, 1993); and the essays in Robert A. Gross and Mary Kelley, eds., *A History of the Book in America,* vol. 2, *An Extensive Republic: Print, Culture, and Society in the Early Republic* (Chapel Hill: University of North Carolina Press, 2010); and Scott E. Casper and Jeffrey D. Groves et al., eds., *A History of the Book in America,* vol. 3, *The Industrial Book, 1840–1880* (Chapel Hill: University of North Carolina Press, 2009).

3. For more on late-Enlightenment intellectual culture in the early national United States, see John Fea, *The Way of Improvement Leads Home: Philip Vickers Fithian and the Rural Enlightenment in Early America* (Philadelphia: University of Pennsylvania Press, 2008).

4. Martin Brückner, *The Geographic Revolution in Early America: Maps, Literacy, and National Identity* (Chapel Hill: University of North Carolina Press, 2006), 3.

5. See, for example, William Guthrie, *A New System of Modern Geography: or, A Geographical, Historical, and Commercial Grammar; and Present State of the Several Nations of the World* (Philadelphia: Mathew Carey, 1794–95). Carey employed Morse to revise Guthrie's text for an American audience. For a later example of a British work Americanized by Morse, see John Bigland and Jedidiah Morse, *A Geographical and Historical View of the World: Exhibiting a Complete Delineation of the Natural and Artificial Feature of Each Country; And a Succinct Narrative of the Origin of the Different Nations, Their Political Revolutions, and Progress in Arts, Sciences, Literature, Commerce, &c., With Notes, Correcting and Improving the Part Which Relates to the*

American Continent and Islands (Boston: T. B. Wait and Co., 1811), which was also printed in Philadelphia in 1812 by W. W. Woodward. For more on the Americanization of British texts, see James N. Green, "The Rise of Book Publishing," in *A History of the Book in America,* vol. 2, ed. Gross and Kelly, 75–127.

6. Jedidiah Morse, *Geography Made Easy: Being a Short, but Comprehensive System of that Very Useful and Agreeable Science* (New Haven: Meigs, Bowen and Dana, 1784), advertisement.

7. Ralph H. Brown, "The American Geographies of Jedidiah Morse," *Annals of the Association of American Geographers* 31, no. 3 (September 1941): 145–217.

8. A comprehensive bibliography of the print culture of geographical knowledge is outside the scope of this work, but see, for example, Joseph Scott, *The United States Gazetteer* (Philadelphia: F. & R. Bailey, 1795); Joseph Scott, *The New and Universal Gazetteer; Or, Modern Geographical Dictionary* (Philadelphia: F. & R. Bailey, 1799–1800); Joseph Scott, *A Geographical Dictionary of the United States of North America* (Philadelphia: Archibald Bartram, 1805); Joseph Scott, *Elements of Geography, For the Use of Schools* (Philadelphia: Kimber, Conrad and Co., 1807); Nathaniel Dwight et al., *A Short but Comprehensive System of the Geography of the World, By Way of Question and Answer. Principally Designed for Children and Common Schools* (Northampton, MA: S. & E. Butler, 1805); Susanna Rowson, *An Abridgment of Universal Geography, Together with Sketches of History Designed for the Use of Schools and Academies in the United States* (Boston: John West, 1804); and Susanna Rowson, *Youth's First Step in Geography; Being a Series of Exercises Making the Tour of the Habitable Globe* (Boston: Wells and Lilly, 1818). See also Brückner, *Geographical Revolution in Early America,* 146–48.

9. Susanna Rowson, *An Abridgment of Universal Geography, Together with Sketches of History, Designed for the Use of Schools and Academies in the United States* (Boston: John West, 1806), 11.

10. Jedidiah Morse, *The American Gazetteer* (Boston: S. Hall, and Thomas & Andrews, 1797), iii.

11. Scott, *United States Gazetteer,* iv.

12. Morse, *The American Gazetteer,* iii.

13. Morse, *American Geography,* iii.

14. As the earliest and most prolific American geographical author, Morse in particular drew controversy (see James Freeman, *Remarks on the American Universal Geography* [Boston: Belknap and Hall, 1793]; and St. George Tucker, *A Letter to the Rev. Jedediah Morse, A. M., Author of the "American Universal Geography"* (Richmond: Thomas Nicholson, 1795).

15. Morse, *The American Geography,* iii. For more on civic culture and commitment to the public good among "men of letters" outside of politics in the 1790s and the early 1800s, see Catherine O'Donnell Kaplan, *Men of Letters in the Early Republic: Cultivating Forums of Citizenship* (Chapel Hill: University of North Carolina Press, 2008).

16. Scott, *United States Gazetteer,* iv–v.

17. Morse, *Geography Made Easy,* dedication.

18. Joseph Churchman, *Rudiments of National Knowledge, Presented to the Youth of the United States, and to Enquiring Foreigners* (Philadelphia: E. L. Carey & A. Hart, 1833).

19. Thomas Salmon, *A New Geographical and Historical Grammar: Wherein the Geographical Part is Truly Modern; and the Present state of the Several Kingdoms of the World is so Interspersed, as to Render the Study of Geography both Entertaining and Instructive* (London: William Johnston, 1754), 7. In the preface to his American edition of Guthrie's *New System of Modern Geography*, the most popular British geographical grammar of the late eighteenth century, Carey traced a lineage for the genre that stretched back to 1716, through Thomas Salmon's 1754 work to that of Patrick Gordon, entitled *Geography Anatomiz'd: Or, the Geographical Grammar, Being a Short and Exact Analysis of the Whole Body of Modern Geography, After a New and Curious Method* (London: J. Nicholson, 1716) (see Guthrie, *New System of Modern Geography*, 3).

20. Jedidiah Morse, *Elements of Geography: Containing a Concise and Comprehensive View of that Useful Science, as Divided Into, 1. Astronomical, 2. Physical or Natural, 3. Political Geography, on a New Plan* (Boston: I. Thomas and E. T. Andrews, 1795), vii.

21. Morse, *American Geography*, vi.

22. Robert C. White, "Early Geographical Dictionaries," *Geographical Review* 58, no. 4 (October 1968): 652–59, 658–59.

23. Scott, *United States Gazetteer*, iii

24. The Enlightenment figure of the "encyclopedist" is delineated in Roger Chartier, "The Man of Letters," in *Enlightenment Portraits*, ed. Michel Vovelle (Chicago: University of Chicago Press, 1997), 142.

25. Jedidiah Morse, *Geography Made Easy: Being an Abridgement of the American Geography* (Boston: Isaiah Thomas & Ebenezer T. Andrews, 1790), iii.

26. Rowson, *Abridgement of Universal Geography*, iii.

27. Morse, *Geography Made Easy*, iv.

28. The term "booster" was a nineteenth-century word that described speculators who sought to increase the value of their investments by promoting them, or "boosting" them, in print (see William Cronon, *Nature's Metropolis: Chicago and the Great West* [New York: Norton, 1991], 34).

29. Jack Larkin, "'Printing Is Something Every Village Has in It': Rural Printing and Publishing," in *A History of the Book in America*, ed. Gross and Kelley, 2:145–60; John Tebbel, *A History of Book Publishing in the United States*, vol. 1, *The Creation of an Industry, 1630–1865* (New York: Bowker, 1972), 203–7.

30. John C. Pease and John M. Niles, *A Gazetteer of the States of Connecticut and Rhode-Island: Written with Care and Impartiality, From Original and Authentic Materials* (Hartford: William S. Marsh, 1819), iii. See also David Pease and Austin S. Pease, *A Genealogical and Historical Record of the Descendants of John Pease, Sen., Last of Enfield, Conn.* (Springfield, MA: Samuel Bowles & Co., 1869), 141.

31. Horatio Gates Spafford, *A Gazetteer of the State of New-York, Carefully Written from Original and Authentic Materials, Arranged on a New Plan, in Three Parts* (Albany: H. C. Southwick, 1813), 14, 16, 49, 36, 24. See also Julian Boyd, "Horatio Gates Spafford: Inventor, Author, Promoter of Democracy," *Proceedings of the American Antiquarian Society at the Annual Meeting Held in Worcester* 51 (1941): 279–50.

32. John Kilbourn, *The Ohio Gazetteer: Or, Topographical Dictionary, Containing a Description of the Several Counties, Towns, Villages and Settlements in the State of Ohio* (Columbus: J. Kilbourn, 1816). See also Charles Chester Cole, *A Fragile Capital: Identity and the Early Years of Columbus, Ohio* (Columbus: Ohio State University Press, 2001), 139.

33. Alphonso Wetmore, *Gazetteer of the State of Missouri* (St. Louis: C. Keemle, 1837). See also Mary Barile, *The Santa Fe Trail in Missouri* (Columbia: University of Missouri Press, 2010), 49; and F. F. Stephens, "Missouri and the Santa Fe Trade," *Missouri Historical Review* 11 (April–July 1917): 289–312, 294.

34. See Nicolas Trübner et al., *Trübner's Bibliographical Guide to American Literature, A Classed List of Books Published in the United States of America during the Last Forty Years* (London: Trübner and Co., 1859), 317–51.

35. John T. Flanagan, "A Look at Some Middle Western Gazetteers," *Indiana Magazine of History* 61, no. 4 (1965): 283–304, 303–4; J. B. Newhall, *A Glimpse of Iowa in 1846* (Iowa City: State Historical Society of Iowa, 1957), iii–xix.

36. Newhall, *Glimpse of Iowa*, 8.

37. For more on the transatlantic origins of guidebooks, see John Vaughan, *The English Guide Book, C.1780–1870; An Illustrated History* (Newton Abbot, UK: David & Charles, 1974); James Buzard, *The Beaten Track: European Tourism, Literature, and the Ways to Culture, 1800–1918* (New York: Oxford University Press, 1993); Richard Gassan, "The First American Tourist Guidebooks: Authorship and the Print Culture of the 1820s," *Book History* 8 (2005): 51–74; and Will B. Mackintosh, "The Prehistory of the American Tourist Guidebook," *Book History* 21 (2018): 89–124.

38. David M. Ellis et al., *A History of New York State* (Ithaca: Cornell University Press, 1967), 150–87.

39. Larkin, "Printing Is Something Every Village Has in It"; Green, "The Rise of Book Publishing," 119–23.

40. Richard H. Gassan, *The Birth of American Tourism: New York, the Hudson Valley, and American Culture, 1790–1830* (Amherst: University of Massachusetts Press, 2008), 35–44.

41. See Dona Brown, *Inventing New England* (Washington, DC: Smithsonian Institution Press, 1995), 28; Gassan, "First American Tourist Guidebooks," 52–53; and Mackintosh, "Prehistory of the American Tourist Guidebook."

42. Davison's guidebook changed titles several times and was translated into French for a European audience, but the content remained relatively stable. See, for example, Gideon M. Davison, *The Fashionable Tour; Or, A Trip to the Springs, Niagara, Quebeck and Boston in the Summer of 1821* (Saratoga Springs: G. M. Davison, 1822); Gideon M. Davison, *Tournée à la mode dans les États-Unis: Ou, voyage de Charleston à Québec et d'Albany à Boston par la route de Philadelphia, New-York, Saratoga, Ballston-Spa, Mont-Réal, et autres villes ou lieux remarquables* (Paris: Arthus Bertrand, 1829); and Gideon M. Davison, *The Traveller's Guide through the Middle and Northern States, and the Provinces of Canada* (Saratoga Springs: G. M. Davison, 1833).

43. Gassan, *Birth of American Tourism*, 44–46; Theodore Corbett, *The Making of American Resorts: Saratoga Springs, Ballston Spa, Lake George* (New Brunswick: Rutgers University Press, 2001), 59–63, 125–68.

44. Gideon M. Davison, *The Fashionable Tour, in 1825. An Excursion to the Springs, Niagara, Quebec and Boston* (Saratoga Springs: G. M. Davison, 1825), 50.

45. Robert J. Vandewater, *The Tourist, or, Pocket Manual for Travellers on the Hudson River, the Western Canal and Stage Road Comprising Also the Routes to Lebanon, Ballston and Saratoga Springs* (New York: J. & J. Harper, 1830), 3.

46. See Edwin Williams and John Disturnell, *New-York As It Is: Containing a General Description of the City of New-York* (New York: T. R. Tanner, 1833), 184; O. L.

Holley, *The New York State Register for 1845* (New York: J. Disturnell, 1845), 26; and E. Porter Belden, *New-York, Past, Present, and Future: Comprising a History of the City of New-York, a Description of Its Present Condition, and an Estimate of Its Future Increase* (New York: Prall, Lewis & Co., 1850), 79.

47. See *Documents of the Senate of the State of New-York. Eighty-First Session.—1858*, vol. 3, nos. 111–39 (Albany: C. Van Benthuysen, 1858), no. 118, 11–12; and William Richard Cutter, *Genealogical and Family History of Western New York: A Record of the Achievements of Her People in the Making of a Commonwealth and the Building of a Nation* (New York: Lewis Historical Publishing, 1912), 321.

48. Samuel De Veaux, *The Falls of Niagara, Or Tourist's Guide to This Wonder of Nature, Including Notices of the Whirlpool, Islands, & C, and a Complete Guide Thro' the Canadas* (Buffalo: W. B. Hayden, 1839), iii.

49. Samuel De Veaux, *The Traveller's Own Book, to Saratoga Springs, Niagara Falls and Canada: Containing Routes, Distances, Conveyances, Expenses, Use of Mineral Waters, Baths, Description of Scenery, Etc.* (Buffalo: Faxon & Read, 1841).

50. Brown, *Inventing New England*, 41–74; John F. Sears, *Sacred Places: American Tourist Attractions in the Nineteenth Century* (New York: Oxford University Press, 1989), 72–86.

51. Allen H. Bent, *A Bibliography of the White Mountains* (Boston: Houghton Mifflin, 1911), 1–10.

52. John H. Spaulding, *Historical Relics of the White Mountains: Also, A Concise White Mountain Guide* (Mt. Washington, NH: J. R. Hitchcock, 1855); see also Frank Hunt Burt, *Mount Washington; A Handbook for Travellers* (Boston: G. H. Ellis, 1906), 27–29.

53. Charlene M. Boyer Lewis, *Ladies and Gentlemen on Display: Planter Society at the Virginia Springs, 1790–1860* (Charlottesville: University Press of Virginia, 2001).

54. Thomas Goode, *The Invalid's Guide to the Virginia Hot Springs: Containing an Account of the Medical Properties of These Waters, with Cases Illustrative of Their Effects* (Richmond: P. D. Bernard, 1839).

55. William Burke, *The Mineral Springs of Western Virginia: With Remarks on Their Use, and the Diseases to Which They Are Applicable* (New York: Wiley and Putnam, 1842), 12–13.

56. Oren F. Morton, *A History of Monroe County, West Virginia* (Dayton, VA: Ruebush-Elkins, 1916), 209, 216.

57. J. J. Moorman, *The Virginia Springs: With Their Analysis, and Some Remarks on Their Character, Together with a Directory for the Use of the White Sulphur Water, and an Account of the Diseases to Which It Is Applicable* (Philadelphia: Lindsay & Blakiston, 1847), 216–19.

58. See, for example, William Burke, *The Mineral Springs of Virginia; With Remarks on Their Use, the Diseases to Which They Are Applicable, and in Which They Are Contra-Indicated* (Richmond: Morris & Brother, 1851); William Burke, *The Virginia Mineral Springs: With Remarks on Their Use, the Diseases to Which They Are Applicable, and in Which They Are Contra-Indicated: Accompanied by a Map of Routes and Distances* (Richmond: Ritchies & Dunnavant, 1853); J. J. Moorman, *A Guide to the Virginia Springs: Giving, in Addition to the Routes and Distances, a Description of the Springs, and Also of the Natural Curiosities of the State* (Staunton, VA: R. Cowan, 1851); J. J. Moorman, *The Virginia Springs: with Their Analysis; And Some Remarks on*

Their Character, Together with a Directory for the Use of the White Sulphur Water and an Account of the Diseases to Which It Is Applicable (Richmond: J. W. Randolph, 1857); and J. J. Moorman, *The Virginia Springs, and Springs of the South and West* (Philadelphia: J. B. Lippincott & Co., 1859). Moorman also lent his name to a promotional effort for a similar spring in Ohio (see J. J. Moorman, and William Wirt Dawson, *The Ohio White Sulphur Springs* [Cincinnati: Moore, Wilstach, Keys & Co., printers, 1859]). Several of these Richmond firms would go on to be the most important publishers of the Confederate States of America (see Tebbel, *History of Book Publishing in the United States*, 474–76).

59. Tebbel, *History of Book Publishing in the United States*, 221. See also Larkin, "Printing Is Something Every Village Has in It"; and Green, "The Rise of Book Publishing."

60. Walter W. Ristow, *American Maps and Mapmakers: Commercial Cartography in the Nineteenth Century* (Detroit: Wayne State University Press, 1985), 179–90; John R. Short, *Representing the Republic: Mapping the United States, 1600–1900* (London: Reaktion, 2001), 127–43.

61. John Melish, *The Traveller's Directory through the United States: Containing a Description of All the Principal Roads through the United States with Copious Remarks on the Rivers, and Other Objects* (Philadelphia: John Melish, 1822), iii. For more on Melish and his road books in the 1810s and 1820s, see Mackintosh, "The Prehistory of the American Tourist Guidebook."

62. Ristow, *American Maps and Mapmakers*, 191–206; Short, *Representing the Republic*, 146–54.

63. Ristow, *American Maps and Mapmakers*, 303–313; Short, *Representing the Republic*, 155–60; Walter W. Ristow, *Maps for an Emerging Nation: Commercial Cartography in Nineteenth-Century America: An Exhibition at the Library of Congress* (Washington, DC: Library of Congress, 1977). See S. Augustus Mitchell, *Mitchell's Traveller's Guide through the United States, Containing the Principal Cities, Towns &C. Alphabetically Arranged; Together with the Steam-Boat, Canal, and Railroad Routes, with the Distances, in Miles, from Place to Place* (Philadelphia: S. Augustus Mitchell, 1832); and S. Augustus Mitchell, *Mitchell's New Traveller's Guide through the United States and the Canadas Containing the Principal Cities and Towns Alphabetically Arranged* (Philadelphia: C. Desilver, 1864).

64. Wayne Franklin, *James Fenimore Cooper: The Early Years* (New Haven: Yale University Press, 2007), 248–54, quotation on 252.

65. See, for example, John Melish, *The Traveller's Directory through the United States; Containing a Description of All the Principal Roads through the United States, with Copious Remarks on the Rivers and Other Objects* (New York: A. T. Goodrich, 1825). This same volume contains an advertising catalogue of geographical works at the end, listing a wide range of genres of geographical knowledge at prices ranging from twenty-five cents to an impressive $8.50.

66. In the mid-1820s, Goodrich identified his shop, at 124 Broadway, as a "geographical establishment" on the title page of the works that he issued there. Gassan has substantiated the claim that Goodrich was the first New York bookseller to carry Davison's guidebook using newspaper advertisements (see Gassan, "The First American Tourist Guidebooks," 54). The business of selling geographical knowledge was evidently good to Goodrich; an 1830 city directory listed him as residing in an elegant

house in the fashionable middle-class neighborhood of Brooklyn Heights (see Clay Lancaster and Edmund Vincent Gillon, *Old Brooklyn Heights: New York's First Suburb; Including Detailed Analyses of 619 Century-Old Houses* [New York: Dover, 1979], 151).

67. *The North American Tourist* (New York: A. T. Goodrich, 1839), 53, 127, 100.

68. Ristow, *American Maps and Mapmakers*, 313–26.

69. See, for example, J. H. Colton, *Colton's Traveler and Tourist Guide-Book through the United States of America and the Canadas: Containing the Routes and Distances on the Great Lines of Travel, by Railroads, Stage-Roads, Canals, Lakes and Rivers* (New York: J. H. Colton & Co., 1850).

70. See Lawrence Martin, "John Disturnell's Map of the United Mexican States," in *A La Carte: Selected Papers on Maps and Atlases*, ed. Walter W. Ristow (Washington, DC:, Library of Congress, 1972), 204–21, 210; and Ristow, *American Maps and Mapmakers*, 318.

71. Samuel L. Knapp, *The Picturesque Beauties of the Hudson River and Its Vicinity: Illustrated in a Series of Views* (New York: J. Disturnell, 1835); John Disturnell, *New-York As It Is, in 1835: Containing, a General Description of the City and Environs, List of Officers, Public Institutions, and Other Useful Information; for the Convenience of Citizens, As a Book of Reference, and a Guide to Strangers. With Correct Maps of the City, and Its Vicinity. Also, the Hudson River Guide, Accompanied by a Map* (New York: J. Disturnell, 1835).

72. John Disturnell, *The Traveller's Guide through the State of New York, Canada, & C: Embracing a General Description of the City of New-York; the Hudson River Guide, and the Fashionable Tour to the Springs and Niagara Falls; with Steam-Boat, Rail-Road, and Stage Routes* (New York: J. Disturnell, 1836)

73. Disturnell's guides to the Fashionable Tour included O. L. Holley, *The Picturesque Tourist: Being a Guide through the Northern and Eastern States and Canada: Giving an Accurate Description of Cities and Villages, Celebrated Places of Resort, Etc.* (New York: J. Disturnell, 1844); John Disturnell, *Tourist's Guide to Niagara Falls, Lake Ontario, and St. Lawrence River; Also a Guide to Lakes George and Champlain; Ottawa and Saguenay Rivers* (New York: J. Disturnell, 1857); and John Disturnell, *The Picturesque Tourist: Being a Guide through the State of New York and Upper and Lower Canada, Including a Hudson River Guide; Giving an Accurate Description of Cities and Villages, Celebrated Places of Resort, Etc.* (New York: J. Disturnell, 1858.). His regional guides included John Disturnell, *The Northern Traveller: Containing the Hudson River Guide and Tour to the Springs, Lake George and Canada, Passing through Lake Champlain; With a Description of All the Places on the Route Most Worthy of Notice* (New York: J. Disturnell, 1844); John Disturnell, *The Western Traveller Embracing the Canal and Railroad Routes from Albany and Troy to Buffalo and Niagara Falls: Also the Steamboat Route from Buffalo to Detroit and Chicago* (New York: J. Disturnell, 1844); John Disturnell, *Disturnell's Guide through the Middle, Northern, and Eastern States Containing a Description of the Principal Places, Canal, Railroad, and Steamboat Routes, Tables of Distances, Etc.* (New York: J. Disturnell, 1847); John Disturnell, *The Eastern Tourist; Being a Guide through the States of Connecticut, Rhode Island, Massachusetts, Vermont, New Hampshire, and Maine: Also, a Dash into Canada, Giving a Brief Description of Montreal, Quebec, Etc.* (New York: J. Disturnell, 1848); and John Disturnell, *A Trip through the Lakes of North America Embracing a Full Description*

of the St. Lawrence River, Together with All the Principal Places on Its Banks, from Its Source to Its Mouth: Commerce of the Lakes, Etc., Forming Altogether a Complete Guide for the Pleasure Traveler and Emigrant (New York: J. Disturnell, 1857).

74. John Disturnell, *Springs, Water-Falls, Sea-Bathing Resorts and Mountain Scenery of the United States and Canada; Giving an Analysis of the Principal Mineral Springs: With a Brief Description of the Most Fashionable Watering-Places, Mountain Resorts, &C.* (New York: J. Disturnell, 1855).

75. See, for example, John Disturnell, *Disturnell's Railroad, Steamboat and Telegraph Book Being a Guide through the United States and Canada: Also Giving the Ocean Steam Packet Arrangement, Telegraph Lines and Charges, List of Hotels, &C.: With a Map of the United States and Canada Showing All the Canals, Railroads, &C* (New York: J. Disturnell, 1851).

76. Goodrich established this neighborhood as the center of New York geographical publishing with his shop at 124 Broadway in the 1820s. By 1848, Disturnell operated at 102 and 233 Broadway, Colton at 86 Cedar Street, and Henry Tanner at 5 Barclay St. The engraving firm of Sherman & Smith, whose partnership included J. Calvin Smith, a prolific gazetteer and guidebook author, was at 122 Broadway (see John Doggett, *Doggett's New-York City Directory, Illustrated with Maps of New York and Brooklyn, 1848–1849* [New York: John Doggett, 1848], 124, 96, 396, 368).

77. John Kirtland Wright, *Geography in the Making, the American Geographical Society, 1851–1951* (New York: American Geographical Society, 1952), 15–17, 403.

78. Wright, *Geography in the Making*, 16; Tebbel, *History of Book Publishing*, 1:299–312.

79. George Putnam, *The Tourist in Europe; Or, A Concise Summary of the Various Routes, Objects of Interest, &C in Great Britain, France, Switzerland, Italy, Germany, Belgium, and Holland; with Hints on Time, Expenses, Hotels, Conveyances, Passports, Coins, &C; Memoranda during a Tour of Eight Months in Great Britain and on the Continent, in 1836* (New York: Wiley & Putnam, 1838). See also Daniel Kilbride, *Being American in Europe, 1750–1860* (Baltimore: Johns Hopkins University Press, 2013), 4–5.

80. See, for example, Roswell Park, *A Hand-Book for American Travellers in Europe, Collated from the Best Authorities: Designed As an Introduction to the European Guide-Books* (New York: G. P. Putnam & Co., 1853); and *Galignani's New Paris Guide for 1873* (New York: G. P. Putnam, 1873).

81. Tebbel, *A History of Book Publishing*, 288.

82. Willis P. Hazard, *The American Guide Book, Being a Hand-Book for Tourists and Travellers through Every Part of the United States . . . Part I. Northern and Eastern States and Canada* (Philadelphia: G. S. Appleton, 1846), v–vi.

83. "The Late George Appleton," *American Bookseller* 6, no. 2 (July 15, 1878): 76.

84. Willis P. Hazard, *Hazard's Cheap Book Store, No. 19 South Fifth Street, (East Side, First Door above Chesnut) Philadelphia, April 20th, 1849* (Philadelphia, 1849).

85. Ristow, *American Maps and Mapmakers*, 126; Kenneth Myers, *The Catskills: Painters, Writers, and Tourists in the Mountains, 1820–1895* (Yonkers, NY: Hudson River Museum of Westchester, 1987), 177.

86. Tebbel, *A History of Book Publishing in the United States*, 283–85.

87. Tebbel, *A History of Book Publishing in the United States*, 284–88.

88. T. Addison Richards, *Appleton's Illustrated Hand-Book of American Travel; A Full and Reliable Guide to the United States and the British Provinces* (New York: D. Appleton & Co., 1860), 10.

89. Susan Schulten, *The Geographical Imagination in America, 1880–1950* (Chicago: University of Chicago Press, 2001), 70, 94–99.

2 / Yesterday the Springs, To-day the Falls

1. E. Polk Johnson, *A History of Kentucky and Kentuckians; The Leaders and Representative Men in Commerce, Industry and Modern Activities,* vol. 3 (Chicago: Lewis, 1912), 1153; William Richardson, *Travel Diary of William Richardson from Boston to New Orleans by Land, 1815,* ed. William Bell Wait (New York, 1938), 19; William Richardson, *River, Road and Rail: William Richardson's Journey from Louisville to New York in 1844,* ed. William Bell Wait (New York: Valve Pilot Corporation, 1942). For more on Richardson's background, see Alfred Sereno Hudson, *The History of Sudbury, Massachusetts, 1638–1889* (Sudbury: Town of Sudbury, 1889), 449.

2. George Rogers Taylor, *The Transportation Revolution, 1815–1860* (New York: Rinehart, 1951), 132. More recently, scholars have harnessed Taylor's paradigm to produce valuable new insights into economic and political history (see, for example, John Majewski, *A House Dividing: Economic Development in Pennsylvania and Virginia before the Civil War* [New York: Cambridge University Press, 2000]; and John Lauritz Larson, *Internal Improvement: National Public Works and the Promise of Popular Government in the Early United States* [Chapel Hill: University of North Carolina Press, 2001]). For an overview of the historiography of the transportation revolution, see Carol Sheriff, *The Artificial River: The Erie Canal and the Paradox of Progress, 1817–1862* (New York: Hill and Wang, 1996), 223–25.

3. See Taylor, *Transportation Revolution,* 132, 58.

4. Only a handful of historians have dug more deeply into travelers' changing experiences during the first half of the nineteenth century. In the American context, see Sheriff, *The Artificial River*; and Lewis Perry, *Boats against the Current: American Culture between Revolution and Modernity, 1820–1860* (New York: Oxford University Press, 1993). In the European context, see Alan Trachtenberg, foreword to Wolfgang Schivelbusch, *The Railway Journey: The Industrialization of Time and Space in the 19th Century* (Berkeley: University of California Press, 1987); and Michael J. Freeman, *Railways and the Victorian Imagination* (New Haven: Yale University Press, 1999).

5. See Elizabeth Stordeur Pryor, *Colored Travelers: Mobility and the Fight for Citizenship before the Civil War* (Chapel Hill: University of North Carolina Press, 2016); John D. Cox, *Traveling South: Travel Narratives and the Construction of American Identity* (Athens: University of Georgia Press, 2005); Amy G. Richter, *Home on the Rails: Women, the Railroad, and the Rise of Public Domesticity* (Chapel Hill: University of North Carolina Press, 2005); and Patricia Cline Cohen, "Safety and Danger: Women on American Public Transport, 1750–1860," in *Gendered Domains: Rethinking Public and Private in Women's History,* ed. Dorothy O. Helly and Susan M. Reverby (Ithaca: Cornell University Press, 1992): 109–22.

6. Richardson, *Travel Diary of William Richardson,* ed. Wait, 4, 5, 9.

7. Richardson, *Travel Diary of William Richardson,* ed. Wait, 11.

8. Richardson, *Travel Diary of William Richardson,* ed. Wait, 12, 13.

9. Richardson, *Travel Diary of William Richardson,* ed. Wait, 6, 9.

10. William Richardson, *Journal from Boston to the Western Country and down the Ohio and Mississippi Rivers to New Orleans*, ed. William Bell Wait (New York: Valve Pilot Corporation, 1940), 9, 10

11. Richardson, *River, Road and Rail*, ed. Wait, 8.

12. According to William Wait, the editor of Richardson's manuscript, "'The Good Intent Line,' one of the stage lines [operating on the National Road between Wheeling and Cumberland], operated in conjunction with the Baltimore & Ohio Railroad and handled its passengers west of the terminus at Cumberland." It is unclear if the Richardsons took the Good Intent Line, but clearly stagecoach and railroad operations were closely coordinated over this heavily traveled route (see Wait, *River, Road and Rail*, 15; see also James D. Dilts, *Great Road: The Building of the Baltimore and Ohio, the Nation's First Railroad, 1828–1853* [Stanford: Stanford University Press, 1996], 292).

13. Richardson, *River, Road and Rail*, ed. Wait, 13, 15, 20.

14. Richardson, *Travel Diary of William Richardson*, ed. Wait, 19.

15. Richardson, *River, Road and Rail*, ed. Wait, 25. The Baltimore and Ohio company advertised "through tickets from Philadelphia to Wheeling" for thirteen dollars in 1849, which suggests that Richardson had purchased a similar ticket in 1844 (see *American Railroad Journal* 5, no. 20 [May 19, 1849]: 319).

16. See, for example, Richardson, *Travel Diary of William Richardson*, ed. Wait, 4.

17. John H. White, *Wet Britches and Muddy Boots: A History of Travel in Victorian America* (Bloomington: Indiana University Press, 2013), 23, 51.

18. White, *Wet Britches and Muddy Boots*, 490, 430.

19. See William Cronon, *Nature's Metropolis: Chicago and the Great West* (New York: Norton, 1992), 97–147; Stuart Thayer, *Traveling Showmen: The American Circus before the Civil War* (Detroit: Astley and Ricketts, 1997); and Gregory J. Renoff, *Big Tent: The Traveling Circus in Georgia, 1820–1930* (Athens: University of Georgia Press, 2012).

20. Thomas Loraine McKenney, *Sketches of a Tour to the Lakes, of the Character and Customs of the Chippeway Indians, and of Incidents Connected with the Treaty of Fond du Lac* (Baltimore: F. Lucas, 1827), 9–10.

21. McKenney, *Sketches of a Tour to the Lakes*, 14.

22. McKenney, *Sketches of a Tour to the Lakes*, 435–37. As Charles Sellers, Harry Watson, James Henretta, and others have argued, economic actors like McKenney frequently turned to older systems of economic regulation based on personal acquaintance and reputation, especially when market systems of regulation broke down (see Harry L. Watson, "The Market and Its Discontents," *Journal of the Early Republic* 12, no. 4 [Winter 1992]: 464–70; and James A. Henretta, "The 'Market' in the Early Republic," *Journal of the Early Republic* 18, no. 2 [Summer 1998]: 289–304).

23. McKenney, *Sketches of a Tour to the Lakes*, 116, 140.

24. McKenney, *Sketches of a Tour to the Lakes*, 218.

25. McKenney, *Sketches of a Tour to the Lakes*, 397.

26. John McCabe, *Grand Hotel, Mackinac Island* (Sault Ste. Marie: Unicorn, 1987).

27. John Sherman, *A Description of Trenton Falls, Oneida County, New York* (Utica, NY: William Williams, 1827), 3.

28. American Scenic and Historic Preservation Society, *Annual Report of the American Scenic and Historic Preservation Society to the Legislature of the State of New York* (Albany: J. B. Lyon, 1916), 302.

29. Joseph Story and William Wetmore Story, *Life and Letters of Joseph Story, Associate Justice of the Supreme Court of the United States, and Dane Professor of Law at Harvard University* (Boston: Little and Brown, 1851), 460. Story's exaggerated description was penned in a letter from Joseph Story to William Pettyplace, Esq., on July 10, 1825.

30. Nathaniel Parker Willis, *Trenton Falls, Picturesque and Descriptive; Embracing the Original Essay of John Sherman, the First Proprietor and Resident* (New York: G. P. Putnam, 1851), 10. Willis's promotional essay, encompassing Sherman's pamphlet, was republished in expanded editions for Moore, the proprietor of the hotel, by N. Orr & Co. of New York in 1865 and 1868.

31. Willis, *Trenton Falls, Picturesque and Descriptive*, 10.

32. "Mary Scollay Bigelow Diary, 1825: Voyage to Niagara Falls," Manuscript Collection, Ms. N-1841, Massachusetts Historical Society, Boston. The Massachusetts Historical Society's ABIGAIL online catalogue entry for this document notes that it was "probably kept by Mary Scollay Bigelow, 14 June–29 July 1825, while on a trip from Boston, Mass. to Niagara Falls, New York." There are actually two diaries in two different hands in this file, both recording the same trip, both of which are quoted here (see Massachusetts Historical Society, "ABIGAIL: MHS Online Catalog," balthazaar. masshist.org).

33. Theodore Dwight, *The Northern Traveller: Containing the Routes to Niagara, Quebec, and the Springs; With Descriptions of the Principal Scenes, and Useful Hints to Strangers* (New York: Wilder & Campbell, 1825), 31.

34. "Mary Scollay Bigelow Diary, 1825." The Bigelows' observation that the hotel was "unfinished" but kept by a "Gentleman" was echoed by Joseph Story, the Supreme Court justice who visited the falls in the same year. The falls "were brought into notoriety principally, by Mr. Sherman, formerly a clergyman in Connecticut, who had the misfortune to write a very sensible book against the Trinity, about twelve or fourteen years ago, and was compelled to quit his profession and his State," Story recorded. "He now resides near the Falls, and keeps a hotel there, which is as yet incomplete, but accommodates strangers pretty well for a few hours" (see Story, *Life and Letters of Joseph Story*, 461).

35. Gideon Davison, *The Fashionable Tour; An Excursion to the Springs, Niagara, Quebec, and through the New-England States: Interspersed with Geographical and Historical Sketches* (Saratoga Springs: G. M. Davison, 1828), 131.

36. John Disturnell, *The Travellers' Guide through the State of New-York, Canada, &c.: Embracing a General Description of the City of New-York, the Hudson River Guide and the Fashionable Tour to the Springs and Niagara Falls: With Steam-boat, Railroad and Stage Routes, Accompanied by Correct Maps* (New York: J. Disturnell, 1836), 47. Essentially the same guidebook was published in Britain under the title of *The Stranger's Guide through the United States and Canada: With Maps* (Edinburgh: J. Sutherland, 1838). Thus geographical knowledge about how to get to Trenton Falls was available to buyer in marketplaces both near and far.

37. C. D. Arfwedson, *The United States and Canada, in 1832, 1833, and 1834*, vol. 2 (London: R. Bentley, 1834), 292.

38. James Silk Buckingham, *America, Historical, Statistic, and Descriptive* (New York: Harper and Bros., 1841), 259. Other travelers agreed that the road was bad but the scenery was delightful (see, for example, Frances Milton Trollope, *Domestic Manners*

of the Americans [London: Whittaker, Treacher, 1832], 297; Eliza R. Steele, *A Summer Journey in the West* [New York: J. S. Taylor and Co., 1841], 32; and Robert Playfair, *Recollections of a Visit to the United States and British Provinces of North America, in the Years 1847, 1848, and 1849* [Edinburgh: T. Constable & Co., 1856], 49–50).

39. Taylor, *Transportation Revolution*, 29–31.

40. Willis's 1851 *Trenton Falls, Picturesque and Descriptive* merely mentions that "a plank road has been laid from Utica hither, over which travel is about two hours," without mentioning precisely when it was constructed. However, Charlotte Pitcher, in her 1915 popular history of Trenton Falls, fixes the date of its construction as 1851, which means it must have been being finished when Willis penned his description (see Willis, *Trenton Falls* [1851], 12; and Charlotte A. Pitcher, *The Golden Era of Trenton Falls* [Utica: C. A. Pitcher, 1915], 23).

41. From Newman Hall, "Notes of Travel in America," cited in Pitcher, *Golden Era*, 94.

42. Willis, *Trenton Falls* (1851), 12.

43. Henry V. Poor, *History of the Railroads and Canals of the United States* (New York: J. H. Schultz & Co., 1860), 236.

44. Nathaniel Parker Willis, *Trenton Falls, Picturesque and Descriptive* (New York: N. Orr & Co., 1865), 12.

45. *The All-Round Route Guide: The Hudson River, Trenton Falls, Niagara, Toronto, the Thousand Islands and the River St. Lawrence, Ottawa, Montreal, Quebec, the Lower St. Lawrence and the Saguenay Rivers, the White Mountains, Ortland, Boston, New York* (Montreal: Montreal Printing and Publishing Company, 1869), 27.

46. Willis, *Trenton Falls* (1865), 85–86.

47. "Henrietta M. Goddard Diary, 1830," Manuscripts Collection, Ms. N-114 Box 17, Massachusetts Historical Society, Boston.

48. For example, upon arriving in Schenectady, Goddard recorded that "we were again beset by the drivers + proprietors of old line + new line stages + boats, we made our selection of the pioneer line canal boat + went quietly below finding it would be an hour before we left, as the passengers take dinner here, we thought we would take a walk + see the town." This local act of "selection," which required the Goddard party to employ their own geographical knowledge as well as their own judgment of the character of the various travel purveyors, was improvisational in its nature (see "Henrietta M. Goddard Diary, 1830").

49. Poor, *History of the Railroads and Canals of the United States*, 219–20.

50. Willis, *Trenton Falls* (1851), 61, 54.

51. "A Letter from the Falls," *Ladies' Repository* 25, no. 5 (November 1856): 164–68, 164.

52. Mrs. N. T. Munroe, "Days of Exodus, No. III," *Ladies' Repository* 37, no. 12 (December 1867): 411–17, 411.

53. Munroe, "Days of Exodus," 413. The guidebook to which she referred in Utica was likely the second edition of Willis's *Trenton Falls, Picturesque and Descriptive*, because the description of Utica as "flourishing" and "the great thoroughfare of this region" was taken verbatim from Sherman's 1827 *Description of Trenton Falls*, which Willis reproduced in its entirety.

54. Munroe, "Days of Exodus," 413.

55. "The Coblou Cataract," *Southern Literary Messenger* 16, no. 7 (July 1850): 439–40, 439. The turnpike to which the author referred was most likely the Lexington and

Richmond Turnpike, which ran east from Lexington, Virginia, through White's Gap in the Blue Ridge Mountains, and the Coblou Cataract itself was likely on the western edge of Amherst County (see Oren Frederic Morton, *A History of Rockbridge County, Virginia* [Staunton, VA: McClure, 1920], 164).

56. Wellington Williams, *Appleton's Northern and Eastern Traveller's Guide: With New and Authentic Maps, Illustrating those Divisions of the Country. Forming, Likewise, A Complete Guide to the Middle States, Canada, New Brunswick, and Nova Scotia . . . Illustrated with Numerous Maps and Plans of Cities, Engraved on Steel, and Several Wood Engravings* (New York: D. Appleton & Company, 1850), 3–4, 5.

3 / I Find Myself a Pilgrim

1. John Tebbel, *A History of Book Publishing in the United States*, vol. 1, *The Creation of an Industry, 1630–1865* (New York: Bowker, 1972), 352.

2. *Our Summer Retreats: A Handbook to All the Chief Waterfalls, Springs, Mountain and Sea Side Resorts: and Other Places of Interest in the United States: with Views Taken from Sketches by Washington Friend, Esq., and from Photographs* (New York: T. Nelson & Sons, 1859).

3. *Our Summer Retreats*, 32. This quotation gets used frequently by scholars of early American tourism because it elegantly captures the regimented energy of the Saratoga social season as it was entering its heyday (see, for example, Thomas A. Chambers, *Drinking the Waters: Creating an American Leisure Class at Nineteenth-Century Mineral Springs* [Washington, DC: Smithsonian Institution Press, 2002], 88; Jon Sterngass, *First Resorts: Pursuing Pleasure at Saratoga Springs, Newport, and Coney Island* [Baltimore: Johns Hopkins University Press, 2001], 37; and Tammis Kane Groft et al., *Hudson River Panorama: A Passage through Time* [Albany: State University of New York Press, 2009], 105). The same phrase was borrowed by other contemporary authors as well (see, for example, *The Report of the New York State Cheese Manufacturers' Association* [Utica, NY, 1864], 152).

4. *Our Summer Retreats*, 14, 20, 50, 46.

5. Pierre Bourdieu, "The Forms of Capital," in *Handbook of Theory and Research for the Sociology of Education*, ed. John G. Richardson (New York: Greenwood, 1986), 241–58.

6. See Theodore Corbett, *The Making of American Resorts: Saratoga Springs, Ballston Spa, Lake George* (New Brunswick: Rutgers University Press, 2001), 27–39; and Richard H. Gassan, *The Birth of American Tourism: New York, the Hudson Valley, and American Culture, 1790–1830* (Amherst: University of Massachusetts Press, 2008), 9–33.

7. See Carl Robert Keyes, "A Revolution in Advertising: 'Buy American' Campaigns in the Late Eighteenth Century," in *We Are What We Sell: How Advertising Shapes American Life . . . and Always Has*, ed. Danielle Sarver Coombs and Bob Batchelor (Santa Barbara: Praeger, 2014), 1–25; and T. H. Breen, "'Baubles of Britain': The American and Consumer Revolutions of the Eighteenth Century," *Past & Present* 119, no. 1 (1988): 73–104.

8. "Miscellany: Ballston or Milton Springs," *Port Folio* 2, no. 43 (October 30, 1802): 340.

9. See Oliver W. Holmes and Peter T. Rohrbach, *Stagecoach East: Stagecoach Days in the East from the Colonial Period to the Civil War* (Washington, DC: Smithsonian

Institution Press, 1983); Andrew K. Sandoval-Strausz, *Hotel: An American History* (New Haven: Yale University Press, 2007); and Kym Rice, *Early American Taverns: For the Entertainment of Friends and Strangers* (Chicago: Regnery Gateway, 1983).

10. Alice Morse Earle, *Stage-Coach and Tavern Days* (New York: Macmillan, 1900), 236.

11. *Virginia Gazette*, Purdie and Dixon, October 3, 1771, 3. Library of Virginia, Richmond. From www.lva.virginia.gov.

12. Carl Bridenbaugh, "Baths and Watering Places of Colonial America," *William and Mary Quarterly* 3, no. 2 (April 1946): 151–81, 160–64. See also Charlene M. Boyer Lewis, *Ladies and Gentlemen on Display Planter Society at the Virginia Springs, 1790–1860* (Charlottesville: University Press of Virginia, 2001), 13–56.

13. Gideon M. Davison, *The Fashionable Tour, in 1825: An Excursion to the Springs, Niagara, Quebec and Boston* (Saratoga Springs: G. M. Davison, 1825), 71.

14. Theodore Dwight, *The Northern Traveller: Containing the Routes to Niagara, Quebec, and the Springs* (New York: A. T. Goodrich, 1826), 38. See also Roland Van Zandt, *The Catskill Mountain House* (New Brunswick: Rutgers University Press, 1966).

15. William Edmonds Horner, *Observations on the Mineral Waters in the South Western Part of Virginia: In a Series of Letters* (Philadelphia: J. Thompson, 1834), 25, 19.

16. Dwight, *The Northern Traveller*, 249.

17. John Disturnell, *Springs, Water-Falls, Sea-Bathing Resorts, and Mountain Scenery of the United States and Canada* (New York: J. Disturnell, 1855), 87.

18. Nathaniel Parker Willis, *Trenton Falls, Picturesque and Descriptive; Embracing the Original Essay of John Sherman, the First Proprietor and Resident* (New York: G. P. Putnam, 1851), 61–62.

19. See Thomas N. Baker, *Sentiment and Celebrity: Nathaniel Parker Willis and the Trials of Literary Fame* (New York: Oxford University Press, 2001).

20. Disturnell, *Springs, Water-Falls, Sea-Bathing Resorts, and Mountain Scenery*, iii, 163.

21. J. J. Moorman and W. W. Dawson, *The Ohio White Sulphur Springs* (Cincinnati: Moore, Wilstach, Keys & Co., 1859), 21. See also Disturnell, *Springs, Water-Falls, Sea-Bathing Resorts, and Mountain Scenery*, 163.

22. Disturnell, *Springs, Water-Falls, Sea-Bathing Resorts, and Mountain Scenery*, 168.

23. J. J. Moorman, *The Virginia Springs, and Springs of the South and West* (Philadelphia: J. B. Lippincott & Co., 1859), 384. See also Margaret Brown Coppinger, *Beersheba Springs: 150 Years, 1833–1983: A History and a Celebration* (Beersheba Springs, TN: Beersheba Springs Historical Society, 1983), 4–5.

24. Moorman, *The Virginia Springs, and Springs of the South and West*, 383.

25. Willis, *Trenton Falls, Picturesque and Descriptive*, 15.

26. See James Buzard, *The Beaten Track: European Tourism, Literature, and the Ways to "Culture," 1800–1918* (New York: Oxford University Press, 1993); Malcolm Andrews, *The Search for the Picturesque: Landscape Aesthetics and Tourism in Britain, 1760–1800* (Stanford: Stanford University Press, 1989); Angela L. Miller, *The Empire of the Eye: Landscape Representation and American Cultural Politics, 1825–1875* (Ithaca: Cornell University Press, 1993); Beth L. Lueck, *American Writers on the Picturesque Tour* (New York: Garland, 1997); and Richard Gassan, *The Birth of American Tourism:*

New York, the Hudson Valley, and American Culture, 1790–1830 (Amherst: University of Massachusetts Press, 2008). For more on the relationship between taste, refinement, and cultural status in the early national period, see Richard L. Bushman, *The Refinement of America: Persons, Houses, Cities* (New York: Knopf, 1992); and Catherine E. Kelly, *Republic of Taste: Art, Politics, and Everyday Life in Early America* (Philadelphia: University of Pennsylvania Press, 2016).

27. Burke's concepts of sublime and beautiful were key in bringing the philosophy of aesthetics into the era of the Enlightenment (see Edmund Burke, *A Philosophical Enquiry into the Origin of Our Ideas of the Sublime and the Beautiful* [London: J. Dodsley, 1787]; and Koen Vermeir and Michael Funk Deckard, eds., *The Science of Sensibility: Reading Burke's Philosophical Enquiry* [New York: Springer, 2012]). By contrast, William Gilpin was generally less succinct and less precise in theorizing the picturesque; he defined it in multiple contexts and in various ways (see, for example, William Gilpin, *Remarks on Forest Scenery, and Other Woodland Views [Relative Chiefly to Picturesque Beauty]* [London: R. Blamire, 1791]; and William Gilpin, *Three Essays: on Picturesque Beauty; on Picturesque Travel; and on Sketching Landscape; To Which is Added a Poem, on Landscape Painting* [London: R. Blamire, 1792]). For more on the picturesque in the context of eighteenth-century British aesthetic theory, see Walter John Hipple Jr., *The Beautiful, the Sublime, and the Picturesque in Eighteenth-Century British Aesthetic Theory* (Carbondale: Southern Illinois University Press, 1957); Carl Paul Barbier, *William Gilpin, His Drawings, Teaching, and Theory of the Picturesque* (Oxford: Clarendon, 1963); and Andrew Ballantyne, *Architecture, Landscape and Liberty: Richard Payne Knight and the Picturesque* (Cambridge: Cambridge University Press, 1997).

28. John H. Spaulding, *Historical Relics of the White Mountains; Also, A Concise White Mountain Guide* (Mt. Washington, NH: J. R. Hitchcock, 1858), 75–76.

29. Wellington Williams, *The Traveller's and Tourist's Guide through the United States of America, Canada, Etc.* (Philadelphia: Lippincott, Grambo & Co., 1851), 194.

30. Ezra Sampson, *The Youth's Companion; Or, An Historical Dictionary; Consisting of Articles Selected Chiefly from Natural and Civil History, Geography, Astronomy, Zoology, Botany and Mineralogy; Arranged in Alphabetical Order* (Hudson, NY: Printed for the author, 1807), 292.

31. Davison, *The Fashionable Tour, in 1825*, 121–22.

32. Robert J. Vandewater, *The Tourist, or Pocket Manual for Travellers on the Hudson River, the Western Canal and Stage Road to Niagara Falls down Lake Ontario and the St. Lawrence to Montreal and Quebec: Comprising Also the Routes to Lebanon, Ballston, and Saratoga Springs* (New York: Harper & Brothers, 1836), 70; Samuel De Veaux, *The Falls of Niagara, Or Tourist's Guide to This Wonder of Nature, Including Notices of the Whirlpool, Islands, &C, and a Complete Guide Thro' the Canadas* (Buffalo: W. B. Hayden, 1839), 66.

33. Frederick H. Johnson, *A Guide for Every Visitor to Niagara Falls, Including the Sources of Niagara, and All Places of Interest, Both on the American and Canada Side* (Buffalo: Phinney & Co., 1852), 39.

34. Orasmus Turner, *Pioneer History of the Holland Purchase of Western New York: Embracing Some Account of the Ancient Remains . . . and a History of Pioneer Settlement Under the Auspices of the Holland Company; Including Reminiscences of the War of 1812; the Origin, Progress and Completion of the Erie Canal, Etc., Etc., Etc.* (Buffalo: Jewett, Thomas & Co., 1849), 559–60.

35. See, for example, De Veaux, *Falls of Niagara*, 168.

36. William B. Peck and Charles E. Peck, *Peck's Tourist's Companion to Niagara Falls, Saratoga Springs, the Lakes, Canada, Etc.: Containing, in Addition to Full Directions for Visiting the Cataract and Vicinity, the Springs, Etc., Full Tables of Routes and Distances from Niagara Falls to the Principal Places in the United States and Canada* (Buffalo: William B. & Charles E. Peck, 1845), 11–12

37. W. E. Tunis, *Tunis's Topographical and Pictorial Guide to Niagara: Containing, Also, a Description of the Route through Canada, and the Great Northern Route, from Niagara Falls to Montreal, Boston, and Saratoga Springs: Also, Full and Accurate Tables of Distances on All Railroads Running to and from Niagara Falls* (Niagara Falls: W. E. Tunis, 1856), 140.

38. Professor Larrabee, "Miscellania," *Ladies' Repository* 9, no. 4 (April 1849): 105–8, 106.

39. "Pleasant Summer Resorts," *Frank Leslie's Illustrated Newspaper* 8, no. 189 (July 16, 1859): 107.

40. *Harper's Weekly: A Journal of Civilization* 2, no. 79 (July 3, 1858): 431.

41. Edward L. Blanchard, *Heads and Tales of Travellers & Travelling: A Book for Everybody, Going Anywhere* (New York: D. Appleton & Co., 1847), 16

42. "Peregrine Prolix" [Philip Houlbrooke Nicklin], "Letters on Pennsylvania," *Southern Literary Messenger* 2, no. 7 (June 1836): 445.

43. "Peregrine Prolix" [Philip Houlbrooke Nicklin], *Letters Descriptive of the Virginia Springs: The Roads Leading Thereto, and the Doings Thereat* (Philadelphia: H. S. Tanner, 1835), 29–30.

44. "Peregrine Prolix" [Philip Houlbrooke Nicklin], *A Pleasant Peregrination through the Prettiest Parts of Pennsylvania* (Philadelphia: Grigg and Elliott, 1836), 72. Nicklin drew his impressions of Langenschwalbach from Francis B. Head, *Bubbles from the Brunnens of Nassau* (Paris: Baudry's European Library, 1834).

45. Nicklin, *Letters Descriptive of the Virginia Springs*, 36–37.

46. Nicklin, *A Pleasant Peregrination*, 81.

47. Nicklin, *Letters Descriptive of the Virginia Springs*, iii, 51–52, 56.

48. "A New Englander" [pseud.], "Journal of a Trip to the Mountains, Caves and Springs of Virginia," *Southern Literary Messenger* 4, no. 3 (March 1838): 200.

49. "A New Englander" [pseud.], "Journal of a Trip to the Mountains, Caves and Springs of Virginia," *Southern Literary Messenger* 4, no. 5 (May 1838): 306.

50. "Sulphur Springs of New York," *Harper's New Monthly Magazine* 13, no. 73 (June 1856): 3.

51. See Beth Lynne Lueck, *American Writers and the Picturesque Tour: The Search for National Identity, 1790–1860* (New York: Garland, 1997).

52. William Parker Foulke to Eleanor Foulke, dated Harrisburg, February 22, 1848, "William Parker Foulke Papers," American Philosophical Society, Philadelphia.

53. Gideon M. Davison, *The Fashionable Tour, in 1825: An Excursion to the Springs, Niagara, Quebec and Boston* (Saratoga Springs: G. M. Davison, 1825), 121–22.

54. Henry D. Gilpin, *A Northern Tour: Being a Guide to Saratoga, Lake George, Niagara, Canada, Boston, &c. &c., Through the States of Pennsylvania, New-Jersey, New-York, Vermont, New-Hampshire, Massachusetts, Rhode-Island, and Connecticut; Embracing an Account of the Canals, Colleges, Public Institutions, Natural Curiosities, and Interesting Objects Therein* (Philadelphia: H. C. Carey & I. Lea, 1825), 147–48.

55. "Charles Stoddard Travel Diary," Manuscript Collection, Ms. N-973, Massachusetts Historical Society, Boston.

56. "Mary Scollay Bigelow Diary, 1825: Voyage to Niagara Falls," Manuscript Collection, Ms. N-1841, Massachusetts Historical Society, Boston.

57. Michael Jenks, *Notes on a Tour through the Western Part of the State of New York* (Rochester: G. P. Humphrey, 1916), 37. For more on the history and attribution of Jenks's narrative, see K. Kabelac, "The 'Unknown Writer': Authorship of 'A Traveler's View of New York State in 1829' Revealed," *York State Tradition* 22, no. 4 (Fall 1968): 20–23.

58. Theodore Dwight, *The Northern Traveller: Containing the Routes to Niagara, Quebec, and the Springs; With Descriptions of the Principal Scenes, and Useful Hints to Strangers* (New York: Wilder & Campbell, 1825), 84.

59. Willis P. Hazard, *The American Guide Book; Being a Hand-book for Tourists and Travellers through Every Part of the United States* (Philadelphia: G. S. Appleton, 1846), 156, 147. For other examples, see Vandewater, *The Tourist*, 55–60; John Disturnell, *The Travellers' Guide through the State of New-York, Canada, &c.: Embracing a General Description of the City of New-York, the Hudson River Guide and the Fashionable Tour to the Springs and Niagara Falls: with Steam-boat, Rail-road and Stage Routes, Accompanied by Correct Maps* (New York: J. Disturnell, 1836), 54–56; and Henry Schenck Tanner, *The American Traveller; Or Guide through the United States: Containing Brief Notices of the Several States, Cities, Principal Towns, Canals and Rail Roads, &c.* (Philadelphia: Published by the author, 1837), 87.

60. John Alonzo Clark, *Gleanings by the Way* (Philadelphia: W. J. & J. K. Simon, 1842), 149–50.

61. Elizabeth Fries Ellet, *Rambles about the Country* (Boston: Marsh, Capen, Lyon, and Webb, 1840), 255–56.

62. Nicklin, *Letters Descriptive of the Virginia Springs*, 79–80.

63. Ellet, *Rambles about the Country*, 188.

64. Mary Kelley, *Private Woman, Public Stage: Literary Domesticity in Nineteenth-Century America* (New York: Oxford University Press, 1984), 12–13.

65. "Mary Scollay Bigelow Diary, 1825."

66. Catharine Maria Sedgwick, *A New-England Tale; Or, Sketches of New-England Character and Manners* (New York: E. Bliss & E. White, 1822), 48.

67. "Mary Scollay Bigelow Diary, 1825."

68. John F. Sears, *Sacred Places: American Tourist Attractions in the Nineteenth Century* (New York: Oxford University Press, 1989), 10. For a similar argument in a different context, see Suzanne K. Kaufman, *Consuming Visions: Mass Culture and the Lourdes Shrine* (Ithaca: Cornell University Press, 2005). For a more theoretical discussion of the relationship between tourism and pilgrimage, see J. B. Allcock, "Tourism as a Sacred Journey," *Loisir et Société* 11, no. 1 (Spring 1988): 33–48.

69. Charles Fenno Hoffman, *A Winter in the West, By a New Yorker*, vol. 2 (New York: Harper & Bros., 1835), 309, 312.

70. Charles Fenno Hoffman, *A Winter in the West, By a New Yorker*, vol. 1 (New York: Harper & Bros., 1835), 141–42.

71. Frederick Hall, *Letters from the East and from the West* (Washington City: F. Taylor and Wm. M. Morrison, 1840), 39–40.

72. Louis Tasistro, *Random Shots and Southern Breezes*, vol. 2 (New York: Harper & Brothers, 1842), 101.

73. Featherstonhaugh, *Excursion through the Slave States*, 15.

74. Featherstonhaugh, *Excursion through the Slave States*, 13.

75. Featherstonhaugh, *Excursion through the Slave States*, 16.

76. Featherstonhaugh, *Excursion through the Slave States*, 16.

4 / I'll Picturesque It Everywhere

1. See William Dean Howells, *My Mark Twain: Reminiscences and Criticisms* (New York: Harper and Brothers, 1910), 107–12; Larzer Ziff, *Return Passages: Great American Travel Writing, 1780–1910* (New Haven: Yale University Press, 2000); and Jeffrey Alan Melton, *Mark Twain, Travel Books, and Tourism: The Tide of a Great Popular Movement* (Tuscaloosa: University of Alabama Press, 2002), 1–2.

2. Edward L. Blanchard, *Heads and Tales of Travellers & Travelling: A Book for Everybody, Going Anywhere* (New York: D. Appleton & Co., 1847), 15–16.

3. Robert A. Gross and Mary Kelley, eds., *An Extensive Republic: Print, Culture, and Society in the New Nation, 1790–1840* (Chapel Hill: University of North Carolina Press, 2010).

4. James Buzard, *The Beaten Track: European Tourism, Literature, and the Ways to Culture, 1800–1918* (New York: Oxford University Press, 1993).

5. Washington Irving et al., *Salmagundi; Or, The Whim-Whams and Opinions of Launcelot Langstaff, Esq. and Others* (New York: D. Longworth, 1807–8), 60.

6. *Salmagundi* made quite a splash when it appeared in 1807; after its initial publication, it was reissued in almost annual editions through the 1820s, and survived in frequent print in both the United States and Europe through the rest of the nineteenth century. It was originally published serially by David Longworth in 1807, and he reprinted it annually until 1810, and then again three more times through 1820. It remained in print sporadically in the United States for the rest of the early republic, through editions from the big industrial publishing firms of Harper & Brothers and G. P. Putnam in New York and Lippincott in Philadelphia. It was also a steady seller in Europe; after its first London edition in 1811, it went through eleven additional London editions through 1850, as well as multiple editions in Glasgow and Paris.

7. Irving, *Salmagundi*, 60, 58.

8. See Malcolm Andrews, *The Search for the Picturesque: Landscape Aesthetics and Tourism in Britain, 1760–1800* (Stanford: Stanford University Press, 1989).

9. The travel narrators cited by Irving were all British, and many of them wrote about their travels in the United States in the 1790s. These travelers included Isaac Weld, who wrote *Travels through the States of North America, and the Provinces of Upper and Lower Canada, during the Years 1795, 1796, and 1797* (London: John Stockdale, 1800); Richard Parkinson, who wrote *A Tour in America in 1798, 1799, and 1800: Exhibiting Sketches of Society and Manners, and a Particular Account of the America System of Agriculture, with Its Recent Improvements* (London: J. Harding and J. Murray, 1805); and William Priest, who wrote *Travels in the United States of America: Commencing in the Year 1793 and Ending in 1797: with the Author's Journals of His Two Voyages across the Atlantic* (London: J. Johnson, 1802). He also cited British travelers to the British isles and continental Europe to support his flippant truisms such as "a knowing traveller always judges of every thing by the inn-keepers and waiters," including John Carr, who wrote *The Stranger in Ireland; Or, A Tour in the Southern and Western Parts of That Country, in the Year 1805* (London: R. Phillips,

1806); August von Kotzebue, who wrote *Travels through Italy, in the Years 1804 and 1805* (London: Richard Phillips, 1806); and John Moore, who wrote a number of narratives of European travel. Finally, Irving made up a number of authoritative travelers with ridiculous names, such as "Linkum Fidelius" and "Messrs. Tag, Rag, and Bobtail" (see Irving, *Salmagundi*, 61–67, quotation on 62). For more on Irving's Cockloft and satire of British travel narratives, see Joseph Rezek, "Tales from Elsewhere: Fiction at a Proximate Distance in the Anglophone Atlantic, 1800–1850" (Ph.D. diss., University of California at Los Angeles, 2009).

10. Irving, *Salmagundi*, 66.

11. William Priest, *Travels in the United States of America* (Whitefish, MT: Kessinger, 2004), 20.

12. Joachim Heyward Siddons, *Travel, Its Pleasures, Advantages, and Requirements: A Lecture by J. H. Siddons, Delivered at Clinton Hall, New York, February, 1860* (New York: H. H. Lloyd & Co., 1860), 284–86.

13. *American Star* (Petersburg, VA) 1, no. 30 (September 16, 1817), 3.

14. *The Tour of Dr. Syntax* was first published in the United States in Philadelphia by William Charles in 1814. This edition, entitled the "first American from the second London edition," was reissued by the same publisher in 1817. In the 1820s, *The Tour of Dr. Syntax* went through three further editions in Philadelphia, one from Carey and Lea in 1822 and two from John Clark in 1822 and 1829. It then spent a couple of decades out of print in the United States, until it was revived in Philadelphia by J. B. Perry in 1855. John Campbell, also in Philadelphia, released another edition in 1865, and J. Miller in New York published another in 1870s. This schedule of editions suggests that after an initial burst of interest in the 1810s and 1820s, it was a slow but steady seller through the middle part of the century. In addition to appearing as a monograph, *The Tour of Dr. Syntax* was excerpted in newspapers following its initial American edition, such as the *American* (Hanover, NH) 2, no. 5 (March 5, 1817): 4. These editions, as well as almost annual London editions, remained widely advertised throughout the first half of the nineteenth century by booksellers in cities throughout the United States, including Philadelphia, Boston, New York, Charleston, New Orleans, and San Francisco.

15. D. R. Hirschberg, "The Government and Church Patronage in England, 1660–1760," *Journal of British Studies* 20, no. 1 (Autumn 1980): 109–39.

16. William Combe, *The Tour of Doctor Syntax in Search of the Picturesque* (London: Ackerman and Co., 1838), 2, 6–7.

17. Combe, *Tour of Doctor Syntax* (1838), 142, 93, 96

18. Combe, *Tour of Doctor Syntax* (1838), 142, 13–14.

19. William Gilpin to William Mason, February 12, 1785, qtd. in Carl Paul Barbier, *William Gilpin, His Drawings, Teaching, and Theory of the Picturesque* (Oxford: Clarendon, 1963), 72.

20. Paul Erickson, "New Books, New Men: City-Mysteries Fiction, Authorship, and the Literary Market," *Early American Studies: An Interdisciplinary Journal* 1, no. 1 (Spring 2003): 273–312.

21. See Joe Eaton, *The Anglo-American Paper War: Debates About the New Republic, 1800–1825* (New York: Palgrave Macmillan, 2012); and Frank Lauterbach, "British Travel Writing about the Americas, 1820–1840: Different and Differentiating Views," *CLCWeb: Comparative Literature and Culture* 3, no. 2 (2001): dx.doi.org/10.7771/1481-4374.1119.

22. See "Art. III.—*Memorable Days in America, Being a Journal of a Tour to the United States, Principally Undertaken to Ascertain, by Positive Evidence, the Condition and Probable Prospects of British Emigrants; Including Accounts of Mr. Birkbeck's Settlement in the Illinois. By W. Faux, an English Farmer. 1823,*" *Quarterly Review* 58 (July 1823) (London: John Murray, 1823): 338–70, 339, 347. The book the review treated was William Faux, *Memorable Days in America: Being a Journal of a Tour to the United States, Principally Undertaken to Ascertain, by Positive Evidence, the Condition and Probable Prospects of British Emigrants; Including Accounts of Mr. Birkbeck's Settlement in the Illinois* (London: W. Simpkin and R. Marshall, 1823).

23. See "Art. III.—*Memorable Days in America, Being a Journal of a Tour to the United States, Principally Undertaken to Ascertain, by Positive Evidence, the Condition and Probable Prospects of British Emigrants; Including Accounts of Mr. Birkbeck's Settlement in the Illinois. By W. Faux, an English Farmer. 1823,*" *Quarterly Review* 58 (July 1823) (Boston: Wells and Lilly, 1824): 338–39, 339.

24. James Kirk Paulding, *John Bull in America, Or, The New Munchausen* (New York: Charles Wiley, 1825), ix.

25. In 1813, Paulding published "The Lay of the Scottish Fiddle," a parody of Walter Scott's "Lay of the Last Minstrel," which was roundly criticized in the *Quarterly Review*. This rebuff, following as it did on the heels of Paulding's most successful work, *The Diverting History of John Bull and Brother Jonathan*, suggests that Paulding had an axe to grind with the *Quarterly Review*. This sense of grievance did not translate into strong sales; after simultaneous 1825 editions in New York and London, *John Bull in America* was not reprinted before the Civil War (see James Grant Wilson and John Fiske, *Appletons' Cyclopædia of American Biography* [New York: D. Appleton & Co., 1898], 680–81; and William B. Cairns, "British Republication of American Writings, 1783–1833," *PMLA* 43, no. 1 [March 1928]: 303–10).

26. Paulding, *John Bull in America*, 3, 13, 24, 174, 12.

27. Marryat was a popular writer in Britain, and his seafaring tales were widely excerpted by American editors, especially in port towns like Salem and Charleston. The *Metropolitan Magazine* was edited by Marryat himself and was published in London by Saunders and Otley throughout the 1830s and 1840s. Although a British publication, it was widely available for sale at booksellers around the United States and was also widely excerpted by American editors. "How to Write a Book of Travels" was later collected with a number of Marryat's other short works in a volume entitled *Olla Podrida*, published in 1840, which seems to have had little circulation in the United States. For more on Captain Marryat, see Tom Pocock, *Captain Marryat: Seaman, Writer and Adventurer* (Mechanicsburg, PA: Stackpole, 2000).

28. Frederick Marryat, "How to Write a Book of Travels," in *Olla Podrida*, vol. 3 (London: Longman, Orme, Brown, Green, & Longmans, 1840), 213, 216, 218. See also Jeffrey Alan Melton, *Mark Twain, Travel Books, and Tourism: The Tide of a Great Popular Movement* (Tuscaloosa: University of Alabama Press, 2002), 23.

29. Marryat, "How to Write a Book of Travels," 219, 233.

30. Marryat, "How to Write a Book of Travels," 231.

31. For more on Asa Greene, see Steven H. Gale, ed., *Encyclopedia of American Humorists* (New York: Garland, 1988), 181–86.

32. Although the publication of *Travels in America* was enough of a phenomenon to have inspired reviews in the "Literary Notices" sections of magazines, the book

must not have sold well, because it only lasted in print for one edition. See, for example "Travels in America, by George Fibbleton, Esq. Ex-Barber to His Majesty, the King of Great Britain," *New-England Magazine* 5 (December 1833): 516–17; and "List of New Books for October 1833," *American Monthly Review* 4, no. 5 (November 1833): 427.

33. Asa Greene, *Travels in America, by George Fibbleton, Esq., Ex-Barber to His Majesty, the King of Great Britain* (New York: William Pearson, 1833), 9–10.

34. Frederick William Shelton, *The Trollopiad, Or, Travelling Gentlemen in America: A Satire* (New York: C. Shepard, 1837), xi.

35. "Travels in America, by George Fibbleton, Esq. Ex-Barber to His Majesty, the King of Great Britain," 427.

36. See chapter 2 for an in-depth discussion of the scientific analysis of the waters in antebellum guidebooks treating Saratoga Springs.

37. Greene, *Travels in America*, 172–74.

38. The *De Witt Clinton*, built in Albany in 1828, had twice been enlarged by 1833. At her largest, she was 233 feet long, 28 feet wide at the waterline, and drew 4 feet 6 inches of water fully loaded. Although she "was one of the leading early Hudson River steamboats," Greene clearly intended Fibbleton's account of her to be a gross exaggeration (Samuel Ward Stanton, *American Steam Vessels* [New York: Smith & Stanton, 1895], 37).

39. Greene, *Travels in America*, 121, 146–47.

40. Greene, *Travels in America*, 94, 184. The British travel narratives cited by Fibbleton include Thomas Ashe's *Travels in America Performed in 1806, For the Purpose of Exploring the Rivers Alleghany, Monongahela, Ohio, and Mississippi, and Ascertaining the Produce and Condition of Their Banks and Vicinity* (London: R. Phillips, 1808); Henry Bradshaw Fearon's *Sketches of America: A Narrative of a Journey of Five Thousand Miles through the Eastern and Western States of America* (London: Longman, 1818); Basil Hall's *Travels in North America in the Years 1827 and 1828* (Edinburgh: Cadell and Co., 1829); Frances Milton Trollope's *Domestic Manners of the Americans* (London: Whittaker, Treacher, & Co., 1832); and Rev. Isaac Fidler's *Observations on Professions, Literature, Manners, and Emigration in the United States and Canada, made during a Residence there in 1832* (London: Whittaker, Treacher, and Co., 1833).

41. Greene, *Travels in America*, 125, 129.

42. Although both volumes contain aspects of both travel narratives and of satire, neither contains the precise events that Greene claims that they do (see Paulding, *John Bull in America*; and James Kirke Paulding, *The Dutchman's Fireside: A Tale; in Two Volumes* [1831; New York: Harper, 1837]).

43. Carolyn S. Brown, *The Tall Tale in American Folklore and Literature* (Knoxville: University of Tennessee Press, 1987).

44. Henry B. Wonham, "In the Name of Wonder: The Emergence of Tall Narrative in American Writing," *American Quarterly* 41, no. 2 (June 1989): 284–307, 288.

45. Wonham, "In the Name of Wonder," 297–98.

46. Henry B. Wonham, *Mark Twain and the Art of the Tall Tale* (New York: Oxford University Press, 1993), 41.

47. See David C. Estes, "Revising Southern Humor: William Tappan Thompson and the Major Jones Letters," in *The Humor of the Old South*, ed. M. Thomas Inge and Edward J. Piacentino (Lexington: University Press of Kentucky, 2001): 154–60; and Hennig Cohen and William B. Dillingham, eds., *Humor of the Old Southwest* (Athens: University of Georgia Press, 1994), 152–53.

48. See, for example, Johnson Jones Hooper, *Simon Suggs' Adventures and Travels. Comprising All the Scenes, Incidents and Adventures of His Travels, in a Series of Sketches of His Life; with Widow Rugby's Husband, and Twenty-Six Other Humorous Tales of Alabama. Being the Most Laughable and Side-Splitting Stories That Have Ever Appeared in Print* (Philadelphia: T. B. Peterson and Bros., 1848); and Charles Farrar Browne, *Artemus Ward; His Travels* (New York: Carleton, 1865).

49. William Tappan Thompson, *Major Jones's Sketches of Travel, Comprising the Scenes, Incidents, and Adventures in his Tour from Georgia to Canada* (Philadelphia: T. B. Peterson, 1848), 7, 9.

50. Thompson, *Major Jones's Sketches of Travel*, 38, 162.

51. Thompson, *Major Jones's Sketches of Travel*, 46, 53.

52. Thompson, *Major Jones's Sketches of Travel*, 41.

53. Thompson, *Major Jones's Sketches of Travel*, 41, 151.

54. Thompson, *Major Jones's Sketches of Travel*, 183, 156, 159.

55. Thompson, *Major Jones's Sketches of Travel*, 192, 167, 165.

56. Mark Twain, *The Innocents Abroad, Or the New Pilgrims' Progress* (Hartford: American Publishing Company, 1869), v.

57. Twain, *The Innocents Abroad*, 20, 22, 23.

58. Twain, *The Innocents Abroad*, 20, 23, 24, 26, 27.

59. Twain, *The Innocents Abroad*, 70–71, 110–11, 87.

60. F. Xavier Medina, "Eating Cat in the North of Spain in the Early Twentieth Century," in *Consuming the Inedible: Neglected Dimensions of Food Choice*, ed. Jeremy MacClancy, C. J. K. Henry, and Helen M. Macbeth (New York: Berghahn, 2009): 151–62, 155.

61. Twain, *The Innocents Abroad*, 40, 41, 364.

62. Thompson, *Major Jones's Sketches of Travel*, 8.

5 / Traveling to Good Purpose

1. Elizabeth Baigent, "Stocqueler, Joachim Hayward (1800–1885)," in *Oxford Dictionary of National Biography*, vol. 52 (New York: Oxford University Press, 2004), 841.

2. Joachim Heyward Siddons, *Travel, Its Pleasures, Advantages, and Requirements: A Lecture by J. H. Siddons, Delivered at Clinton Hall, New York, February, 1860* (New York: H. H. Lloyd & Co., 1860), 284–86.

3. See Stewart Fraser, "Count Leopold Berchtold: Eighteenth Century Educational Travel Counselor," *Peabody Journal of Education* 40, no. 1 (July 1962): 4–11, 5.

4. Thomas Hartwell Horne, *A Catalogue of the Library of the College of St. Margaret and St. Bernard, Commonly Called Queen's College, in the University of Cambridge* (London: S. and R. Bentley, 1827), 675–76. The earliest evidence of such cataloging in a library in the United States was in the 1856 catalogue of the holdings of the Library Company of Philadelphia, which included a subheading in the "Voyages and Travels" category for "Treatises on Travelling." The library held five titles under this heading, all published in London or Philadelphia between 1838 and 1851 (see *A Catalogue of the Books Belonging to the Library Company of Philadelphia*, vol. 3 [Philadelphia: Printed for the Company, 1856], 1367; see also John M. Horton, *Catalogue of the Books Belonging to the Young Men's Association of the City of Chicago*, vol. 1 [Chicago: Rounds & James, 1865], 110).

5. Siddons, *Travel, Its Pleasures, Advantages, and Requirements*, 300.

6. Charlene M. Boyer Lewis, *Elizabeth Patterson Bonaparte: An American Aristocrat in the Early Republic* (Philadelphia: University of Pennsylvania Press, 2012), 65–68; Richard L. Bushman, *The Refinement of America: Persons, Houses, Cities* (New York: Vintage, 1993).

7. See Sean Wilentz, *Chants Democratic: New York City and the Rise of the American Working Class, 1788–1850* (New York: Oxford University Press, 1984): 61–103; Catherine McNicol Stock, *Rural Radicals: Righteous Rage in the American Grain* (Ithaca: Cornell University Press, 1996): 15–86; and Tony Allan Freyer, *Producers Versus Capitalists: Constitutional Conflict in Antebellum America* (Charlottesville: University Press of Virginia, 1994).

8. See Joanna Cohen, *Luxurious Citizens: The Politics of Consumption in Nineteenth-Century America* (Philadelphia: University of Pennsylvania Press, 2017).

9. Siddons, *Travel, Its Pleasures, Advantages, and Requirements*, 286–87.

10. Timothy Dwight, *Travels in New-England and New-York* (New Haven: T. Dwight, 1821), 129–30.

11. Richard Gassan, "The First American Tourist Guidebooks: Authorship and the Print Culture of the 1820s," *Book History* 8 (2005): 51–74, 56–57.

12. Theodore Dwight, *Sketches of Scenery and Manners in the United States* (New York: A. T. Goodrich, 1829), preface, 179–80.

13. Dwight, *Sketches of Scenery and Manners*, 176, 182.

14. Dwight, *Sketches of Scenery and Manners*, 176.

15. Dwight, *Sketches of Scenery and Manners*, 176.

16. For more on the gendering of sympathy in early American novels and its complex political valences, see Elizabeth Barnes, *States of Sympathy: Seduction and Democracy in the American Novel* (New York: Columbia University Press, 1997); and Julia A. Stern, *The Plight of Feeling: Sympathy and Dissent in the Early American Novel* (Chicago: University of Chicago Press, 1997).

17. See Ann Douglas, *The Feminization of American Culture* (New York: Noonday Press/Farrar, Straus and Giroux, 1998); and Cathy N. Davidson, *Revolution and the Word: The Rise of the Novel in America* (New York: Oxford University Press, 2004), 110–50.

18. Mary Kelley, *Learning to Stand & Speak: Women, Education, and Public Life in America's Republic* (Chapel Hill: University of North Carolina Press, 2006), 155–60, quotation on 158.

19. See Mary Louise Pratt, *Imperial Eyes: Travel Writing and Transculturation* (New York: Routledge, 2008); and David N. Livingstone and Charles W. J. Withers, eds., *Geographies of Nineteenth-Century Science* (Chicago: University of Chicago Press, 2011).

20. See Linda K. Kerber, "Science in the Early Republic: The Society for the Study of Natural Philosophy," *William and Mary Quarterly*, 3rd ser., 29, no. 2 (April 1972): 263–80.

21. Stocqueler's intellectual debt to Jackson is obvious because the categories of inquiry he listed as necessary for useful observation were almost a mirror image of Jackson's table of contents (see Siddons, *Travel, Its Pleasures, Advantages, and Requirements*, 301–3; and J. R. Jackson, *What to Observe; Or, the Traveller's Remembrancer* [London: James Madden & Co., 1841], v–xvii).

22. See A. S. Goudie, "Colonel Julian Jackson and His Contribution to Geography," *Geographical Journal* 144, no. 2 (July 1978): 264–70, 264.

23. See Felix Driver, *Geography Militant: Cultures of Exploration and Empire* (Oxford: Blackwell, 2001), 49–67.

24. Driver, *Geography Militant*, 64.

25. See John F. W. Herschel, *A Manual of Scientific Enquiry; Prepared for the Use of Officers in Her Majesty's Navy; and Travellers in General* (London: J. Murray, 1859), iii, iv.

26. See *United States Magazine, and Democratic Review* 1, no. 1 (July 1841): 99; *Christian Advocate and Journal* 36, no. 16 (April 18, 1861): 127; and *American Publishers' Circular and Literary Gazette* 7, no. 24 (June 15, 1861): 206. *What to Observe* was available at the Mercantile Library of New York by 1844 and at the Library Company of Philadelphia and the Free Public Library of New Bedford by the mid-1850s at the latest (see the *Catalogue of the Mercantile Library in New York* [New York: E. O. Jenkins, 1844], 107; *Catalogue of the Books Belonging to the Library Company of Philadelphia*, 1367; and *Catalogue of the Free Public Library, New Bedford, Mass.* [New Bedford: B. Lindsey, 1858], 163).

27. The unrealized Carey and Hart edition was announced in the *United States Magazine, and Democratic Review* 9, no. 38 (August 1841): 202.

28. *Appleton's Library Manual: Containing a Catalogue Raisonné of Upwards of Twelve Thousand of the Most Important Works in Every Department of Knowledge, in All Modern Languages* (New York: D. Appleton and Company, 1847), 352.

29. Goudie, "Colonel Julian Jackson," 265, 266, 268.

30. Jackson, *What to Observe*, iv.

31. See Driver, *Geography Militant*, 50.

32. Jackson, *What to Observe*, iii.

33. Driver, *Geography Militant*, 51.

34. Jan Golinski, "The Care of the Self and the Masculine Birth of Science," *History of Science* 40, pt. 2, no. 128 (June 2002): 125–45, 140, 139.

35. Siddons, *Travel, Its Pleasures, Advantages, and Requirements*, 297–98.

36. See Renée Bergland, *Maria Mitchell and the Sexing of Science* (Boston: Beacon, 2008), 42–52; Margaret W. Rossiter, *Women Scientists in America: Struggles and Strategies to 1940* (Baltimore: Johns Hopkins University Press, 1982), 51–72; and Ruth Watts, *Women in Science: A Social and Cultural History* (New York: Routledge, 2007), 99–133.

37. The membership of the "association" behind the "How to Observe" series, and its relationship to the SDUK, remain unclear; the volumes' introductory materials were intentionally obfuscating, written in the passive voice and attributed only by initials. Its attribution to "an association of philanthropic geniuses of both sexes" was made in a review of Martineau's volume in the *London Quarterly Review*, which claimed that "This association seems to be an offset from the illustrious 'Society for the diffusion of Useful Knowledge,' and means, we understand, to publish a complete encyclopedia *de omnibus rebus et quibusdam aliis.*" The involvement of the SDUK seems clear; Felix Driver makes this attribution, pointing out that both extant volumes were issued by Charles Knight, SDUK's publisher of choice in the late 1830s. However, it is unclear if the "association of philanthropic geniuses" and the SDUK were the same thing or not (see "ART. II.—*How to Observe—Morals and Manners.* By Harriet Martineau. Charles Knight. London. 1838," *London Quarterly Review* 63, no. 125 [January 1839]: 34; and Driver, *Geography Militant*, 61).

38. Mead T. Cain, "The Maps of the Society for the Diffusion of Useful Knowledge: A Publishing History," *Imago Mundi* 46 (1994): 151–67, 151. See also Harold Smith, *The Society for the Diffusion of Useful Knowledge 1826–1846: A Social and Bibliographical Evaluation* (Halifax: Dalhousie University School of Library Service, 1974).

39. Henry T. De La Beche, *How to Observe: Geology* (London: Charles Knight, 1836), iv–vi.

40. "ART. II.—*How to Observe—Morals and Manners*," 34.

41. De La Beche, *How to Observe*, 5.

42. Harriet Martineau, *How to Observe: Morals and Manners* (New York: Harper and Brothers, 1838), 62.

43. "ART. II.—*How to Observe—Morals and Manners*."

44. See Harriet Martineau, *Society in America* (New York: Saunders and Otley, 1837).

45. Martineau, *How to Observe*, 44.

46. Kelley, *Learning to Stand and Speak*, 17.

47. Martineau, *How to Observe*, 44–45, 48.

48. Martineau, *How to Observe*, 52–53, 53–54, 56, 57.

49. Martineau, *How to Observe*, 58.

50. Martineau was comfortable distinguishing the gender of a body from the gender of a mind; as Roger Cooter has argued, she "was often regarded as 'one of the finest examples of a masculine intellect in a female form which . . . [has] distinguished the present age'" (see Roger Cooter, "Dichotomy and Denial: Mesmerism, Medicine and Harriet Martineau," in *Science and Sensibility: Gender and Scientific Enquiry, 1780–1945*, ed. Marina Benjamin [Oxford: Basil Blackwell, 1991], 145).

51. See Marina Benjamin, "Elbow Room: Women Writers on Science, 1790–1840," in *Science and Sensibility: Gender and Scientific Enquiry, 1780–1945*, ed. Benjamin (Oxford: Basil Blackwell, 1991), 29.

52. See G. J. Barker-Benfield, *The Culture of Sensibility: Sex and Society in Eighteenth-Century Britain* (Chicago: University of Chicago Press, 1992), xvii, 395. For more on the relationship between sympathy, sensibility, sentiment, and sentimentality, see Kelley, *Learning to Stand and Speak*, 50–55.

53. For more on women's use of sympathy to claim authority in medicine and the social sciences, see Regina Markell Morantz-Sanchez, *Sympathy and Science: Women Physicians in American Medicine* (New York: Oxford University Press, 1985). Indeed, the link between Martineau's notion of sympathy and the foundations of the social sciences of sociology and anthropology is even tighter than in the medical sciences; in 1962 Seymour Lipset called *How to Observe—Morals and Manners* "the first book on the methodology of social research in the then still unborn disciplines of sociology and anthropology" (see Harriet Martineau, *Society in America, Edited, Abridged and with an Introductory Essay by Seymour Martin Lipset* [Garden City, NY: Anchor, 1962], 7). Martineau's place in the pantheon of methodological founders of the discipline of sociology has become firmer since Lipset first pointed out her pioneering importance (see Michael R. Hill and Susan Hoecker-Drysdale, eds., *Harriet Martineau: Theoretical and Methodological Perspectives* [New York: Routledge, 2001]).

54. Martineau, *How to Observe*, 45.

55. Dwight, *Sketches of Scenery and Manners*, 181–83.

56. Theodore Dwight, *Things As They Are; Or, Notes of a Traveller through Some of the Middle and Northern States* (New York: Harper & Bros., 1834), 227, 233.

57. For more on Phelps's biography and her career as a textbook author, see Emma L. Bolzau, *Almira Hart Lincoln Phelps: Her Life and Work* (Lancaster, PA: Science Press Printing, 1936); and Sally Gregory Kohlstedt, "Parlors, Primers, and Public Schooling: Education for Science in Nineteenth-Century America," *Isis* 81, no. 3 (September 1990): 425–45.

58. Almira Hart Lincoln Phelps, *Caroline Westerley; Or, The Young Traveller from Ohio: Containing the Letters of A Young Lady of Seventeen, Written to Her Sister* (New York: J. & J. Harper, 1833), 3, 34–35.

59. Phelps, *Caroline Westerley*, 135, 182.

60. Hale qtd. in Bolzau, *Almira Hart Lincoln Phelps*, 363–64.

61. See Stephen Dow Beckham, *The Literature of the Lewis and Clark Expedition: A Bibliography and Essays* (Portland, OR: Lewis & Clark College, 2003); Edward C. Carter II, "Living with Lewis & Clark: The American Philosophical Society's Continuing Relationship with the Corps of Discovery from the Michaux Expedition to the Present," in *Lewis & Clark: Legacies, Memories, and New Perspectives*, ed. Kris Fresonke and Mark Spence (Berkeley: University of California Press, 2004); and Frank Bergon, "Wilderness Aesthetics," in *Lewis & Clark*, ed. Fresonke and Spence, 43.

62. See, for example, Zebulon Montgomery Pike and Nicholas King, *An Account of a Voyage up the Mississippi River, from St. Louis to Its Source* (Washington, 1807); William Darby et al., *A Geographical Description of the State of Louisiana, the Southern Part of the State of Mississippi, and Territory of Alabama: Presenting a View of the Soil, Climate, Animal, Vegetable, and Mineral Productions, Illustrative of Their Natural Physiognomy, Their Geographical Configuration, and Relative Situation, with an Account of the Character and Manners of the Inhabitants* (New York: James Olmstead, 1817); Henry Rowe Schoolcraft, *Narrative Journal of Travels through the Northwestern Regions of the United States: Extending from Detroit through the Great Chain of American Lakes, to the Sources of the Mississippi River; Performed as a Member of the Expedition under Governor Cass in the Year 1820* (Albany: E. & E. Hosford, 1821); and Ross Cox, *Adventures on the Columbia River: Including the Narrative of a Residence of Six Years on the Western Side of the Rocky Mountains, among Various Tribes of Indians Hitherto Unknown: Together with a Journey across the American Continent* (New York: J. & J. Harper, 1832).

63. "Tourists, at Home and Abroad," *United States Magazine and Democratic Review* 28, no. 156 (June 1851): 528–31, 528, 531.

64. Timothy Dwight, *Travels in New England and New York*, ed. Barbara Miller Solomon (Cambridge: Belknap Press of Harvard University Press, 1969), xlv–xlvii.

65. Benjamin Silliman, *Remarks Made on a Short Tour between Hartford and Quebec, in the Autumn of 1819* (New Haven: S. Converse, 1820), 3.

66. See Donald De B. Beaver, "Altruism, Patriotism, and Science: Scientific Journalism in the Early Republic," *American Studies* 12, no. 1 (Spring 1971): 5–19; and S. W. Jackman, "The Tribulations of an Editor: Benjamin Silliman and the Early Days of the American Journal of Science and the Arts," *New England Quarterly* 52, no. 1 (March 1979): 99–106

67. Silliman, *Remarks* (1820), 3.

68. Sally Gregory Kohlstedt, "The Geologists' Model for National Science, 1840–1847," *Proceedings of the American Philosophical Society* 118, no. 2 (April 19, 1974): 179–95.

69. Silliman, *Remarks* (1820), 3

70. Silliman, *Remarks* (1820), 3.

71. Benjamin Silliman, *Remarks Made on a Short Tour between Hartford and Quebec in the Autumn of 1819* (New Haven: S. Converse, 1824), 5.

72. Henry D. Gilpin, *A Northern Tour: Being a Guide to Saratoga, Lake George, Niagara, Canada, Boston, &C., &C.: Through the States of Pennsylvania, New-Jersey, New-York, Vermont, New-Hampshire, Massachusetts, Rhode-Island, and Connecticut, Embracing an Account of the Canals, Colleges, Public Institutions, Natural Curiosities, and Interesting Objects Therein* (Philadelphia: H. C. Carey & I. Lea, 1825), iv.

73. William Parker Foulke to Eleanor Foulke, dated Harrisburg, February 22, 1848, "William Parker Foulke Papers," American Philosophical Society, Philadelphia. See also Charles Trego's *A Geography of Pennsylvania: Containing an Account of the History, Geographical Features, Soil, Climate, Geology, Botany, Zoology, Population, Education, Government, Finances, Productions, Trade, Railroads, Canals &c. of the State: With a Separate Description of Each County, and Questions for the Convenience of Teachers: To Which Is Appended, A Travellers' Guide, or Table of Distances on the Principal Rail Road, Canal and Stage Routes in the State* (Philadelphia: Edward C. Biddle, 1843).

74. For more on Hall's biography, see Rossiter Johnson and John Howard Brown, *The Twentieth Century Biographical Dictionary of Notable Americans* (Boston: Biographical Society, 1904).

75. See *Daily National Intelligencer* (Washington, DC), October 3, 1838, 2.

76. Frederick Hall, *Letters from the East and from the West* (Washington, DC: F. Taylor and W. M. Morrison, 1840), v–vi.

77. Hall, *Letters from the East and from the West*, 8.

78. Hall, *Letters from the East and from the West*, 39, 90, 108, 140.

79. Hall, *Letters from the East and from the West*, 137.

80. See Susan Clair Imbarrato, *Traveling Women: Narrative Visions of Early America* (Athens: Ohio University Press, 2006), 10.

81. Anne Newport Royall, *Sketches of History, Life, and Manners in the United States* (New Haven: Printed for the author, 1826), 13.

82. Royall, *Sketches of History, Life, and Manners*, "To the Public," 228–29, 222.

83. Sarah Harvey Porter, *The Life and Times of Anne Royall* (Cedar Rapids: Torch Press Book Shop, 1909), 68, 85, 89. For more on Royall's career, see Elizabeth J. Clapp, "Black Books and Southern Tours: Tone and Perspective in the Travel Writing of Mrs. Anne Royall," *Yearbook of English Studies* 34 (2004): 61–73; Alice S. Maxwell and Marion B. Dunlevy, *Virago! The Story of Anne Newport Royall (1769–1854)* (Jefferson, NC: McFarland, 1985); and Patricia Cline Cohen, *The Murder of Helen Jewett: The Life and Death of a Prostitute in Nineteenth-Century New York* (New York: Knopf, 1998), 156–65.

84. Royall, *Sketches of History, Life, and Manners*, 157. See also Elizabeth J. Clapp, "'A Virago-Errant in Enchanted Armor?': Anne Royall's 1829 Trial as a Common Scold," *Journal of the Early Republic* 23, no. 2 (Summer 2003): 207–32.

85. See Donna Dickenson, *Margaret Fuller: Writing a Woman's Life* (London: Macmillan, 1993), 49; and Charles Capper, *Margaret Fuller: An American Romantic Life* (New

York: Oxford University Press, 1992), 155. Not only did Fuller seek intellectual guidance from Martineau; the older woman also engineered one her most important intellectual introductions: Ralph Waldo Emerson. Even though relations between the two women turned frosty in the late 1830s, Martineau remained an important intellectual link for Fuller; in 1846, Martineau arranged for her to visit the English Lake District, where she met a number of important figures, including Wordsworth (see Dickenson, *Margaret Fuller*, 47–52; Meg McGavran Murray, *Margaret Fuller, Wandering Pilgrim* [Athens: University of Georgia Press, 2008], 86–93; and Capper, *Margaret Fuller*, 153–55).

86. Margaret Fuller, *Summer on the Lakes, in 1843* (Boston: C. C. Little and James Brown, 1844), 1, 41, 28.

87. Fuller, *Summer on the Lakes*, 104, 58, 60–61.

88. Elaine Showalter, *Inventing Herself: Claiming a Feminist Intellectual Heritage* (New York: Simon and Schuster, 2001), 46.

89. Fuller, *Summer on the Lakes*, 245, 30, 178.

90. "Literary Notices and Miscellanies," *Brownson's Quarterly Review* 1, no. 4 (October 1844): 546.

91. "Notices of Recent Publications," *Christian Examiner and Religious Miscellany* 37, 4th ser., no. 2 (September 1844): 274.

92. "Literary Notices," *Brownson's Quarterly Review*, 546. Another later observer recorded that it had "attained wide consideration" upon its publication (see *The Whig Almanac and United States Register for 1851* [New York: Greeley & McElrath, 1851], 42).

93. For a sample of library holdings from the first ten years after the book's publication in 1844, see *Catalogue of the Mercantile Library in New York*, 234; John L. Tillinghast and George Wood, *Catalogue of the New York State Library, January 1, 1846* (Albany: C. Wendell, 1846), 240; *Alphabetical and Analytical Catalogue of the New York Society Library* (New York: R. Craighead, 1850), 166; *Catalogue of the Library of the Providence Athenaeum* (Providence: Knowles, Anthony & Co., 1853), 149; *A Catalogue of Books of the Mercantile Library Association, of Boston* (Boston: Damrell & Moore, 1850), 63; and *A Catalogue of the Mercantile Library Company of Philadelphia* (Philadelphia: Mercantile Library Company, 1850), 188.

94. "Literary Notices," *Harper's New Monthly Magazine* 12, no. 72 (May 1856): 838. For more on Fuller's posthumous reception, see Charles Capper, *Margaret Fuller: An American Romantic Life*, vol. 2 (Oxford: Oxford University Press, 2007), 515–16.

95. John Seely Hart, *The Female Prose Writers of America, with Portraits, Biographical Notices, and Specimens of Their Writings* (Philadelphia: E. H. Butler, 1852), 238.

96. Margaret Fuller et al., *Memoirs of Margaret Fuller Ossoli*, vol. 2 (Boston: Brown, Taggard and Chase, 1860), 152. The *Memoirs* were originally published by Phillips, Sampson and Co. in Boston in 1852.

97. "Margaret Fuller Ossoli," *Russell's Magazine* 1, no. 3 (June 1857): 229.

98. "Pleasing narrative" was the assessment of the *American Whig Review* in 1852 (see "Margaret Fuller Ossoli," *American Whig Review* no. 88 [April 1852]: 362).

99. Hart, *Female Prose Writers of America*, 239.

100. *Christian Examiner and Religious Miscellany* 60, 4th series, 25, no. 11 (March 1856): 6.

101. See Sarah Margaret Fuller Ossoli and Arthur B. Fuller, *At Home and Abroad; or, Things and Thoughts in America and Europe* (Boston: Crosby and Nichols, 1856).

Other editions were issued in Boston by Brown, Taggard and Chase in 1860; by Roberts Brothers in 1874 and 1895; and in New York by the Tribune Association in 1869.

102. Fuller, *At Home and Abroad*, iii–iv.

103. Fuller, *At Home and Abroad*, iv–v.

104. Crosby, Nichols, & Company echoed Arthur Fuller's argument in their advertising when making a case for the work's continuing relevance. Since, "in the language of the author, 'it aims to communicate the poetic impression she received of the country at large,' and not to give a statistical account of her journey, it is as valuable to-day as when first published." Fuller's travels had a continuing relevance due to their profundity, which their publisher clearly thought was a valuable selling point (see *Christian Examiner and Religious Miscellany* 60, 4th series, 25, no. 11 [March 1856]: 6).

105. Fuller, *At Home and Abroad*, v.

106. See Charles Capper, *Margaret Fuller: An American Romantic Life* (New York: Oxford University Press, 1992), ix.

Epilogue

1. Lisa Kearns, "Gift Guide 2001: *Not For Tourists, 2002*." *New York Press*, www.notfortourists.com.

2. Ariel Teplitsky, "Guides Help Real Travellers Rush in Where 'Tourists' Fear to Tread," *Toronto Star*, October 21, 2006, www.notfortourists.com.

3. Teplitsky, "Guides Help Real Travellers Rush in Where 'Tourists' Fear to Tread."

4. "About Fodor's," www.fodors.com; "About Frommer's," www.frommers.com.

5. "Our History—Let's Go," www.letsgo.com.

6. Tony and Maureen Wheeler, *Unlikely Destinations: The Lonely Plant Story. How Two Backpackers Trekked Across Asia—And Revolutionized the World of Independent Travel!* (Singapore: Periplus Editions, 2005).

7. Thomas A. Chambers, *Drinking the Waters: Creating an American Leisure Class at Nineteenth-Century Mineral Springs* (Washington DC: Smithsonian Institution Press, 2002), 184–225; Charlene Boyer Lewis, *Ladies and Gentlemen on Display: Planter Society at the Virginia Springs, 1790–1860* (Charlottesville: University Press of Virginia, 2001), 209–11.

8. Cindy Sondik Aron, *Working at Play: A History of Vacations in the United States* (New York: Oxford University Press, 1999), 45–100; Dona Brown, *Inventing New England: Regional Tourism in the Nineteenth Century* (Washington, DC: Smithsonian Institution Press, 1995), 75–104, 135–67; Catherine Cocks, *Tropical Whites: The Rise of the Tourist South in the Americas* (Philadelphia: University of Pennsylvania Press, 2013); David E. Goldberg, *The Retreats of Reconstruction: Race, Leisure, and the Politics of Segregation at the New Jersey Shore, 1865–1920* (New York: Fordham University Press, 2016).

9. Richard H. Gassan, "Tourists and the City: New York's First Tourist Era, 1820–1840." *Winterthur Portfolio* 44, no. 2/3 (Summer/Autumn 2010): 221–46; Catherine Cocks, *Doing the Town: The Rise of Urban Tourism in the United States, 1850–1915* (Berkeley: University of California Press, 2001).

10. Marguerite S. Shaffer, *See America First: Tourism and National Identity, 1880–1940* (Washington, DC: Smithsonian Institution Press, 2001), 7–92.

11. Shaffer, *See America First*, 93–129; Michael Berkowitz, "A 'New Deal' for Leisure: Making Mass Tourism During the Great Depression," in *Being Elsewhere:*

Tourism, Consumer Culture, and Identity in Modern Europe and North America, ed. Shelley Baranowski and Ellen Furlough (Ann Arbor: University of Michigan Press, 2001): 185–212.

12. Lizabeth Cohen, *A Consumers' Republic: The Politics of Mass Consumption in Postwar America* (New York: Vintage, 2003); Susan Sessions Rugh, *Are We There Yet?: The Golden Age of American Family Vacations* (Lawrence: University Press of Kansas, 2008).

13. Daniel Boorstin, "From Traveler to Tourist: The Lost Art of Travel," in *The Image: A Guide to Pseudo-Events in America* (New York: Harper and Row, 1961), 78–79.

14. This evocative phrase is drawn from Henry Miller's 1936 description of Coney Island, which shows that Boorstin's sense of inauthenticity well predated his postwar moment (Henry Miller, *Black Spring* [New York: Grove Press, 1963], 159).

Index

ABOUT THE AUTHOR

Will B. Mackintosh is an Associate Professor of History at the University of Mary Washington, where he teaches and writes about early American history, cultural and intellectual history, the history of travel and tourism, and the history of capitalism.

Lightning Source UK Ltd.
Milton Keynes UK
UKHW011513280820
368968UK00003B/728/J

9 781479 889372